UNFINISHED
BUSINESS

UNFINISHED BUSINESS

A DEMOCRAT AND A REPUBLICAN
TAKE ON THE 10 MOST IMPORTANT
ISSUES WOMEN FACE

Dr. Julianne Malveaux
and Deborah Perry

A PERIGEE BOOK

A Perigee Book
Published by the Berkley Publishing Group
A division of Penguin Putnam Inc.
375 Hudson Street
New York, New York 10014

First edition: September 2002

Visit our website at www.penguinputnam.com

LIBRARY OF CONGRESS CATALOGING-IN-PUBLICATION DATA

Malveaux, Julianne.
    Unfinished business : a Democrat and a Republican take on the
10 most important issues women face / Julianne Malveaux and
Deborah L. Perry.
        p. cm.
    Includes index.
    ISBN 0-399-52808-3
    1. Women—United States—Social conditions. 2. United States—
Social conditions—1980- I. Perry, Deborah L., 1952- II. Title.

HQ1421 .M34 2002
305.42'0973—dc21

                                                2002025801

Printed in the United States of America

10 9 8 7 6 5 4 3 2 1

CONTENTS

ACKNOWLEDGMENTS

This book could not have been produced without the strong support of our agent, Claudia Cross, and our editor, Jennifer Repo. Claudia has been an absolute joy to work with, a wonderful, focused, delightful, and committed woman who believed that this book was an important addition to the discourse on women, participation, and public policy. Jennifer has gently shaped and guided this book into the volume that it is, helping to turn our disparate voices into a unit, making suggestions about content, common ground, and commonality that have been valued and appreciated. Jennifer also provided an adept eye, not to mention unwavering support, during all phases of this book from inception to completion, and we are so grateful and proud that she has been the editor for our first book project. Thank you for caring about this book as much as we did. We would be remiss if we did not acknowledge Soledad O'Brien's enthusiasm to step up to the plate and write the foreword for this book. We suspect she had great fun writing about the first time we were on-air together on her former MSNBC television show, since Soledad was the one who first had to cautiously steady the flames of hostility between us. Words cannot fully express our thanks to Claudia, Jennifer and Soledad!

JULIANNE MALVEAUX

First of all, I give honor to God from whom all blessings flow. I have not always acknowledged the divine in my work, and certainly I always should. This time, though, it has been clear that an "invisible hand" has guided this undertaking which may have, so many times, been abandoned were it not for a sense that there was greater good in this work. The Landmark Forum and Howard Ross have also provided me with lessons, blessings, and insights that affirmed the benefits and challenges of collaborative work.

When I asked Deborah Perry to work with me on *A Room Full of Women*™, I had no idea that our work would lead to this book project. She has been an enthusiastic and energetic partner who has always pushed the envelope on our collaboration and I am (mostly) grateful to her for her forward thinking and the vision that made this book a reality.

I am also grateful for the friends and supporters who helped the *A Room Full of Women*™ project become the springboard for this book. Esther Silver Parker at AT&T, Clyde Rucker at Burger King, Anna Perez (then at Chevron), Glegg Watson (then at Xerox), and Stacey Davis at the Fannie Mae Foundation provided corporate support for the Room Full. Dean Kathleen Hall Jameson at the Annenberg School for Communications at the University of Pennsylvania and her amazing team extended themselves in ways we could not have anticipated. We got similar help and extraordinary technical support from Geoffrey Cowan. Dean of the Annenberg School for Communications at the University of Southern California, and his team. Not only did they provide us with a venue, but they also helped us with outreach, student participation, technical support, production offices, and general goodwill. We had a dozen or so outstanding women appear on our program, including Marcia Ann Gillespie, Gloria Allred, and Melanie Campbell. Their enthusiastic support for our work convinced us to move forward together. My policy friends and allies were a great help in providing sources for and reviews of my work. I am especially grateful to Leslie Wolfe at the Center for Women Policy Studies, Heidi Hartmann at the Institute for Women's Policy Research, and Max Sawicky at the Economic Policy Institute for their input to my parts of this work. Legislators, litigators, policy wonks, and editors who have helped me with background information include the many members of the Congressional Black Caucus; Dr. Dorothy Irene Height; C. Delores Tucker of the National Political Congress of Black Women; and Carlottia Scott, formerly of the Democratic National Committee, all of whom I consider lodestones of policy.

Thank you, John Wiley Price (Dallas), Chris Askew (Atlanta), and Carl Nelson (Los Angeles) for making me a regular guest on your radio shows. The opportunity to talk is also an opportunity to refine ideas. I am indebted to Maxine Waters, Barbara Lee, Nan Orrock, Minyon Moore, and other women in politics for insight, vision, and support. I serve on the Board of Directors of the Center for Policy Alternatives, and appreciate their present and former staff and leadership (especially Renee Redwood and Linda Tarr Whelan) for sharing data, especially Women's Voices poll results. I have also been blessed with wonderful and supportive research staff, especially Reginna Green, an extraordinarily talented young writer and researcher. Evangeline Gray did yeoman's work in compiling a first draft of this book. Trina Holmes was part of the early development of this project, and worked tirelessly to ensure that the Room Full was a success in Philadelphia and Los Angeles. Brandice Allen, on my staff since 1999, is an exceptional administrative staffer. She will be a brilliant physician, but I wish I could clone her and keep part of her in the office. My friends and family have been patient and forbearing as I have groused, cussed, and agonized about this book. Marcia Ann Gillespie, Cora Barry, Barbara Skinner, Eddie Arnold, Cheryl Poinsette Brown, Delores Sennette and my amazing sisters Antoinette, Mariette, and Marianne Malveaux have been especially helpful. Faye Williams and Cassandra Burton, owners of D.C.'s own Sisterspace and Books have always been warm and encouraging. At Fox News, we are especially grateful to Donovan Grannum; at MSNBC we argued election politics and refined our book concept thanks to Terry Keaney. I appreciate my many opportunities to provide commentary on CNN and on local television. Bonnie Erbe, the godmother of women's issue programming, provided me with an opportunity to appear on *To the Contrary* for nearly a decade, which honed my ability to debate women's issues. Though I no longer appear on her program, I am grateful to her.

My first feminist is my mother, Proteone Marie Malveaux. She is a bold woman who has emboldened me to take risk, listen to my inner voice, and fear no backlash but God's. She has also, always, emphasized history and context. In 1984, as I ran for public office, she shared a 1963 clipping of herself testifying before the San Francisco Commission on the Status of Women. A photograph of her in one of those Jackie Kennedy pillbox hats accompanied the article. She was quoted speaking of hidden voices. This apple don't fall far from the tree (the Ebonics and Levert lyricism are intentional here). My fabulous, fine, feminist mama is my greatest love and my most enduring role model. Her grandsons, and my nephews, Anyi Malik Howell and Armand Marcus Howell, along with my godchild Matthew Elijah Brown, are also the impetus for me writing this book. When the men "get it" they will stand shoulder to shoulder with women, helping us finish our business.

DEBORAH PERRY

The idea for this book, in part, came from the television pilot Julianne and I taped and cohosted at the 2000 political conventions called *A Room Full of Women*™. This taping brought together many skillful women including Prime Minister Kim Campbell, U.S. Rep. Juanita Millender-McDonald, *The View*'s Lisa Ling, lawyer Gloria Allred, and activist Arianna Huffington. Not only was the experience exceptionally gratifying, but also it helped fuel our passion to continue raising women's voices in politics and advocacy.

In truth, the undertaking of this book was one of the more arduous challenges I've ever embarked on. Numerous policy and non-policy experts inspired me to think outside of the boundaries and beyond contemporary conservative views such that I sometimes modified my own point of view. I reflect on the drafting of this book, and the numerous individuals who influenced me here, in and around Washington, D.C., and abroad in Italy.

In Washington, I was continuously challenged by the gathering brilliant minds at Grover Norquists' Center-Right Coalition meetings. Most notably Dave Murray and, of no relation, Iain Murray, and Howard Feinberg of Statistical Assessment Service who reached out to me, and steered me away from erroneous statistics and misuse of commonly referred to data, and diligently canvassed many of my chapters for truths. To all of the staff at Americans for Tax Reform, most notably Ryan Horn, who not only reviewed related chapters, but put up with my badgering over my need to speak with more experts.

Also, I owe homecooked meals to Dr. Christine Stolba, of the Independent Women's Forum, and Danielle Doane, of Citizens for a Sound Economy, who read my chapters on Equal Pay and Retirement Programs, respectively. Roger McClure, who didn't even know me, but offered to walk me through the more perplexing sections of our tax code, and scrutinized my chapter on tax. Paul Heinold, whose keen eye in foreign policy fostered me to rethink a U.S. role in a global economy. To Daniel Corrin, who volunteered to do valuable research for me on women's figures. To Jonathan Blyth, who is not only a friend—but a walking encyclopedia—and someone I can count on when I need to know the most innocuous stuff on anything . . . and everything. To Sarah Taylor, who kept me intact during the commonplace trials and tribulations of writing a book.

In Chestertown, Maryland, Vida Morley and Bob Fox insisted that I escape the noise of Washington to write in an environment more conducive for concentration, and were the best hosts. And, I would be remiss if I did not acknowledge a certain park bench in the middle of a forest at Potomac Overlook Park that provided the most sensational backdrop for writing.

Then there are these places that pushed me beyond my comfort zone on so many levels, and forced me to think about American politics from a different vantage point—thank you Capri, Ischia, and Bagni di Lucca (Tuscany), Italy. Camille Seigel, who first joined me in Capri, is the dearest friend anyone could hope for, not to mention a consummate editor of my work. While suffering from nothing (perhaps a little writer's block), high up in a castle in Ischia, along came the Brownstone family—Hugh, Laura, Sydney, and Maggie—who tempted me to join them on a voyage to Tuscany. Without knowing me, they took a risk, as did I, and this one experience for me rekindled the meaning of life and of the human spirit. You are exceptional people and I thank you from the bottom of my heart.

A special recognition is for Jenny Rider, who helped mold this book and always tests the mold I have for other projects. Despite our similarities in age and professions, you have provided tremendous vision, and I am thankful for our willingness to challenge one another.

Without Julianne Malveaux, this journey would not be nearly as rewarding. You are more like family to me than a business partner, and you have extended yourself to me in ways that no one else has, and I am forever indebted. From our humble beginnings, we have accomplished so much more than professional success together. You have taught me the value of friendship, commitment, and created a greater awareness of race relations in the United States.

To my mother and father who provided me with foundation to want to conquer the world. And to my adoring and adored love of my life, Dino Piscione: Thank you for being you, for being a part of my life, and for always putting a smile on my face.

FOREWORD

It was a Sunday morning during the long, hot summer of 1998, and I was working—anchoring MSNBC's *Morning Blend*. In our headquarters, we were all complaining—about the heat and about having to report on what seemed like the never-ending scandal involving President Bill Clinton and White House intern Monica Lewinsky. At the same time, in our studio in Washington, D.C., our two female guests were seated next to each other, just minutes away from the start of my interview via satellite. Both were well-known experts—"talking heads," as we called them—on the Clinton impeachment process. Julianne Malveaux, an economist, is a vocal supporter of the liberal left, and Deborah Perry, a former Bush administration appointee, put forth as a spokeswoman by the Republican National Committee. In the interest of a lively debate they were appearing together, since they were also known to be at polar opposites of the political spectrum. Deborah and Julianne had both been guests on MSNBC—but never next to each other, at the same time.

The interview began smoothly—each woman, dressed somewhat dramatically in bright red was well-spoken and gracious, making a point and then allowing the other to respond. The genial tone lasted for about ten seconds—then off came the gloves and the sparks started to fly. Julianne and Deborah tried to out-talk, out-debate and sometimes just plain drown out each other on every point. It was evident how passionately each felt about her position on the issues, and crystal clear just how much they disagreed.

I made several fairly futile attempts to break in with questions, but it was as if they'd forgotten they were on television—they debated ideologies, the law, matching each other point for point. My *Morning Blend* producer contemplated "unplugging" them—killing their mikes—just so I could get a word in edgewise. For an anchorwoman, it was chaos—but for our audience, it was not only great television but an illuminating, smart debate. And, no surprise, even once we were off air, their argument continued. The combativeness wasn't faked for the sake of compelling television—they disagreed on *everything*; neither had any intention of giving an inch, they genuinely seemed to dislike each other—and it showed. When it was over each felt there was much more to say.

Years later these two passionate, outspoken women—who between them commandeered in excess of ten minutes of airtime on national television, are now co-authors of *Unfinished Business: A Democrat and A Republican Take on the 10 Most Important Issues Women Face*. Two women could not be less alike, but their passion has found commonality on women's issues. Over time Deborah and Julianne have turned their dislike into respect, and respect into a professional relationship. And while they will probably never agree on everything—hey, they'll never agree on most things—their back-and-forth debate in *Unfinished Business* illuminates the critical and salient issues that matter to women today. What's more, Julianne and Deborah have nurtured a strong female relationship based on their common interest, that has fueled over time, I daresay, a friendship.

For my part, I am proud to have been, to a small degree, the catalyst that brought them together. Regardless of your political leanings or your perspectives on the role of women on all fronts, you will see your viewpoint represented, debated, and dissected, as Deborah and Julianne examine and explain the intellectual economic and political agendas that encompass and affect today's women. Read their takes on the impact of technology on the lives of working women (and men), their disagreement on the notion of the "glass ceiling," their insights into the failings of our country's education system, and their debate over the inequalities that women face, as compared to men. A resource section ends every chapter for women of either political affiliation and is a useful starting point on how to get involved in these issues that we care about.

This much is certain: As they did when I first met them, Julianne and Deborah always have much to say, and we have much to learn by listening.

—SOLEDAD O'BRIEN
Anchor, NBC News
April 2002

INTRODUCTION: WHERE WOMEN ARE NOW

JULIANNE MALVEAUX

THE STATUS OF WOMEN—HOW DO WE MEASURE?

Remember the Virginia Slims ad with the tag line "You've come a long way, baby"? Well, yes, we've come a long way. Where corporate boardroom photos used to be dreary and gray, women's jewel-colored plumage now provides a smattering of diversity in corporate governance. Both Democratic and Republican presidents now routinely appoint women to their cabinets, and count them among their senior advisors. The sorority of women who head our nation's major corporations is growing, though you can still serve tea to all the sorority sisters and get change from a twenty-dollar bill. Our graduate and professional school enrollments are growing to the point where nearly half of all incoming law and business students are women. And the number of women college professors, though low, is growing. While more women than men now earn associate's, bachelor's, and master's degrees, that is in large part due to a decline in men's enrollment in postsecondary education. In addition, women now earn 42 percent of the Ph.D. degrees granted in the United States, but we are still concentrated in education and the humanities.

However, we've not come this far because somebody sprayed magic dust over women and said, "Go for it." Women's progress has been a direct result of the pressure that they have put on structures and systems in our society. We shouldn't be fooled into thinking that letting up on the pressure we apply will result in continued progress. Instead, absent pressure, our pace will be two steps forward, one step back. Although the status of women has changed in the last two generations (if you count a generation as a twenty-year period), some of the very gaps that sparked the women's movement still exist.

For example, even as women's enrollments have increased in graduate and professional schools, there is an absolute ossification of male power in some of the professions. It's possibly worse in politics, where women make up more than half of the voters but less than 15 percent of elected officials at the federal level. San Francisco was once called a "nanny city" by England's Prince Philip when Mayor (now Senator) Dianne Feinstein and six of the city's eleven supervisors (the equivalent of a city council in most localities) were women. Except for places like San Francisco, though, men dominate politics, and their domination shapes the political discourse. Of course, a handful of women do shatter glass ceilings. In February 2002, for example, San Franciscan Nancy Pelosi was elected the first woman Democratic whip in Congress!

Still, women hold just a fraction of the nation's political offices, are near invisible among corporate leadership ranks, and are far too often culturally depicted in ways that can only be defined as blatantly sexist and misogynist. I cringed when people celebrated the twentieth anniversary of MTV since, in my opinion, MTV has added nothing to the culture but a focus on soft pornography. It and its imitators (including VH1 and BET) subscribe to the dehumanizing "Kentucky Fried Chicken" view of women. In other words, when you get pieces of chicken in a bucket the legs, breast, thighs, and wings don't always come from the same chicken. Likewise, when you see body parts undulating in music videos, they don't always come from the same woman. Why? Much of our nation's culture is directed by men. They are the decision-makers in television, film, and music and they decide which women are sexy, attractive, or shapely enough to be featured. To be sure, there are a few women who have, against all odds, made inroads. But we still live in a patriarchal society, and in the words of abolitionist Frederick Douglass, "Power concedes nothing without a demand."

Images of women are sexualized and dehumanized. Women's bodies are used to sell everything from automobiles to power tools. We talk of women's progress and the statistics show inching inroads into bastions of men's power. But I wonder how seriously women are taken in our culture when our naked behinds are used to peddle consumption for both women and men.

Women get the short end of the stick in politics, economics, education, and culture, and some are happy to take the short end. These are the folks who are so enamored with our progress that they trust the "gradual process" to make everything equal. They are the women who don't like to talk about structural inequality, about the "isms" like sexism, racism, and classism, which shape women's lives and opportunities. Many of them have stories to tell, compelling stories, about their own success. Like donkeys with blinders, they have been so focused on themselves and their success that they don't realize that many other women lack the same opportunities from which they have benefited.

When I think of women's progress, and the ways we measure it, I am reminded of the ways that history is written and developed. Many people learn history through the lens of those pivotal and important figures of an era, learning about feminism by examining the life of Elizabeth Cady Stanton, and about the Civil War by reading a Lincoln biography. Certainly, these rich lives offer many historical lessons, but they offer an incomplete picture of the ways people lived in those eras. In *A People's History of the United States: 1492 to Present*, Howard Zinn depicts history from the vantage point of factory workers, fugitive slaves, labor leaders, war resisters, and working women. So, too, when I think about the status of women, I'm dazzled by the data that suggest enormous progress, but mindful of how most women currently live.

The aggregate story suggests that women have made some progress, but there is still a long way to go. The median income for a woman who works full-time, full year, in 1999 was $27,370, according to the Current Population Survey from the Department of Commerce. This median income rose to $41,747 for women with a bachelor's degree or higher. But less than a third of all women over twenty-five had bachelor's degrees. Women without that degree earned less than $25,000 a year, or less than $2,000 a month.

Who are these women? What are their family circumstances? How do they make it? And why aren't their stories as well-known as the stories of success we are so fond of discussing? Somehow, when we tell the story of the status of women, it has to be a story that speaks of more than the statistic. Yes, the number of businesses owned by women is rising, and women-owned businesses, to cite a popular statistic, employ more people than Fortune 500 companies. Who are their workers? How are they paid? Is their employment also a story of women's success, or is it a story of making ends meet?

Time-deprived professional women are often interviewed by awestruck journalists who wonder how they juggle everything. Coyly, some admit that they have "help." Who is their help? How are they paid? Is this a complete story of women's success?

How will we see this juncture in women's history—through the eyes of historians and pundits, or through the eyes of the people? Even as I spend much of my space in this book using statistics to make a few points, I'd like to use this opening chapter to plead that we look at the flesh and blood behind the statistics, that we pay as much attention to the sticky floor as we do to the glass ceiling, and that the nuances of women's progress are considered.

Women's Stories

Two years ago, Maria moved to the United States from El Salvador. She speaks little English, but has a pleasing enough personality to have put together a dozen clients whose homes she cleans two or three times a month. She prefers to be paid in cash, charges one hundred dollars to clean a home, and takes washing and folding home with her for an extra fee. She supports two children on the roughly two thousand dollars she earns each month, and relies on public health clinics to provide health care for herself and her children. Maria has tried to find more regular, and better paying employment, but her poor English is a barrier to her employment. Like Maria, hundreds of thousands of immigrant women are stuck at the bottom of the pay scale, without benefits or amenities. Though many would qualify for food stamps or other assistance if they were citizens, because they are not citizens, they cannot get help.

Consider a fifty-three-year-old woman I'll call Carletta. She has been working as an attendant in a Dover, Delaware, nursing home for the past five years, earning a whopping eight dollars an hour for a job she describes as "backbreaking." In my opinion, her struggle to pay her bills and to survive each month is even more backbreaking than her job. Carletta is divorced, and her children are grown, with her oldest daughter, a teacher, contributing two hundred dollars a month to help her mother make ends meet. Carletta says she is one of the lucky ones—the starting pay at her nursing home is about six dollars an hour, and she earns near the top of the pay scale. The health attendant job is one of the fastest growing, but its pay is at the lowest end of the economic spectrum. The women (and more than 90 percent of those who hold these jobs are women) employed in these jobs take care of our aging parents and the disabled, but they earn so little they can barely take care of themselves.

Sarah is a secretary. She earns $25,000 a year in San Francisco, California. The single woman attended college for two years, but dropped out because, even with student loans, she couldn't afford tuition and expenses. She'd like to go back to school, but can't even get a transcript because of the money she owes the university. One of four children, Sarah says she is not "doing too badly" economically—she shares an apartment with two roommates, but can't afford a car. "I just can't seem to get ahead," she says, adding that she has been passed up for promotion twice on her job, and that her boss, who often makes leering comments to her, seems to be holding her back. Women are more likely to hold the clerical job than any other.

Adrienne and her three children left her husband, an abusive truck driver, for a battered women's shelter. She left the shelter for subsidized housing and public assistance. Adrienne is a high school graduate who "would love to work" but her youngest child, who is disabled, requires nearly constant care. Adrienne is concerned that her public assistance eligibility will run out soon, and that she has not been able to obtain the training she needs to find a job that pays a living wage. Millions of women who receive public assistance are challenged by lifetime eligibility limits, by regulations that make it difficult for them to improve themselves by going to school or learning a skill.

For some of us, especially those who count numbers, equality will come when women get half of the pie that is called our society. For others, though, success will come when we change the recipe for pie, when the status of women is expanded to include not only statistical equity, but also some balances in the quality of our lives. For some, success will come not when women behave like men, but when women are able to influence culture and behavior in a greater way than they do now.

Deborah will tell you that women should stop being victims and just step up to the plate and compete with men. I'll tell you that there are millions of women, the majority, who are doing all they can to support their families and survive. It is the status of these women that we must constantly consider when we attempt to measure women's success and look at women's issues.

The lens through which we look at women has influenced my choice of political affiliation. I am a far left–leaning Democrat, a Jesse Jackson Democrat, if you will. I believe that our system is broken, and that government intervention can sometimes fix it. Democrats believe in paying attention to gender gaps and passing legislation designed to close them. Democrats believe in tinkering with markets so that they can deliver fairer outcomes. The Democratic Party tends to be the part of the "little people." We tend to focus more on workers than managers, more on raising the minimum wage than protecting corporate property.

Of course, Democrats aren't perfect. Politics is a boys' club, no matter what the party. And it's a white boys' club that isn't always open to people of color or sensitive to the concerns of people of color. Still, the party recently established the Women's Vote Center, naming political veteran Ann Lewis its chair (Lewis's brother, Barney Frank, represents Massachusetts in Congress). The Women's Vote Center is committed to involving women in the political process.

Still, we stumble. Thanks to former President Bill Clinton, who did quite a bit to advance women's rights (and I say this facetiously), we have welfare reform legislation that is so bad I call it "welfare deform" legislation. Things like this frequently tempt me to step outside my party and consider viable third parties like the Green Party or New York's Working Family Party. But as far left as I am, I'm also mindful of issues like access and influence. There just aren't enough folks in third parties to make them viable just yet, and some third-party actions (like the Nader run) have cost us so much (like a Gore victory) that they give third parties a bad name.

If you share my concerns about the status of women and things politicians might do to make things better for women, you, the reader, can get involved. At election time, most political organizations are looking for helping hands, but there are so many gender gaps that you can get involved year-round. Join a political party. Attend party meetings. Volunteer to chair a committee. Circulate petitions about issues of concern. Read chapter Twelve, "Seven Ways to Lift Your Voice," for some ideas. Women have come a long way. But we have a long way to go and we won't get there until and unless more of us get involved.

DEBORAH PERRY

In the winter of 2000, Julianne and I attended the annual National Association of Television Production Executives (NAPTE) convention, where anyone and everyone in television assemble to do business. We were there to market our television pilot, *A Room Full of Women*™, to the executives floating around in search of new programming for their networks and stations. The NAPTE convention also holds many panels featuring leading industry executives and on-air talent.

We were jazzed up to attend the "Women of TV" panel, which was moderated by television host Leeza Gibbons. These top-notch women, including Whoopi Goldberg, Judith Sheindlin (Judge Judy), Gloria Allred, and Cristina Saralegui, talked about what it took to work in television, and it was empowering to learn of their stories, particularly to hear about how the minority panelists broke the mold in the industry and made it "big time." But the encouragement was short-lived. The conversation took a nosedive as most of them rallied together over their inhibitions to take a seat at the table in television's male-dominated boardrooms. Instantaneously, my feelings of "you go, girl" turned into ennui, and I thought . . . here we go again!

Whoopi Goldberg, fortuitously, broke ranks and I will forever remember her sizzling retort. She first scoffed at the remark of the last panelist, and with emphatic passion said something in the tune of "Where have I been? I have always just walked up to the board table and sat down." The audience was overcome with laughter, and I admired her tenacity for standing up for her convictions in light of being surrounded by some women who appear to let the men in the boardroom jolt them. I suspect that Whoopi thought it was downright ridiculous to ever feel inferior to anyone. I agree!

We're all familiar with the adage "You are what you eat," but women who harbor an inferiority complex should adopt something in the order of "You are what you project." I will not play the victim, and for those who do, they shall be treated as victims. This is the predominant reason why I identify with the Republican Party. I take responsibility for who I am, and government cannot mandate my place in society or in work. I have to work hard, just like everyone else. Republicans believe in the equality of all people, and that individuals should be judged by their abilities, not whether you are a man or woman, or of Native American, Hispanic, African-American, European, or Asian descent. All people are to be treated equally, period!

In addition to equality, the Republican Party embodies a pragmatic balance between government and individuals, and offers a platform of positions that are in sync with the way I want to live my life: less government, lower taxes, protection of the family, a stronger educational system, and tougher criminal laws. Less government means living in a society free of a Big Brother–style government, and allowing me more freedom to pursue my American dream. Lower taxes means that Republicans trust you to do a much better job managing the money you earn, more so than the government can. We know what happens when Americans take more money home in their paychecks. It makes the economy flourish.

Taking responsibility also means protecting the sanctity of human life, and when my family ages, Republicans want a Social Security and Medicare system that ensures me to get the best return on my investment. A stronger public educational system through the control of local government is what the Republican Party believes in, and not through some massive bureaucracy that applies a one-size-fits-all approach to your child's education whether you live in Miami, Florida, Painesville, Iowa, or anywhere else on the map. Republicans want you and your family to be safe at home, on the streets, and in your communities, and they believe in tough law enforcement, with stiff penalties, no loopholes, and judges who respect the rights of law-abiding citizens. As these and other issues reflect my conservative values throughout my sections of the book, I hope you will find how women are better served by the pragmatic approaches of the Republican Party. Because we are the party that says, "Take responsibility for yourself, work hard, and you will excel."

In the short time that women have been in the mainstream workforce, we have bolstered to the uppermost ranks in politics and business. Unlike the plight of so many women around the world, nothing prevents us from doing anything we want to do. Our great democratic society fosters freedom of choice, whether that choice is to persevere and run for president as Shirley Chisholm and Elizabeth Dole did in the years 1972 and 2000, respectively, become chairman of a major Fortune 500 company like Hewlett Packard CEO Carly Fiorina, triumph into a media mogul like Oprah Winfrey, or stay at home and raise children. These women and countless others serve as valiant role models.

One of my heroines in politics is Jeannette Rankin, a less well-known early pioneer of women's suffrage who was the first woman elected to Congress in 1916. Representative Rankin was a Republican from Montana, and arrived at the U.S. Congress four years before women even had the right to vote. At thirty-six, Representative Rankin's agenda included a women's suffrage amendment, an eight-hour workday for women, better health care for mothers and children, and prohibition. What inspires me so much about her is not only did she have the courage to serve as the first woman in national politics, but she believed in herself for the person she was and did not feel she needed special preferences because she was a woman.

Fast-forward to the twenty-first century election cycles, and an unprecedented number of women are being sent to Congress. Shortly after the book *Nine and Counting: The Women of the Senate* was released mid-2000, an addendum had to be added for the four more female senators who were sworn into office in January 2001. These 13 out of 100 U.S. Senators represent a diverse geographic mix across the country: Maria Cantwell (D-WA), Hillary Rodham Clinton (D-NY), Debbie Stabenow (D-MI), and Jean Carnahan (D-MO) joined ranks with Barbara Mikulski (D-MD), Kay Bailey Hutchison (R-TX), Dianne Feinstein (D-CA), Barbara Boxer (D-CA), Patty Murray (D-WA), Olympia Snowe (R-ME), Susan Collins (R-ME), Mary Landrieu (D-LA), and Blanche L. Lincoln (D-AR).

The U.S. House of Representatives has had similar gains as a historic 60 women serve out of 435 seats in 2002. Overall, women represent 13.6 percent of Congress, and if this sounds like a small piece of the pie, keep in mind it is because women tend not to run for political office, and not because they don't win. Women have been making significant gains in the U.S. Congress as each election cycle progresses.

Statewide electoral politics are also seeing noteworthy gains in women's presence. In 2002, 88 women hold statewide elected executive offices across the country, or 27.4 percent of the 321 available positions. In 1998 in Arizona, five women were elected to the top state offices, including governor, secretary of state, treasurer, attorney general, and superintendent of public instruction. The same story can be told in state legislatures where women, in 2002, occupy 1,663, or 22.4 percent, of the 7,424 seats. According to the Center for American Women and Politics, since 1969 the number of women serving in state legislatures has increased fivefold.

Electoral politics is not the only realm where women are flexing their muscle. We are making headway in the business world. Throughout the twentieth century, many legal, economic, and social changes altered the employment landscape for American women, and revolutionized the way America does its business. Historians look back at the droves of women who entered into the workforce during World War II and credit them with breaking the iron grip of American trade unions, and giving a new lease on life to the economy. During the World War II era, women provided a more superior engine to the locomotive, theoretically speaking—better, faster, and more dependable. Women made the workforce more competitive, and everyone—most especially men—had to work harder in order to keep their jobs. American businesses recognized the value of women in the workforce, and this has become one of America's greatest secret weapons for economic prosperity.

Here's a snapshot of how women have exploded onto the business scene today: *Fortune* magazine states we are 46.5 percent of the labor force, 49.5 percent of managers and professionals, and 12.5 percent of corporate officers. According to the Department of Labor, from 1964 to 1999, for every two jobs added for men in government, five were added for women. For every two jobs in services and retail sales, three were added for women. During this time period, women's jobs doubled in every industry except manufacturing. And we're getting the education, too. According to the Department of Education, women now acquire more degrees in undergraduate and graduate school than men. In 1999, women represented 44 percent of the freshman class at Yale Medical School.

In addition to the gains women have made in the workforce, female entrepreneurs show more progress. The Center for Women's Business Research finds that the number of women-owned businesses continues to grow at twice the rate of all U.S. firms. In 2002, there are 6.2 million female-owned, privately held firms, employing more than 9.2 million people and gathering receipts of $1.5 trillion in sales. These figures are up 30 percent since 1997. Even more attention-grabbing is that the greatest growth in the number of women-owned firms is seen in the nontraditional career paths of construction and agricultural services, which had a gain of 36 and 27 percent, respectively. Women are starting businesses at twice the rate of men according to the National Foundation of Women Business Owners. So, what's all the whining about?

Many Democratic women, including my colleague, still lecture about women suffering in the workplace. Don't they understand that their monikers, including the "glass ceiling," "old boy network," and "sexual harassment," ends up harming women in the workplace? This negative perception actually discourages employers from hiring women in the first place, and holds women back from thinking they can progress beyond the first stumbling block that comes in their way. Men face stumbling blocks in their careers, too. When there is so much negative reporting about women's growth in corporate America, I suppose it is easy to fall prey to women's distortion of progress. Are there few women CEOs in corporate America? Yes, there are, but there are also few men, because it typically takes a master's of business administration (M.B.A.), and about thirty years of consistent work to grow anyone into a CEO. Thirty years ago women were just entering the professional workforce, and also dropped out to have children. Besides, most people don't have any desire to be a corporate CEO, and prefer to have a life more conducive for family with less of an interest to be married to a job. The bottom line is that women's progress in business and entrepreneurship in the short time we have been acting as full participants in the workforce is nothing short of monumental.

These triumphs in women's progress are also well documented in American popular media culture. Now, in all fairness, some might say that pop culture doesn't reflect women's business statistics, but rather chooses a media diet of women's figures, literally. We live in a society obsessed with body image and because we exist in a world dominated by American popular culture, this narrow-minded portrayal is transmitted everywhere. Sure, our leg-, breast-, and butt-obsessed culture is part of a path of least resistance—a dumbing down in America—as advertisers and promoters of sorts are fully cognizant that sex sells . . . and that will never change. This is not misogyny, as some liberal women may suggest . . . this is what makes money. But, if we look at the glass as half full instead of half empty we may just realize how empowering American women's depiction in pop culture really is. Across the board, communication mediums have not only revolutionized the American woman throughout the last five decades, but also have come full range in her portrayal—from housewife to powerhouse CEO—which reflects the various roles that women have the ability to choose from today.

In the early 1950s, when the small screen became a staple in every household, television advertising focused on women's role as domestic caregivers. In the late '60s and '70s, TV ads started showcasing women in the workplace, and some ads even portrayed women in activist roles when it was cool and intellectually provocative to have a cause of action. Charlie perfume ads in the '70s reflected the change in the way women were viewed. The ad conveyed, "Now, you can climb the corporate ladder, buy yourself perfume, and never have to wait for your husband to buy it for you ever again."

In the '80s, commercials advanced women from secretaries to executives so "the boys" of the workplace became her peers, not her bosses. Charlie perfume made a comeback in the late '80s and played up role reversals, where the woman dressed up in a man's business suit, carried a briefcase, and invaded the male colleague's space. In the '90s, Vice President Dan Quayle attacked television sitcoms like *Murphy Brown* for glamorizing the life of single motherhood. While Vice President Quayle may have been demonized for being "too provincial," he was right on the money, as our postfeminist era has shown a backlash against the antifamily crusade, and made it very "in vogue" for women to be married and either have a high-powered career or stay at home and raise her children. Supermodels like Cindy Crawford, mega-entertainers like Faith Hill, high-powered officials like former Massachusetts Governor Jane Swift, and countless others have opted for "true-to-self" careers, marriage, and babies.

If you want to carry your convictions forward, then surround yourself with positive role models. In 1989, I worked as a congressional staffer for Representative Ileana Ros-Lehtinen (R-FL), the first Cuban-American in Congress. At that time, there were two women in the U.S. Senate and twenty-nine women in the House, representing less than 6 percent of Congress. Ileana taught me three valuable life lessons. First, she instilled in me that anything is possible. Second, it doesn't matter how many men there are in the room, just keep your eye on the prize. Third, believe in yourself and what you're doing, work hard, and you will persevere.

After less than three years of working for Ileana, I received a political appointment in the first Bush administration at the U.S. Agency for International Development at the Department of State. I was the youngest policymaker in my office, and not once did I ever feel discriminated against because of my young age or gender. In fact, I found being a woman in the male-dominated world of foreign policy worked to my advantage. I worked hard, and believed in what I was doing. If I ever felt exhausted, I used Ileana as my model of a "just do it" trailblazer. Rep. Ileana Ros-Lehtinen had such a profound impact on my outlook in life and my place in the workforce. (Thanks, Ily!)

To the early role models like Elizabeth Cady Stanton and Lucretia Mott, who organized the women's rights convention in Seneca Falls, New York, on July 19, 1848, we are forever indebted. Just twenty-one years later in May 1869, Elizabeth Cady Stanton and Susan B. Anthony created the National Woman Suffrage Association in New York City, and Lucy Stone started the American Woman Suffrage Association to help define a women's liberation agenda and advocate to the nation that women were just as capable as men. These women and countless others exuded insurmountable courage and planted the seeds for generations of women's voices to be heard in American society. They even traveled abroad to radiate influence in other countries. They were a force to be reckoned with then, and laid the groundwork for women today.

Can we, as women, do better and make ourselves more visible around Congress or state legislatures, in corporate boardrooms, or have a greater impact on pop culture? Certainly, we can and need to. Look around, because while there is so much to be thankful for, there is always much more that needs to be done. September 11 taught us not to take our egalitarian society for granted. Get involved and become active in issues on the local, statewide, and national levels. Contact your local women's volunteer group such as the Junior League, or another nonprofit organization of interest, and find out how you can give an hour a month to help someone get back on their feet.

If you read in your local paper about a bill before your state senate that you vehemently oppose, do something! Don't just sit on your duff and complain when the bill passes your state legislature and is signed into law by your governor. Start a letter campaign or petition, set up a meeting with your local officials or their aides, or write a letter to the editor in your local newspaper. Don't wait until April 15 to express your outrage over the excessively taxed society we live in; Congress wants to hear your views. So does President George W. Bush. As a former legislative aide in Congress, I know how much letters, e-mails, and phone calls influence the way a member of Congress votes. If your member of Congress or state representatives do not hear from you, they have no way of knowing how you feel.

If you do something, you may just make a difference like seventeen-year-old Leah Kuchinsky. She drafted a bill for the 2002 session of the Virginia General Assembly that would require Virginia's health care providers to report to police if they suspect a patient might be involved in terrorism. Leah's idea evolved over the dinner table months before the September 11 attacks. She vetted her idea with scientists and counterterrorism experts and drafted the bill. "I've been raised with the belief that you can change the world for the better," Leah said. And, to you, Leah, I say, "You are an inspiration to us all!"

1

EQUAL PAY

DEBORAH PERRY

A couple of years ago, Julianne and I had a contract negotiation with television producer, and now friend, Beth Mandel. We were somewhat familiar with Beth's credibility in the television production business (I had worked with her on *The McLaughlin Group* when I was a guest), and we wanted to meet with her about working on our television pilot, *A Room Full of Women*™, which we were shooting at the 2000 political conventions in Philadelphia and Los Angeles.

Beth came to the meeting armed with notepad and pen and rapidly took notes as we fired away over the layout of the production. In less than twenty minutes, Beth emphatically stated that she wanted to work with us. And, before Julianne and I got to say a word, Beth said, "And with regards to the money, I want $15,000 for the month, plus my expenses paid to Philadelphia and Los Angeles." If I could have replayed that moment, I am sure that my mouth must have dropped, as our budget for a producer peaked out at $7,500. To make a long story short, after some hard back-and-forth negotiations with Beth, we hired her and ever so slightly negotiated her down. I can say that Julianne and I are robust negotiators, and

Beth, to her credit, did not back down from knowing her financial worth to the project.

About a year later, I reminded Beth about that negotiation conversation. I asked her if she was always that fervent in her contract dealings. With an air of candidness, she replied, "Oh, I was easy on you guys. I am usually much tougher. We had so little time to put that pilot together, and it was just a win-win for everyone to just move forward." This time, I am sure I raised an eyebrow, as I would not describe our negotiations as easy by any means. "What are your strategies for getting what you want?" I asked. Beth's response went something like this: "What I first do is assess the character of the people I am negotiating with, and figure out how far they're willing to go, and who between the two of us is going to hold our cards closest to the table. Once I've assessed that, then it becomes a barometer for me as to how far I can go in my negotiating tactics. Often, timing is more of a factor than anything, and if I feel that a deal will be lost by too much maneuvering, I'm willing to make a little less to do a deal I find important."

Because Beth Mandel works as an independent producer, she does not have to subject herself to the in-house politics of negotiations between the employee and employer, which tend to favor the employer more often than not. However, she is constantly on the front lines and has to negotiate fee-based contracts for herself all the time. My point is that Beth is characteristic of the very few women and men who know what they want, believe in themselves, and go for it.

Unlike the Beth Mandels of the world, there remains a widespread belief among many liberal women that their contribution and worth in the workforce is somewhat less than men's. It is this counterproductive mindset that allows many women to settle on the first employment offer they receive rather than negotiate for what they want or hold out for another job that provides higher pay or greater flexibility.

While there was a time in history when it was socially acceptable to pay women less than a male in the same position with the same level of education and experience, women's median earnings have risen over 14 percent since 1979. Men's median earnings, on the other hand, have dropped

7 percent during that same period. And, as older women who have less education and experience continue to retire, younger women who have greater opportunities than their mothers could have dreamed of are now virtually equal to their male counterparts. You have to ask to get in life. So, if you feel you deserve a higher salary or hourly wages—ask for it! Besides, employers know that unequal pay is against the law, and being sued for gender discrimination is too costly—in more ways than just financial—for any company.

UNEQUAL PAY IS ILLEGAL

Prior to the 1963 passage of the Equal Pay Act, it was socially acceptable for men to be the breadwinners and heads of household, and therefore they were entitled to make more money. Only one state, Wyoming, had enacted equal pay legislation for state employees in 1869. While many other states did pass minimum wage laws for women, the U.S. Supreme Court declared it unconstitutional in *Adkins v. Children's Hospital* in 1923.

At the recommendation of the Commission on the Status of Women, Congress passed the Equal Pay Act, which protected women from workplace discrimination. It made it illegal to pay unequal wages to uniformly qualified workers who performed the exact same job, and prohibited employers from lowering the wages of one sex in order to avoid raising the wages of the other sex. The only circumstances where exceptions in the law could be made were in the differences of a worker's seniority, merit, or production output. Otherwise, women were granted equal parity in pay.

Women have advanced enormously since the passage of the Equal Pay Act and Title VII of the Civil Rights Act of 1964, which also protected women from workplace discrimination and set up the Equal Employment Opportunity Commission (EEOC). This government agency provides women and men the opportunity to file a complaint if they believe they have been discriminated against. Since the EEOC started compiling statistics in 1986, discrimination charges under the Equal Pay Act have fallen by 20 percent, and only about 18 percent of the Equal Pay Act charges resulted in a liable settlement. Irrespective of the antidiscriminatory laws in place in our judicial system, one assumption continues to be heavily mulled over in liberal women's circles—the infamous wage gap.

THE "SEVENTY-SIX CENTS TO THE DOLLAR" MYTH

Seventy-six cents, sixty-four cents, fifty-five cents; it's like a cheerleading chant, but it's not. It is the mantra of many liberal women who seem to relish in misrepresenting comparative statistics of a woman's dollar to a man's dollar. Enough already! Let me tell you why these statistics are so off base, not to mention damaging to the credibility of women's progress. Consider the Department of Labor statistics, which these women so frequently refer to, stating that in the year 2000 women earned seventy-six cents to the man's dollar. First of all, the report compares men and women's wages listing a small handful of occupations such as waiter and waitresses or manicurist, which is fallible considering the thousands of career positions available in our workforce.

Second, in an unbelievable misstep, the study only contrasts women and men's earnings, and does not incorporate factors such as the differences and types of education, experience and tenure, ages, special training and skills, and time away from the workforce to raise children that would all account for differences in salaries. For example, in the position of accountant, the study found that women averaged 72.4 percent of a man's earnings, and does not state the percentage of master's degrees for either the men or the women or their respective years in the workforce. No worthy economist in the world who studies the wage gap would draw a comparison without examining the differentials in a person's background.

When comparing apples to apples, and adjustments for qualifications are considered, women earn ninety-eight cents on the man's dollar, according to the National Longitudinal Survey of Youth for childless people ages 27–33. It is true that some women's salaries may be lower than that of a man's because the average woman has less work experience, and typically chooses a job to give her greater flexibility for family responsibilities. But, no one is twisting women's arms into lower-paying careers. The fact is that 80 percent of women bear children at some point in their lives, and unless we choose for men to stay at home and care for the children, many women take years out of their careers. In addition, according to Diana Furchtgott-Roth and Dr. Christine Stobla, of the Independent Women's Forum, women are five times as likely to change careers, and don't stay around long enough to grow from within a given firm. This is not discrimination . . . this is freedom of choice.

STILL NOT HAPPY . . . SO NOW YOU WANT COMPARABLE WORTH?

So with their "wage gap" moniker intact, liberal women now lobby Congress for "comparable worth" or "pay equity" legislation, otherwise known as wage setting. This means that these liberal women want the bloated bureaucracy of government to rank dissimilar occupations and calculate each job's value. And just who is qualified to determine which job is worth what? The president? The secretary of labor or defense? Democrats believe that the wages of a female-dominated occupation, such as a manicurist, should be artificially inflated to those of a male-dominated job such as a construction foreman just to make their pay equal. Does this not jettison the free market principles on which this country is based and move more toward a socialist way of governing?

This is one of the more ridiculous ideas I've heard and has been continuously tested and rejected in our courts. Even officials in Canada and the United Kingdom, where comparable worth policies have been tried, state that attempts by the government to determine the intrinsic worth of any job undermines the laws of supply and demand and ultimately leads to lower rates of employment for women.

So with these facts in mind, these liberal women are not advocating equal pay for equal work. If employers were forced to pay female-dominated positions beyond what the market bears, then few women would get hired in the first place. Like a centrally controlled economy, comparable worth denies the course of supply and demand. Even absent market forces, the idea of setting equality to different jobs is arbitrary, and it is impossible to set standards as few jobs ever remain stagnant. Comparable worth actually works against women, as it assumes a woman is incapable of doing a job on her own, and needs special protections to be effective in the workforce.

THE FREEDOM TO CHOOSE

Luckily, we live not in a socialist state, but in a great democracy, allowing us the freedom to choose. There are also times when a woman or a man may have to make employment choices based on life-changing circumstances. For example, someone may choose to take a less demanding job with less pay because of the birth of a child or to care for an ailing parent. Other times, we may be going through an economic recession and are forced to take any position we can get. I, on two occasions, in my first job and in a new city, have accepted positions for less pay because it was beneficial for my long-term career goals.

My first job, as a congressional staffer on Capitol Hill, paid $17,000 a year. As a receptionist for a U.S. Senator, entry-level salaries were low regardless of your gender, where you went to college, who your parents were, or your political affiliation. We political wanna-bes would do just about anything for a $17,000-a-year receptionist position for a U.S. Senator. I struggled to make ends meet and worked a second job to helped ease the financial pressures of monthly living expenses. Looking back, I would not have changed a thing because this one job was my purview to want to reach for the stars.

Later in my career, I accepted a position with lower pay due to the special circumstances of moving to a new city and needing to be settled.

I took the first low-paying job I was offered at a philanthropic foundation. But that was my legitimate choice, and I could have waited for higher-paying employment opportunities. Notwithstanding, the contacts that I made in this particular position—at very low pay—helped me to foster other relationships, which then catapulted my career in other directions. At that point in my work life, surrounding myself in an environment with individuals who stimulated my mind and inspired me to new heights was more important to me than any salary differential I could have been making in a higher-paying position.

Women's dramatic gains in the workforce over the last three decades are well documented, but you have to wonder how much more women would have progressed absent the liberal cries for further government action. The argument of wage discrimination marketed by liberal women is a deliberate scare tactic and underestimates the choices and rights women have in the workplace and the home. Sometimes wage discrimination is often blamed when we truly don't have the same level of experience as the person in the next office.

While cries about "wage gap" continue to sound loudly, it tends to cause women to think they are pitiful, weak beings, and are incapable of fighting for what they want. Do we really need big government to protect us from big, strong men? We have tremendous free market opportunities in this country, and if we want to get ahead in life, then we have to get the best education possible, and work hard throughout our entire careers. Striving for comparable worth policies and artificially inflating women's wages is not the answer, but taking responsibility for oneself is.

While on a press trip in Jamaica, Beth Mandel and I got into a rousing, competitive game of Ping-Pong. I already knew Beth was a resilient negotiator, but I did not know how competitive she is in Ping-Pong (and I'm a pretty good Ping-Pong player myself). While she was whipping my butt, I inadvertently swung at the Ping-Pong ball as if it were more of a racquetball, and that sucker drove high into the jungle backdrop behind Beth. But that didn't stop Beth. She then proceeded to swipe the Ping-Pong ball from the table next to us where there were three young boys taking a momentary break from their Ping-Pong game. The boys and I looked at each other in complete disbelief. Again my mouth dropped and Beth said, "Look, it's not how you play the game, it's all about winning." At that point, we promptly returned the ball to its rightful users and ran away laughing.

RESOURCES FOR THE RIGHT

INDEPENDENT WOMEN'S FORUM
This organization affirms women's participation in and contributions to a free, self-governing society.
P.O. Box 3058
Arlington, VA 22203-0058
703-558-4991
www.iwf.org

EMPLOYMENT POLICY INSTITUTE
This organization provides high-quality research and education on living standards of working people in order to promote a prosperous, fair, and sustainable economy.
1775 Pennsylvania Avenue, NW
Washington, DC 20006
202-463-7650
www.epinet.org

NATIONAL INSTITUTE FOR LABOR RELATIONS RESEARCH
This organization's primary function is to act as a research facility for the general public, scholars, and students on labor relations.
5211 Port Royal Road
Suite 510
Springfield, VA 22151
703-321-9606
www.nilrr.org

JULIANNE MALVEAUX

When I teach seminar classes, I love the strands of conversation that are woven into a quilt of exploration. I enjoy the flow, the dialogue, and also the discordance that sometimes comes when opinions collide. Sometimes my mind sees the conversation in colors, red for conflict, soothing green for concurrence. When a conversation is rich enough, my mind wanders and comes back; the rich quilt is my reward for the facilitating that I'm doing.

I taught a "Women and Work" class one year at San Francisco State University, and it was one of the most rewarding classes I ever taught. It stands out in my mind because of the differences between the women (and one man) enrolled in the class. The youngest student was nineteen, the oldest over sixty. They were African American, Latino, Asian, Caucasian, and Native American. Almost all were opinionated, and even the most reticent would venture to say something during the weekly three hours we spent together.

We'd just finished digesting labor market statistics and reading a set of articles on equal pay, and had saved the last hour of class for discussion. I perched on the edge of the desk, anticipating meaty conversation from this diverse group. I liked all my students but was especially drawn to Vera, a sixty-something white woman who, with four grown children, had worked as a waitress, a telephone operator, and a teacher's aide. Vera was thick around the middle, had a shock of gray hair, and meaty hands that reflected her life of hard work. After her husband's death, with an unexpected insurance windfall, she'd decided to earn the bachelor's degree she couldn't get four decades before. She tackled every reading suggestion I made by devouring professional journals and pulp fiction with equal enthusiasm. And she added a needed voice of experience and realism to classroom discussions.

I was least drawn to a young, white woman who was a nineteen-year-old senior on a determined path to graduate school. She was as smart as Vera, but much less enthusiastic, frequently wondering aloud why some selections had made it to the reading list. Kathy was a slight girl who almost always wore pressed jeans, a silk blouse, a matching blazer, and brown loafers. Vera and Kathy were the poles in the room, and depending on the topic, students seemed to gravitate between one and the other. I worked hard to not favor either in discussion, but a betting student could have had a hunch that Vera's words carried more weight with me.

We were talking about the issue of unequal pay and Kathy, naive as ever, asserted that no one could be exploited unless they allowed themselves to be. She gave a great set of examples of individuals who had been able to bargain their way to a fair pay deal and suggested that women should emulate them, and "stop whining." In the three or four minutes she spoke, she scolded me for skewing the reading toward my own ideological point of view and suggested that students read writings by conservative women who denied a pay gap. I struggled to respond gently, conscious of the fact a sharp retort wouldn't be fair in the teacher-student context. Before I could say a word, though, Vera growled in, with a laugh as guttural as some "down-home blues." She literally growled for ten or fifteen seconds, then wiped tears from her eyes as if she had nearly bust a gut with her laughter. Students looked at her as if she'd lost her mind, wondering why she'd been so amused by Kathy's comment.

"Sometimes," Vera told Kathy, "I can tell that you've not lived long, and that you've read too many books. When you go to work as a waitress, you don't sit and bargain with the people over whether you'll get two dollars or two and a half dollars an hour. Usually you take what you are offered, because you need to work. The phone company posts their pay, and it has already been collectively bargained. The jobs aren't bad jobs, and the benefits are decent, but they'd as soon hire me as hire you, so if I want to stand out like a sore thumb and pass up on a good job opportunity, I'll start haggling about my pay. High-profile individuals with unique skills can bargain for their money, but those of us who are seen as cogs in a wheel, interchangeable, don't have that opportunity."

Despite my ideology, I had some sympathy with Kathy's point. I always tell women that the most powerful words in a negotiation are "Is that all?" People will offer you anything, but if you are properly situated, you don't have to take it. As a speaker, I get calls every day from someone who thinks that I should talk for free because I'm black, female, progressive, and committed. I have to remind them, most of the time, that I talk for a living, and committed politics don't put food on my table. When they come up with a small honorarium, the words "Is that all?" often push them to another level.

That's fine for me, but Vera had a point, too. I don't see a former welfare recipient, being pushed to find employment, any employment, having the freedom to ask, "Is that all?" She pretty much has to take what she can get, and in some cases be glad for it. I love the flow of a seminar, the way people build on each other's ideas and use their experiences to see the many ways that women approach issues.

A discussion of the pay gap has to have some flow. Women's employment differences are shaped by class, race, occupation, opportunity, and family circumstance. Women with children often have less flexibility than those who are childless. Those with hierarchical status (read corporate executives) get concessions that others don't. It was delicious to watch Massachusetts Lt. Governor Jane Swift bring her twins to cribs in her State House office. But it was also sobering to note that she didn't favor the same kind of flexible work arrangements for state employees that she enjoyed herself. This is, perhaps, a comment that might be better made in another chapter, but when we talk about the pay gap, it's about the flow, about the work women do, the way they are paid, and the inherent discrimination in the pay scale.

THE WAGE GAP

Here's the wage gap in a nutshell. Using the most recent data from the Bureau of Labor Statistics, men who work full-time, full-year earn $646 per week, while women with the same work schedule earn $491 per week, or 76 percent of what men earn. According to the Institute for Women's Policy Research these numbers vary by state, with women in Washington, D.C., earning a high 85.7 percent of what men earn, while women in Louisiana earn a paltry 64.8 percent of what men earn. According to the Economic Policy Institute, more than a quarter of all white women, more than a third of African-American women, and fully half of Latina women work full-time and still earn wages that fall below the poverty line. Many of these women have children and head households, but they can't get equal pay.

OCCUPATIONAL SEGREGATION

Those who can't quite see a pay gap will tell you that the reason that women earn unequal pay is because they work in different jobs than men do. So some suggest that women should work in different jobs. We should. Meanwhile, though, occupational segregation is a way of life for working women, who are more likely to work as secretaries or administrative support workers than any other occupation, a fact that has not changed in three decades. Women, especially poor, immigrant women, are also heavily represented as food, health, and cleaning service workers, and in light manufacturing. Their bargaining power in these occupations is low, though somewhat enhanced by their membership in unions. When women are part of collective bargaining organizations, their pay level jumps by 30 percent over women in the same occupations who are not unionized. Thus, the conservative exhortation that women should ask for more money is best actualized at the bottom when women join unions.

Women's wages typically increase when they leave segregated occupations, but the dynamics of supply and demand too often constrain women to typically female jobs: Flexibility in certain jobs, for example, is appealing to women who need to work but who want to be with their kids as well. While it is likely that the pay range of certain jobs would change if they were largely occupied by men, the dynamics of occupational shift do not

TABLE 1

The Gender Wage Gap

Earnings Ratio Between Women and Men Employed Full-time Year-round 1997

STATE	PERCENT	RANK	STATE	PERCENT	RANK
Alabama	68.8%	41	Montana	68.9%	40
Alaska	74.1%	17	Nebraska	71.4%	29
Arizona	79.0%	5	Nevada	74.1%	17
Arkansas	72.5%	23	New Hampshire	70.2%	34
California	78.7%	6	New Jersey	70.0%	37
Colorado	74.5%	15	New Mexico	70.2%	34
Connecticut	75.2%	12	New York	79.3%	4
Delaware	71.3%	30	North Carolina	75.2%	12
District of Columbia	85.7%	1	North Dakota	69.6%	39
Florida	76.7%	8	Ohio	70.7%	32
Georgia	76.7%	25	Oklahoma	74.1%	17
Hawaii	83.8%	2	Oregon	67.7%	46
Idaho	74.8%	14	Pennsylvania	71.5%	27
Illinois	68.7%	42	Rhode Island	68.6%	44
Indiana	66.7%	48	South Carolina	68.7%	42
Iowa	76.4%	9	South Dakota	70.9%	31
Kansas	70.2%	34	Tennessee	70.7%	32
Kentucky	72.7%	21	Texas	76.4%	9
Louisiana	64.8%	50	Utah	64.9%	49
Maine	72.7%	21	Vermont	73.8%	20
Maryland	79.8%	3	Virginia	69.9%	38
Massachusetts	77.6%	7	Washington	74.4%	16
Michigan	67.4%	47	West Virginia	72.1%	26
Minnesota	72.4%	24	Wisconsin	68.6%	44
Mississippi	71.5%	27	Wyoming	62.8%	51
Missouri	75.4%	11	United States	73.5%	

suggest that such changes would take place immediately. Thus, many look at the issue of pay equity, or comparable worth, to deal with the unequal pay status of working women. Instead of equal pay for equal work, should we be concerned with equal pay for jobs of equal value? In other words, should tree trimmers be paid more than registered nurses, or guards in a men's prison more than guards in a women's prison? Many suggest that "the market" should determine what wages are paid, but markets are as flawed as the bargaining process, and all too often, it is not markets but complex civil service systems and job evaluation studies that determine wages. In these cases, often, the "compensable factors" of a job are quantified and measured, with workplace characteristics such as caring for people more likely to be found in typically female jobs devalued by the biases that recursively undervalue women's work.

It is especially troubling to look at pay levels in jobs that require caring for people. Home health aids, for example, earn an average of $8.71 an hour. They take care of our parents and grandparents, and enable those of us who have home caretaking responsibilities to maintain our productive jobs when they relieve us of those duties. Yet if these home health workers attempt to support a family, they will find themselves hard-pressed to do it at the level of pay they earn. Our societal rhetoric suggests that we value both children and elders, yet we pay those who care for them a pittance. We describe these jobs as "unskilled" to justify low levels of pay, but anyone who observes a caring worker feeding an incapacitated elderly person would be hard-pressed to suggest that this work is unskilled.

Because so many women hold low-wage jobs, "living wage" campaigns have been a centerpiece of economic justice programs spearheaded by the AFL-CIO and other organizations. A living wage is defined as a wage that yields an above-poverty-line wage for a full-time worker. The wage varies from city to city, but is usually between $6.50 and $8.50 an hour. Economist Chauna Brocht noted that there were more than 162,000 federal contract workers—about 11 percent of the total—who earned less than a living wage. Women can get involved in this fair pay issue by working with groups like ACORN and the AFL-CIO on living wage campaigns. Contact information for these organizations is given at the end of this chapter.

In attempting to explain the wage gap, econometricians have controlled for length of time in the labor force, occupation, and other factors, and generally found that they can explain away about two-thirds of the wage gap with a statistical process that suggests that if women were in the work-force longer (that is, beginning to work during high school like many boys or not taking maternity leave during and after pregnancy), or worked in different occupations, they would earn more. How, then, do they explain that part of the wage gap for which they can't control? Some economists call the unexplained portion the "discrimination coefficient" and suggest this part of the difference is solely a function of gender. While the entire wage gap needs to be addressed, this part of the wage gap should merit particular consideration.

It is also important to note that within occupations women have occupied for many years, women too often earn less than men do. Some of this, undoubtedly, is due to the difference in bargaining skills that women have. Some studies of managers suggest that while women are more likely to take the first job offered, men are likely to bargain, even at entry level. But there also seems to be an element of discrimination in pay, at the bottom and at the top. Our government has been very concerned with the wages of executive women, empaneling a Glass Ceiling Commission when Lynn Martin was labor secretary in 1991. This commission was charged with looking at job advancement and unequal pay at the top, but most women faced a sticky floor, or low-wage work, at the bottom. While many women celebrate whenever a new woman is inducted into the small sorority of executive women, there will be much more to celebrate when wages are raised for women at the bottom.

To this end, it is important to consider how low the minimum wage is, and to understand the impact of the minimum wage on working women. Nearly ten million people earn the minimum wage. More than 70 percent of them are adults, contrary to the myth that most minimum wage workers are teens. Nearly 60 percent are women, and these women are disproportionately black and brown. Many head households. A full-time, full-year minimum-wage worker earns $10,700 a year, much less than the federal poverty line for a household head and two children.

Who earns poverty-level wages? According to Table 2, low-wage earners include waiters and waitresses, maids, hairdressers, home health aides, teacher aides, and nursing aides. The majority of the jobs in Table 2 are jobs that are mostly held by women. These are jobs that provide care for our children and elderly parents, but "the market" values these jobs so poorly that those who work in them must scramble to make ends meet. Of course, an alternative explanation is that many of the people who hold these jobs have few options in other parts of the labor market. Notably, economists argue that labor shortages push up wages, but while demand for home health aides far exceeds supply, with five hundred thousand more people needed in that occupation in the next decade, wages have not risen to accommodate increased demand.

The issue of unequal pay is linked to the jobs women hold, and while women can seek education and training to change their employment profile in the long run, in the short run it makes sense for policymakers to increase the minimum wage and pay attention to the terms and conditions of low-wage work.

THE LAW—EQUAL PAY AND COMPARABLE WORTH

Before Congress passed the Equal Pay Act in 1963, it was legal for employers to pay men and women who did exactly the same job, with exactly the same job title, a different wage. How did employers justify it? Often single working women were told they didn't "need" the money that a "family man" needed. Also, there was a pervasive secrecy about pay levels that many could not "prove" that they were receiving unequal pay. (I often joke that Americans would rather tell someone how many times they had sex last week than how much money they make. I wonder why.)

The passage of the Equal Pay Act didn't make things immediately equal. Indeed, the Equal Employment Opportunity Commission is still routinely called in to enforce equal pay laws, having received 1,270 equal pay claims in 2000. One of the ways that employers get around equal pay laws

TABLE 2

OCCUPATIONS WITH HALF OR MORE OF THE WORKERS PAID POVERTY LEVEL WAGES

OCCUPATIONS	MEDIAN WAGE	OCCUPATIONS	MEDIAN WAGE
Waiters and Waitresses	$5.85	Hotel Desk Clerks	$7.29
Cooks in Fast Food	$5.99	Stock Clerks	$7.31
Farm Workers (Crops)	$6.02	Funeral Home Attendants	$7.34
Manicurists	$6.49	Motion Picture Projectionists	$7.41
Cashiers	$6.58	Sewers (Hand)	$7.46
Child Care Workers	$6.61	Guides	$7.46
Parking Lot Attendants	$6.69	Taxi Drivers/Chauffeurs	$7.48
Maids	$6.85	Cannery Workers	$7.56
Service Station Attendants	$6.90	Sales Persons in Retail	$7.61
Cooks (Short Order)	$6.92	Janitors and Cleaners	$7.66
Vehicle Washers	$6.99	Cooks in Restaurants	$7.81
Hand Packers and Packagers	$6.99	Home Health Aides	$7.81
Pressers (Hand)	$7.09	Meat Cutters and Trimmers	$7.82
Sewing Machine Operators	$7.09	Teacher Aides	$7.83
Personal/Home Care Aides	$7.17	Recreational Workers	$7.93
Crossing Guards	$7.18	Nursing Aides	$7.99
Hairdressers	$7.28		

is to give jobs held by men and those held by women different titles. In Lynn, Massachusetts, for example, women custodians at the public schools were called "house workers," and their jobs were to clean the schools, wash lunch tables, mop floors, and scrub toilets. Their male coworkers, called "junior custodians" were paid $1.50 more per hour for the same duties. That $1.50 an hour adds up to more than $3,000 a year! No wonder women house cleaners sued. It took a year for the Lynn public schools to take the women seriously and settle their case out of court. This is hardly an isolated incident. According to writer Anne Driscoll, the Equal Pay Act is "little known and underutilized." Further, it is time-consuming and costly for workers to tackle employers through litigation.

The law mandates equal pay, but not comparable worth—equal pay for jobs of equal value. The comparable worth movement gained popularity in the 1980s after the extent of occupational segregation made it clear that women could not close the pay gap without closing the occupational gap unless comparable pay measures were implemented. Several states and municipalities have done pay equity studies and passed comparable pay legislation, but momentum for this legislation has slowed in recent years. Research by the Institute for Women's Policy Research buttresses the concept of comparable worth. Their data show that if single mothers were paid the same as men for work of comparable worth, they'd see a pay adjustment of $4,459, and their poverty rates would drop from 15.3 percent to 12.6 percent. This is the argument for equal pay—when women are paid equally, they are able to support themselves and their children, rely less on government, and reduce their poverty levels.

Today, most women work in the paid labor force and many, especially at the bottom, experience pay discrimination. Yet these women do the "backbone" jobs in our society, caring for children and seniors, and staffing those service industries (food, health) that provide essential services for all of us. In order for women to get their due in the labor market, equal pay laws must be enforced and comparable worth laws must be implemented. Educational access for women should also be improved, since the more education women have, the more they tend to earn. Finally, women should be encouraged to consider nontraditional employment and pursue union organizing (which improves pay). While women can certainly hone their bargaining skills, it will take more than bargaining skills to root pay discrimination out of the workplace.

Some discrimination is pernicious. A discussion of occupational segregation reminds us that women are often paid differently when they are
doing different, but equally valuable, work as men. Sometimes, though,
employers violate the Equal Pay Act and pay women less money to do the
same job men do. Why? Because they can get away with it. People don't
much like to talk about their pay. Because women don't tend to bargain,
often accepting the first pay offer they get. Because some folks don't realize
that we are in the twenty-first century, and they've yet to check their biases
at the door. When women and men doing the exact same work are paid
differently, it's lawsuit time. Unfortunately, too many women don't want to
go to court, and go through the process for addressing pay discrimination
that is often cumbersome and time-consuming. The Equal Employment
Opportunity Commission litigates less than 4 percent of the complaints
that are filed with it. Many women who are discriminated prefer to move
on than to fight.

But fight we must, because when women fight they change the terms
and conditions of work for other women, and make it more difficult for
employers to discriminate. Plus they send a warning signal—when companies see women getting six- and seven-figure judgments because of discrimination, they think twice before they pay men more than they pay
women (or they come up with elaborate justifications). Because so many
families depend on women's pay for survival, we simply can't afford to
accept pay discrimination in any form or fashion.

That's why updates to the 1963 Equal Pay Act are especially important.
In 2002, thirty-two bills in sixteen states have been introduced to prohibit
wage discrimination, allow the state to penalize companies, require pay
equity for female state government employees, and institute an equal pay
study. Many states recognize April 13 as equal pay day, since women must
work that long into a second year to earn as much as men do in just one
year. You can get involved in equal pay efforts in your state by hooking up
with groups like the National Committee on Pay Equity or the AFL-CIO's
Working Women's Department listed below.

RESOURCES FOR THE LEFT

NOW: THE NATIONAL ORGANIZATION FOR WOMEN

"NOW is dedicated to making legal, political, social, and economic changes in our society in order to achieve our goal, which is to eliminate sexism and end all oppression."

733 15th Street, NW
2nd Floor
Washington, DC 20005
202-628-8NOW (8669)
www.now.org

NATIONAL WOMEN'S POLITICAL CAUCUS

"The purpose of the National Women's Political Caucus is to increase women's participation in the political process and to identify, recruit, train, and support pro-choice women for election and appointment to public office."

1630 Connecticut Avenue, NW
Suite 201
Washington, DC 20009
202-785-1100
www.nwpc.org

FUND FOR A FEMINIST MAJORITY (FMF)

"The Feminist Majority Foundation, which was founded in 1987, is a cutting-edge organization dedicated to women's equality, reproductive health, and nonviolence."

1600 Wilson Boulevard
Suite 801
Arlington, VA 22209
703-522-2214
www.feminist.org

THIRD WAVE

"Through grant-making, networking, and public education, Third Wave informs and empowers a generation of young women activists. We support young women activists whose innovative social change strategies are often overlooked elsewhere."

116 East 16th Street

7th Floor

New York, NY 10003

212-388-1898

www.thirdwavefoundation.org

NATIONAL CONGRESS OF BLACK WOMEN

"The National Congress of Black Women, Inc., recognizes the need for a nonpartisan political organization that addresses the aspirations and concerns of the African-American community, with special attention to the unique and particular needs of African-American women and youth . . ."

8401 Colesville Road

Suite 400

Silver Spring, MD 20910

301-562-8000

www.npcbw.org

CENTER FOR WOMEN POLICY STUDIES

The Center's "multiethnic and multicultural feminist research, policy analysis, and advocacy bring women's diverse voices to important debates—on women and AIDS, violence against women and girls, welfare reform, access to health care, educational equity, work/family and workplace diversity policies, reproductive rights and health, and much more."

1211 Connecticut Avenue

Suite 312

Washington, DC 20036

202-872-1770

www.centerwomenpolicy.org

CENTER FOR POLICY ALTERNATIVES

The Center for Policy Alternatives is a nonpartisan organization that develops progressive policy models and model legislation for states. The Equal Pay Remedies and Enforcement Act is an especially useful model legislation.

1875 Connecticut Avenue, NW

Suite 710

Washington, DC 20009

202-387-6030

www.stateaction.org

AFL-CIO WORKING WOMEN'S DEPARTMENT

Led by former Women's Bureau Director and 9to5 founder Karen Nessbaum, the AFL-CIO Working Women's Department disseminates data and organizes women around equal pay and other issues.

815 16th Street, NW

Washington, DC 20006

202-637-5000

www.aflcio.org/women

9TO5: NATIONAL ASSOCIATION OF WORKING WOMEN

9to5: National Association of Working Women is the nation's largest nonprofit membership organization of working women and has more than twenty chapters and members in all fifty states. For over twenty-five years, 9to5 has organized to end sexual harassment and discrimination and to win better wages, working conditions, and family-friendly policies.

231 West Wisconsin Avenue

Suite 900

Milwaukee, WI 53203-2308
414-274-09251
www.9to5.org

INSTITUTE FOR WOMEN'S POLICY RESEARCH
Think tank on women's issues.
1707 L Street, NW
Suite 750
Washington, DC 20036
202-785-5100
www.iwpr.org

NATIONAL COMMITTEE ON PAY EQUITY (NCPE)
The National Committee on Pay Equity (NCPE), founded in 1979, is
the national membership coalition of over eighty organizations, including labor unions; women's and civil rights organizations; religious, professional, education, and legal associations; commissions on women,
state and local pay equity coalitions; and individual women and men
working to eliminate sex- and race-based wage discrimination and to
achieve pay equity.
3420 Hamilton Street
Suite 200
Hyattsville, MD 20782
301-277-1033
www.feminist.com/fairpay.htm

2

WORK AND FAMILY

JULIANNE MALVEAUX

Veteran television and radio personality Bev Smith is one of my favorite people. A Black Entertainment Television (BET) staple for several years, Bev now burns the midnight oil at American Urban Radio, spinning her special blend of wit, policy analysis, and cutting-edge interviews. Most of the time I could just sit back and listen to Bev, but every now and then she rattles my cage. Especially when she harks back to the "good old days."

I remember her saying once, "Kids today are a lot less disciplined than we were. But then we knew better than to act up. Because if Miss Sally saw you, she'd come off her porch and whack you one, and then she'd call your mother and tell her, and you'd go home to face another whipping." The image Bev recalls of close-knit, intertwined communities all looking out for each other is a wonderful one. Since she is looking through rose-colored lenses tinted by nostalgia, she's skewed the past, making the "good old days" seems sweet and special, and not nearly as trying as they were way back then.

Miss Sally was probably home because she couldn't find employment or because she was working just a couple of days a week. Mama probably *wasn't* home, instead she was working in somebody's kitchen. After all, back in Bev Smith's good old days of the 1950s, nearly 70 percent of African-American women were maids. So, the good old days were good for some folks, but not for everyone. Bev's not the only American with a bad case of the good-ole-days blues. Conservative women hark back to the days of Ozzie and Harriet to conjure up an image of ideal families. But what's so ideal about an all-knowing father, and a rather inappropriately dressed mother (pearls while cooking—give me a break!) whose suburban life, quiet as it's kept, is a tax-subsidized, segregated invention. Back in the good old days, many women didn't work, most people of color were discriminated against, gay and lesbian folks had to hide in the closet, and white men ruled the roost. Good old days? For whom?

Ozzie and Harriet hit the airwaves in 1952 and stayed there for another fourteen years. They spawned copycat white-bread families, the Andersons of *Father Knows Best, Leave it to Beaver*'s Cleavers, and *The Donna Reed Show*'s Stone family. From where I sit these television programs were a media expression of wishful thinking regarding patriarchal suburban contentment. They were so out of step with the way people lived, that even as these shows were being broadcast, Betty Friedan was writing her groundbreaking book, *The Feminine Mystique*, which challenged the myth that most middle-class American women were content to be homemakers. From a survey of graduates of Smith College, her alma mater, Friedan wrote of "the problem that has no name," the feeling of personal worthlessness that comes when women accept a role that requires an intellectual, economic, and emotional reliance on their husbands. Many credit *The Feminine Mystique* with launching the feminist movement. Certainly those who would click their heels three times and go back to the days of Ozzie and Harriet need to both get a grip and a reminder that things aren't always what they seem.

The Ozzie and Harriet model of a working dad and stay-at-home mom was never a reality for all families. A construct called the "family wage" or a wage that would allow a man to support a family, was available for most, but not all, unionized or professional white men. Men of color, on the other hand, did not have access to such well-paid employment, which pushed about half of married African-American women into the labor force in the 1950s. Working-class white women who were widowed or divorced also worked, and those who were married to "ne'er-do-well" men had no choice but work to support themselves and their children. Of course these women worked without benefit of the Equal Pay Act, without the few social supports for working families offered in our society today. Instead, they cobbled together childcare arrangements, using relatives and friends to take care of children after school—and widows and divorcées were often urged to remarry as soon as possible.

My own mom was divorced when I was six, and worked at the post office for a time because that work paid better than the teaching she was accustomed to doing. She left for work at 4 A.M. and I, as oldest child, had to rise and lock the door behind her. More than forty years later, I credit her for my current early-bird habits and love dawn because it is a special, autonomous time for me. The way my mom handled her divorce is largely responsible for the independent lives her four daughters live. I recall us thinking that the children in the whitewashed sitcoms of the 1950s were horribly spoiled brats and that their mothers might develop drinking problems to cope with their all-day idleness! Indeed, the gender roles projected by Ozzie and Harriet Nelson or Ward and June Cleaver were precisely the roles that the feminist movement rebelled against. They were roles that were restrictive both for women and for men.

When people hold up the 1950s nuclear family model, they forget about family diversity. Marshall Miller, cofounder of the Alternatives to Marriage Project (ATMP) says, "Diverse families, including stepfamilies; single-parent families; gay, lesbian, bisexual, and transgender families; and unmarried cohabitors are here to stay. Our challenge as a society is to end prejudice and discrimination so these relationships and families can continue to be healthy and strong." The old-school model also excludes extended families, where members of more than two generations live under the same roof. Nostalgia for the nuclear family with two parents, two kids, and a pet is little more than an attempt to elevate one model of family formation over many others.

The deification of the traditional family seeps into public policy in ugly and pernicious ways. With the unemployment rate rising in February 2002, the Bush administration has proposed to spend $300 million of public assistance dollars to promote marriage to welfare recipients. Wade F. Horn, assistant secretary of the Department of Health and Human Services, says that programs urging poor couples to marry will "promote the well-being of children." Horn is right when he notes that "on average, kids who grow up in stable, healthy, married two-parent households do better than kids who grow up in some other kind of arrangement." But even a bad statistician will tell you correlation is not causation. In other words, the fact that children in married households "on average" do better than those who are not in married households does not mean you can sprinkle magic dust on unmarried parents, hook them up, and expect poverty to magically disappear. If unmarried parents lack jobs, marriage won't improve their children's economic status. Government helps poor kids when it develops programs to help get their parents paid. Programs to promote or provide education, training, child care, and health services are likely to do more for poor children than programs to promote marriage. An unemployed man and an unemployed woman can't feed their children with their marriage license.

Professor Stephanie Coontz has written extensively about the diversity among families, first in her book *The Way We Never Were: American Families and the Nostalgia Trap,* and more recently in *The Way We Really Are: Coming to Terms with America's Changing Families.* She suggests that instead of attempting to develop a "most favored family" model of a nuclear family with a working dad and stay-at-home mom, we should get realistic about the many ways that families are organized and the many ways in which they differ. It's not public policy's job to decide on a favorite family, Coontz suggests, but instead to work with the strengths and vulnerabilities of today's families and use policy to support them. For example, the daughters of working mothers tend to excel more often in school and the conspicuous absence from the children's lives of the 1950s nuclear family father is something the modern family models do not feature.

Coontz feels that we need high-quality and affordable child care, tax breaks for families with children, family-friendly work policies, job training, child support enforcement, national health insurance, high school programs in child development and community service, and special programs for single mothers. More importantly, she notes that Ozzie and Harriet families evolved from a set of economic, demographic, and political forces, some of which have changed, and suggests that there are many reasons why such a model is impractical now.

The challenge in public policy, then, is to find a way to facilitate the work/family balance that many women and men deal with daily, to make it easier for people to be attentive both to their jobs and to their loved ones. It is important to note that men, too, juggle work and family matters, and that work and family issues aren't restricted to women with small children. Increasingly, the "sandwich generation" deals both with child care, and with elder care. And increasingly men are deciding that they want to play a greater role in family development and are asking for some of the same kind of workplace flexibility that women have been requesting for decades.

WHAT IF WORKING WOMEN STAYED HOME?

Working women are a reality. According to the Bureau of Labor Statistics, 64 percent of women with children under age three are in the labor force, as are 60 percent with children under age six. Women work for one of two reasons: They may need to work, economically, either because they are single moms and don't have the choice to stay at home, even if they wanted to, or, they may want to work. Many well-educated and highly trained women love their children and want to nurture them, but also crave the intellectual stimulation they get from the workplace. Some of them, like Elizabeth Perle McKenna, author of *When Work Doesn't Work Anymore*, have contributed greatly to corporations and feel betrayed when the flexible policies that exist on paper haven't quite been implemented at their companies. Whether women work out of economic need, or out of a need for occupational fulfillment outside of the home, the fact that they have children means that they must balance work and family, which is a challenge in a society that sees the care of children as a low-paying occupation. There are also the culture wars, the tug between feminist principles of self-determination and the conservative notion that women need to stay home and raise children. These culture wars play out in newspaper headlines, on magazine covers, and in studies that are skilled at tugging guilt and concern out of even the most focused careerists. For example, in the summer of 2001, women were battered by a set of studies that offered negative views of child care. One study said that children in day care are more likely to be aggressive than those who are not, and another study said that low pay contributes to high turnover and staffing problems at child care centers. Both stories generated headlines that only induced guilt, causing many women to wonder whether they have made the right choices for their children. And as the culture wars rage, some feel pressure to stay home instead of working. Guess what, though? Many women have no choice but to work. Single moms who are the sole source of support for their children head 20 percent of white families, and more than 40 percent of black ones. What's a working mother to do? To begin with, we ought to read the fine print.

The aggressiveness finding came from a study by the National Institute of Child Health and Human Development, the largest report on child care ever. The sample size—more than thirteen hundred—makes the findings credible. The fact that children were tracked at ten sites since 1991 make the results comprehensive. The headlines focused on the fact that 17 percent of the children in the study who spent more than thirty hours a week in day care exhibited some behavioral problems, while just 6 percent of those who spent less than ten hours a week in day care exhibited the same kinds of problems. Here's the caveat: The fine print shows that these problems fall into "normal" range, and that pushing and grabbing toys are not necessarily pathological behaviors. Further, the majority of the youngsters who spent more than thirty hours a week in day care exhibited no aggressiveness problems.

How did the story get spun out of control? Some say that the researcher who volunteered to be the media spokesperson, Jay Belsky of Birkbeck College in London, had something of an ax to grind. Others say there is a natural bias against child care that the study played into. Certainly, many reporters didn't read the fine print. Some made the easy leap that child care causes aggressiveness, stoking the guilt that working moms already feel about leaving their toddlers with others.

What if more women stayed home? It might be better for their toddlers (and then again, it might not, given the frustration that some mothers might feel), but is it better for the economy? After all, women are 46 percent of the labor force. What if working mothers of children under six (there were nearly ten million of them in 1998) decided to stay home in response to studies that their work lives are bad for their children? Exactly who is going to fill the gap that women workers would leave by withdrawing from the labor force?

Think about it. Women's absence from the workplace would create a labor shortage. It would drive wages up and increase costs. It might force employers to make special considerations for those women with children, considerations like on-site child care and flexible hours. In the long run, if the mothers of small children decided to withdraw from the labor force, the shortage that their absence precipitated might improve the status of other workers. But women leaving the workforce is not a viable solution. Improving child care quality is, though. That's why the other child care–related study of 2001, which focused on conditions in child care centers, is sobering. Prepared by researchers at the University of California at Berkeley and the Center for the Child Care Workforce, the study says that high turnover hurts the quality of childcare. It went on to say that compensation in child care centers has not kept pace with inflation and has contributed to turnover problems. If we know that there is a connection between the quality of child care and the pay that is provided, why haven't pay levels risen for child care workers? This is the case primarily because of the perception that child care work is "easy" work that comes naturally to women—it helps that child care work is considered "unskilled labor."

Good people are leaving child care jobs, though, because they need to be paid a competitive wage. As the quality of child care declines, the pressure on working mothers increases. Some of the best child care centers in urban areas have long waiting lists and high tuitions, yet demand for these services does not abate because so many women have to work. Many mothers are forced to make catch-as-catch-can child care arrangements, leaving their children with friends or relatives because they cannot find structured child care. Some are forced to extreme measures, such as leaving their children home alone or in a locked automobile. Some have been prosecuted for child neglect when pushed to these extreme measures, but if affordable child care is not available and they must work, what are they to do?

It seems to me that if we focus on child care and those who provide it, developing high-quality and affordable child care should be an imperative, even if it has to be subsidized. We say that our human resources are an asset but the way that parents and children are treated belies that point. Some would say that child care is an individual responsibility. I'd say it is a public good, as much as K–12 education is, and that government can play a critical role in making sure that quality child care is available for all parents, regardless of income or occupation.

PAID LEAVE

It would be a mistake to focus solely on child care when looking at the ways women and men can juggle work and family. The very first act of juggling, for a woman, comes with her pregnancy. Fortunately, pregnancy discrimination is now against the law, but it was not until 1978 that such a law was passed. Eliminating discrimination against pregnant women, though, doesn't mean that a woman's pregnancy is encouraged or supported in a corporate setting. The Family and Medical Leave Act, one of President Bill Clinton's first acts in 1993, provides workers with twelve unpaid, job-protected weeks of leave in a twelve-month period for a specific family or medical reason. Because the Family and Medical Leave Act only applies to employers with more than fifty employees, and the number of small businesses is on the rise in the nation, as many as forty million Americans do not qualify for family and medical leave. Many of those who qualify say that twelve weeks is just not enough. It took eight years of lobbying to get the Family and Medical Leave Act passed. We need to get busy and start working on ways to provide women with more paid leave.

Family and medical leave is a step in the right direction. Much of the research on families with children talks about how "time starved" parents are as they attempt to juggle work and family. Part of that time starvation comes from our workaholic culture where some professional workers clock ten or twelve hours a day, and some working-class parents commute an hour or two a day on top of their regular shift because they have to live farther away from their jobs in order to live in affordable housing. Further, while most Americans get two weeks of paid vacation a year, workers in western European countries get many more paid weeks of leave. The law requires employers in Sweden, Spain, Denmark, Austria, Finland, and France to provide at least thirty days of paid vacation. Ireland, Portugal, the Netherlands, Belgium, Norway, and Switzerland require at least twenty days of paid vacation. The average worker in the United States gets sixteen vacation days per year, which is less than the law requires in any of the western European countries on which the Organization for Economic Cooperation and Development reported in 1998.

Enlightened workplaces often offer paid sabbaticals to executive workers, and other perks designed to improve job satisfaction and retention. One might ask if these perks would benefit all workers, from those at the loading dock or at the typewriter, to those who are making executive decisions. When employers don't offer sabbaticals, it is not unusual to find employees making career decisions that fulfill their personal goals, even if it means leaving the structured workplace. One wonders what kind of productivity drain takes place when seasoned workers pick up and leave because they are feeling burned out. We live in a culture of burnout though, where many people compete for bragging rights on their level of busyness. A whole generation of electronic devices has been developed so that we can keep in constant touch with the office. As the U.S. economy has slackened too many workers fear that out of touch means out of mind. Who wants to take off when twelve-hour workdays are part of the office culture? In her book

The Time Bind, sociologist Arlie Hochschild says that even people who have flextime don't take it because they fear career stagnation if they aren't present and visible on the job.

Our hard-driving work culture among professional workers has the most impact on working women with children, who are often forced to make hard choices between career development and child rearing. At issue is the fact that our hard-working culture also distorts the way we make public policy and the efforts we assume that low-wage workers should make to survive. Too many cobble together a living from several part-time jobs, earning little empathy from those who think that twelve-hour workdays are normal. It is worth noting that working several part-time jobs can be worse than working one twelve-hour job because of the time constraints commuting incurs.

PART-TIME EMPLOYMENT AND FLEXIBLE WORK ARRANGEMENTS

In response to corporations that won't develop family-friendly workplace policies, some women have attempted to create an employment situation that reflects their values and lifestyle choices. Most commonly, some women work part-time instead of full-time, sometimes putting together several part-time jobs to create one full-time income. Women represent nearly 70 percent of part-time employees, but what they gain in flexibility they often lose in customary workplace benefits. Thus, part-time employees, even those who work half-time or more, are likely to lack health care and retirement benefits. Some may also lack leave benefits, though it is possible to prorate such benefits to both reflect a part-time worker's employment engagement and the benefits that a corporation provides for others.

Telecommuting, flextime, and job sharing are all touted as ways that workers can better juggle household and family; mounting research suggests that flexible work time and reduced-time work opportunities successfully reduce work/family conflict. In 1977, under the Carter administration, the

federal government actually piloted a flextime and job-sharing program, al
lowing a small number of workers in federal agencies to opt for such working arrangements. This experimentation, while important, is not widespread
either in the federal government or in the private sector, but it is a place
where government can take the lead by setting an example and providing
the tools for private employers to consider this kind of workplace flexibility.

Women can lobby for flextime, job sharing, and telecommuting arrangements both in their own workplaces and in society. Often, human resource
managers have forgotten how to "think outside the box" and an innovative
employee can push a human resource manager into making different kinds
of work arrangements. Of course, unique employees with unusual skills are
frequently the ones who are able to cobble together alternative arrangements, but once a company tries flextime or telecommuting for one worker,
it is easier to consider it for others.

TOWARD A FAMILY-FRIENDLY WORKPLACE

If we look at the families we have, not the ones we used to have, or the
ones we'd rather have, we would accept women's presence in the workforce
as a given and develop policies that support working families. A family-
friendly economy would view workers as having dual roles, both as productivity centers and as family members. We need to structure our entire
society—not just the workplace—to support both of these roles. A
family-friendly company would provide on-site day care, but a family-
friendly society would have community child care and supervised play environments for people who don't work for family-friendly companies. A
family-friendly society would deal with the time crunch so many working
people face. If grocery stores can be open 24-7, what about libraries and
post offices? At the very minimum the provision of services should be more
evenly spread around the clock so that an eight-to-five worker is not trying
to push her work life into an eight-to-five teacher's day and an eight-to-five

doctor's schedule. Will it cost? Probably. But we pay for everything else we want. We can't simply talk about work and family; we must alter our society to be amenable to both people's productivity and their lives. This encompasses a variety of approaches, including universal family and medical leave, child care and elder care tax credit, universal health and child care, and improved pay for child and elder care workers. On second thought, there is no *probably* about it: This will definitely cost. But so do stealth bombers and we have plenty of those.

What must we do, then, to move toward a family-friendly society? We need to encourage every institution to provide amenities like child care as a matter of course. Political events and rallies must have child care to encourage moms to be able to attend. Supermarkets and department stores could have child-friendly areas so that women can leave their children safely while they shop. Few workplaces provide child care, but more could. We must keep libraries open longer so that young people can leave school and continue their educational process. We didn't close libraries during the Depression, but some municipalities began to close them when the federal government started talking about "downsizing" in 1986, cutting funds to cities (which in turn cut "nonessential" services). If people work together, they can turn the family-friendly concept into a competitive advantage, favoring those establishments that are family-friendly in favor of those that ignore families.

RESOURCES FOR THE LEFT

NATIONAL PARTNERSHIP FOR WOMEN & FAMILIES
"The National Partnership for Women & Families is a nonprofit, nonpartisan organization that uses public education and advocacy to promote fairness in the workplace, quality health care, and policies that help women and men meet the dual demands of work and family."
1875 Connecticut Avenue, NW
Suite 710

Washington, DC 20009
202-986-2600
www.nationalpartnership.org

NATIONAL ASSOCIATION FOR THE EDUCATION OF YOUNG CHILDREN

"NAEYC exists for the purpose of leading and consolidating the efforts of individuals and groups working to achieve healthy development and constructive education for all young children. Primary attention is devoted to assuring the provision of high quality early childhood programs for young children."
www.naeyc.org

SEE ALSO NOW (UNDER "EQUAL PAY")

LABOR PROJECT FOR WORKING FAMILIES

"The Labor Project for Working Families is a national advocacy and policy center providing technical assistance, resources, and education to unions and union members addressing family issues in the workplace including child care, elder care, flexible work schedules, family leave, and quality of life issues."
2521 Channing Way
#5555
Berkeley, CA 94720
510-643-7088
www.laborproject.berkeley.edu

NEW WAYS TO WORK

New Ways to Work provides technical assistance, training, customized tools, and facilitated support to employers, schools, community organizations, and community collaboratives interested in developing systems that better prepare young people for their future. New Ways provides a range of services to enhance and improve workplace practices, career

development activities, educational improvement efforts, and collaborative systems development in order to create powerful relationships
and build significant connections between schools, community, and the
workplace.

425 Market Street
Suite 2200
San Francisco, CA 94103
415-995-9860; Fax: 415-995-9867
info@nww.org
www.nww.org

DEBORAH PERRY

Everyone has moments in childhood that bear on our minds like detailed Ansel Adams photographs—a snapshot caught in time, emblematic of simplicity, naivete, and boundless adventure. One of those moments for me was when I was in the first grade and I walked home alone from school for the first time. I remember how each step forward gave me greater confidence to face the challenges of the unknown. When I drew near the walkway of our home, my mother swung open the front door, and I ran to her with all my might and crashed into her arms. We both cheered, and cherished the moment as if I had championed the African bush unscathed. I felt filled with the prowess of the jungle, and thanks to my mother, I felt safe and secure just to know that she was at home for me when I arrived back from school.

My mother and all of her friends were part of the "traditional" family where dad worked and mom stayed at home. This was the late 1960s when women basically had two employment choices—nursing and teaching—and life was a heck of a lot cheaper. If we look back to even earlier decades, the family unit was its strongest ever and deep-rooted in the fabric of American society. In the fifties, Americans backed postwar prosperity, a baby boom, and the stability of marriage that lasted an average of thirty-one years—the highest rate ever. In the forties, 67 percent of households were "traditional" families, as compared to 17 percent today. What does this mean? Perhaps the American family is experiencing a bit of an identity crisis.

Today, life for the American family is not so clearly defined anymore. With nearly two-thirds of American women in the workforce with children under the age of three, the dividing line between the role of a mother versus the role of a father is blurry. Who stays at home with the kids when they're sick? With the 9 A.M. to 5 P.M. workday being a thing of the past for most careers, who prepares dinner when both parents needs to stay at the office late? Who takes the kids to soccer practice?

Divorce in American society is the highest in the world, and a snapshot exposes American families in jumbled forms: single parents, second-time marriages, grandparent- or aunt- or uncle-headed families, people with half siblings and step-siblings or a combination thereof. Today, only 40 percent of American children reach the age of eighteen with a mother and father at home. The consequence of all this confusion is that out-of-wedlock children or children of divorced parents are more likely to experience poverty, crime, abuse, drug and alcohol abuse, behavioral and emotional problems, lower academic achievement, less income over their working lives, and other serious problems.

To add fuel to the fire, we live in the information age, where life's work happens at a frenetic pace. From the moment we wake up in the morning until the time the kids are put to bed, it's just rush, rush, rush. With the development of fax machines, cell phones, the Internet, e-mail, and the like, work, friendships, and shopping take on a whole different rhythm— expediency! Not only are the lines between mom and dad blurred, but also the division between work and family is as well. And, no matter how much technology is supposed to ease our lives, women still tend to feel the greatest crunch between balancing work and family. According to the Families and Working Institute, 83 percent of working mothers are more likely to care for a child than working fathers. Some women are willing to take lower-paying jobs just to have more flexible schedules and other benefits.

So, can government help ease this time crunch or should the twenty-first century employers step up to the plate? The time crunch has captured the attention of lawmakers to enhance the equilibrium between work and family, but before lawmakers continue to poke their noses in private business, let's take a look at how one such labor law has failed to strike the balance for women in the workplace.

The Family and Medical Leave Act (FMLA), which was passed in 1993, has a great title and certainly intended to be well-meaning, but in reality is now costly and ineffective. In 1993, Congress enacted FMLA for businesses with more than fifty employees, and allows up to twelve weeks of unpaid, job-protected leave in a twelve-month period for the attention of a newborn, newly adopted child, the placement of a foster child, and for more serious health care for the employee or the employee's family. FMLA also contains provisions on everything from employer coverage to maintenance of health benefits during leave.

In the nine years since the passage of FMLA, the Society for Human Resource Management (SHRM) finds three main problems:

1. Almost 60 percent of employers admit the difficulties and excessive costs associated in complying with the law;

2. No one ever considered during the debate of FMLA about who covers the workload of an employee out on FMLA leave. What happens is that other employees are reassigned the work of the person on leave. SHRM, in its own survey, admitted to reassigning work 92 percent of the time when an employee is on FMLA leave; and

3. FMLA did nothing to support women in the day-to-day time crunch.

The federal government should keep out of the business of mandating one-size-fits-all approaches to balancing work and family, and allow private industry to take advantage of the advancements in technology, and seek innovative alternatives such as telecommuting, flextime and comp time, and job sharing.

Outside the Box Mentality

In order to find balance in work and family, we first need to change the way we think and act. We need to get past the mentality of managers thinking you're not working just because they can't see you. This is a major shift in the way business has been done for centuries where employers dictated where, when, and how to work. Surprisingly, the federal government was ahead of the curve in family-friendly policies when it pioneered the leave programs in the 1970s. These programs allowed for federal workers to share leave time with another employee for unforeseen emergencies or bank leave for expected events such as the birth of a child or surgery. But private industry has also caught up with clever, flexible work schedules in a cost-effective manner.

Allstate Insurance Company is a great example of ingenuity. It is not only ranked as a top ten company for working women by *Working Mother* magazine, but has excelled at emphasizing policies to encourage a stronger work/life balance. "Our employees can't give their best if they are conflicted, concerned, or worried about their families," says Allstate CEO Edward Liddy. Employees have the option of telecommuting, job sharing, and full benefits for part-time workers. Women represent more than half of Allstate's workforce and many are finding themselves rising through the corporate ranks to top levels and in need of more formable work styles. To buttress this environment, managers' compensation is affected by their ability to assist in employees' career development. This means that Allstate managers have to arrange seminars and training programs that will assist in job promotion.

Fannie Mae Corporation is also a *Working Mother* top ten for working women. This is one company that practices what it preaches. In the business of helping low- and moderate-income families acquire homes by lending trillions of dollars each year, Fannie Mae employees are eligible for loans for down payment and closing costs that are 100 percent forgivable. Borrow $10,000 and you're forgiven $2,000 a year over the course of five years. In addition to encouraging home ownership, Fannie Mae supports its employees through job rotations, full tuition reimbursement, mentoring, and company-sponsored courses. It also participates in job sharing and gives employees up to ten hours of paid time each month to volunteer in their communities.

Every manager in America must recognize that if you are going to generate a productive workforce and keep top employees on the roster, then family-friendly options must be a part of a recruiting package. Employee productivity and commitment go hand-in-hand, and if employers treat employees well in a variety of ways, then employers will find their costs re duced overall. Major studies of family-friendly programs have found they reduce attrition and absenteeism, and help managers accomplish mission objectives. Family-friendly options can also cut recruiting costs because they have proven to reduce attrition rates.

Below are the three most common forms of family-friendly programs in government and the private sector having a positive effect on balancing work and life. Here are the pros (and some cons) of working alternatives, and if you are in the market for greater flexibility in the workplace, talk to your employer about these commonplace options.

Telecommuting

Few ideas in alternative workplaces have caught on with such fire as telecommuting, which allows employees to work from home full- or part-time, and fosters flexibility over their work schedule and control over the pace of work. Most employed telecommuters work from home one to three days a week and go to the office the remaining days.

Even before telecommuting was in vogue, one-quarter of the workforce in the United States consisted of workers who worked away from the main office and alone where their supervisors couldn't see them. The number of homes equipped with personal computers, modems, Internet access, and fax machines has increased dramatically, affording the opportunity for millions of Americans to work from home. According to the Employment Policy Foundation (EPF), more than twenty-one million people performed some work from home in 1997, and if the current trend continues EPF estimates that thirty-five million workers will telecommute by 2008.

There are tremendous benefits to telecommuting for the employer, as well, such as reduced costs for office space and equipment, the ability to conduct business from numerous virtual locales beyond the corporate headquarters, and increased work productivity derived from boosted employee morale. The quality of life increases for everyone, as telecommuting also eliminates the aggravation of driving on America's congestive highways.

The downside to telecommuting is the further blurring of the lines between work and family and the feeling of isolation. Professional inter-action and the bouncing around of ideas with your peers is a critical aspect of productivity and happiness. And then, there is still the old perception of "face time," which still holds a measurable impact on how you and your work are perceived. Without that degree of visibility, you will undoubtedly miss out on "inside" information and opportunities to advance your career.

Flextime/Comp Time

Wouldn't it be ideal to work early morning hours if you are an early riser? Conversely, would it be suitable if you could drop the kids off at school, deal with your ailing mother, and then head into work around 10:00 A.M.? Some 30 percent of Americans enjoy flextime, which allows workers to choose their work hours and is a fitting solution for those needing more accommodating hours to meet their personal lives. Flextime allows em-ployees, for example, to work from 6:30 A.M. to 3:30 P.M. Employees can also work a compressed schedule that allows for traditional five-day, forty-hour workweeks to be compressed into four days or the option to take off a day over a two-week period if employees so choose. Since the Catalyst organization found that 80 percent of working couples would like to set their own hours, and Ernst & Young revealed that flextime is good for employers, too, it is a win-win for everyone.

Comp time is the exchange of overtime pay for time off, and is one of the most popular programs throughout the federal government. There was a time that many of my friends working in federal agencies had every other Friday off due to comp time. Because employers are mandated by the Fair Labor Standards Act (FLSA) to pay workers for any overtime above the forty-hour workweek, it is difficult for employees to "time shift" their hours from week to week, and many would prefer to have a day off than keep slaving away at the job while struggling to keep up on the homefront. Eighty-one percent of women favor comp time as a viable option for flexi-bility according to the Employment Policy Foundation.

Job Sharing

Imagine if you had a terrific career that you did not want to forgo because you just gave birth or adopted a child, but the demands of the job were too incompatible with your family needs. Now, imagine if you could actually split your position with another person who could share the responsibility of the job, and provide for a preferred work/life balance.

Job sharing is probably the least talked about option for family-friendly programs, but is on the rise in the private sector. Job sharing is when two people share one full-time job and therefore have the delivery of a part-time position. According to Nancy Collamer in an article entitled "Making Job Shares Work," job sharing increases flexibility for those in high-level jobs, provides higher pay and benefits compared to part-time positions, and reduces stress for both employees. For the company, it provides a continuum of work production where there is virtually no downtime, and two heads are always better than one. This is a great option for women with children.

As family life in the United States has moved further and further away from the traditional family of earlier generations, there is a heightened need to reduce stress on the working couple, or the single man or woman who is trying to support a family. Senators Judd Gregg, a Republican from New Hampshire, and Kay Bailey Hutchison, a Republican from Texas, introduced the Workplace Flexibility Act, which establishes flextime arrangements, modifies the antiquated Fair Labor Standards Act, and ends discrimination against women in the workforce.

As women continue to dominate the workforce, we can have an enormous influence on family-friendly options if we let our voices be heard. By going to your employer and offering solutions such as telecommuting, flextime and comp time, and job sharing, you can enhance your specialized need to balance your work and family life. Expansion of existing government programs or creating of new ones can only hinder that process. Speak up, and know that with all the technology that is available to us there is no greater time to be able to share the end goal of creating a flexible, family-friendly workforce based on free market principles that is good for you and your employer.

RESOURCES FOR THE RIGHT

EMPLOYMENT POLICY FOUNDATION
This organization promotes "sound employment policy through research on workplace trends and issues."
1015 15th Street, NW
Washington, DC 20005
202-789-8685
www.epf.org

CLARE BOOTHE LUCE POLICY INSTITUTE
This organization looks to the "achievements and philosophy of Clare Boothe Luce for guidance because she was a leader in the free world's opposition to communism, an outspoken advocate of free enterprise, and a woman devoted to her family."
112 Elden Street
Suite P
Herndon, VA 20170
703-318-8867
www.cblpolicyinstitute.org

COMMON GROUND

We both support **telecommuting, flextime/compressed workweeks,** and **job sharing** as viable options for federal and private sector employees to the traditional forty-hour workweek in the headquartered office. These options provide women and men more opportunity for balance between their work and family life, and cuts down on commuting headaches. While Julianne believes that the federal government should take leadership in introducing these measures and implementing them, Deborah believes that it is up to the individuals and government or company managers to determine viable options.

3

EDUCATION

DEBORAH PERRY

Maggie arrived at her fifth grade class at Woodmont Elementary just in the knick of time before an unpredicted, early morning snowfall. Her teacher, Ms. Cherrydale, paced in front of the blackboard with the anticipation of each child secure in his or her assigned seat and out of harm's way of the deteriorating, slippery sidewalks. Ms. Cherrydale wiped the sweat away from her forehead when the last of her fifteen students appeared safe and sound. The morning began with students in groups of three presenting their self-made replica of Tom Sawyer's raft. A week earlier Ms. Cherrydale brought in small wood planks and twine for the students to assemble. She wanted her students not only to read Tom Sawyer, but to bring to life the character of Tom from this narrative. Ms. Cherrydale applied storytelling and practical applications to all of her instruction, and it became apparent that all of her students, past and present, caught the bug to learn.

What is the fundamental message in this fictitious story? The answer is that Ms. Cherrydale instills in her students the inspiration to learn. American author and Pulitzer Prize–winning historian Will Durant (1885–1981) said, "Educators should be chosen not merely for their special qualifications, but more for their personality and character, because we teach more by what we are than by what we teach." While there are certainly motivating teachers in public education, teaching today adheres to a different edification because our culture has forced teachers to spend a disproportionate amount of time assuming other occupations—disciplinary cops, mentors, guidance counselors, and in many cases, more often than not, surrogate parents. It is a tough job, and few can handle the challenge.

Teaching is a small slice of the pie when dissecting the laundry list of modern-day needs in K–12 public education. One of the reasons I think that the education issue sat on the back burner in national politics—until President Bush came along—is because it's a difficult topic to wrap your hands around. Throughout recent years, questions have been raised about the appropriate federal government role in public education. There are those in my party who think that the federal government should have no role other than to provide block grants to local school districts, and that the U.S. Department of Education should be abolished entirely. The Democrats would like to see more money poured into an already failed system, but Republicans know this is the absolute erroneous course of action to take, and here's why.

During the Clinton years, there was a lot of talk of a heightened federal role in education, which makes great lip service and eye-catching news stories for the morning papers, but our public education system is already plagued by a massive federal bureaucracy. It operates like a monopoly and does not foster to serve its customer base—parents and students. There are at least forty different federal agencies, boards, and commissions that oversee more than 760 education programs, and at a cost of about $100 billion a year to the American taxpayer. While this may sound like a lot of money, and it is, a recent study found that as little as sixty-five to seventy cents per federal dollar actually reaches the classroom.

Clinton and the Democrats had also allowed teachers' unions to dictate their education policy agenda The two largest teachers' unions, the National Education Association (NEA) and the smaller American Federation of Teachers (AFT), have become masterful political lobbying operatives in Washington and state legislatures, and the result is publicly run schools controlled by teachers' unions and not by the voices of parents. The unions have an ethos of being the protectorates of mediocrity, and have been more anxious with their own longevity as teachers and less concerned for the children they teach. As they were once set up to highly standardize their profession, teachers' unions have vigorously rejected accountability in their profession and work against the tide of education reform.

Look at the wrath of what teachers unions have left behind. Even though government spending provides each student with an average of more than $7,000 per year, 40 percent of American fourth graders can't read, and American eighth graders rank last in math and science among students from the seven developed nations that administer the International Assessment of Educational Progress. If that doesn't sound bad enough, it gets worse. U.S. twelfth graders are behind 95 percent of the children in other countries, and half of the students in urban schools fail to graduate on time, if at all.

A recent National Assessment of Educational Progress (NAEP) test administered to twelfth graders by the federal government to students across the country revealed that:

- 47 percent could not express the fraction 9/100 as a percent;

- One-third did not know who Abraham Lincoln was;

- 62 percent did not know that the Civil War was in the years between 1850 and 1900;

- One-third did not know that the Mississippi River flows into the Gulf of Mexico; and

- One-third could not identify the countries the U.S. fought against in World War II.

Republicans say let's take public education out of the hands of the teachers' unions and put it into the parents' hands. President Bush believes that when given the right opportunity, all children can learn. Following through on his campaign promise to level the playing field for all children, he signed into law the bipartisan supported No Child Left Behind Act of 2001, cultivating: accountability and testing, flexibility and local control, funding for what works, and expanded parental options. This $26.5 billion commitment to public education overhauled the 1965 Elementary and Secondary Education Act and set a blueprint for school success.

HIGHLIGHTS OF THE NO CHILD LEFT BEHIND ACT OF 2001

- Progress will be measured through annual tests in reading and math for all students in grades three through eight.

- For the first time, most local school districts will have flexibility in determining how to use up to 50 percent of the federal funds they receive. States will have similar flexibility with non–Title I federal funds.

- The law increases federal funding for reading from $300 million in fiscal year 2001 to more than $900 million in fiscal year 2002.

- Approximately $600 to $1,000 per child can be used for supplemental educational services—such as tutoring, after-school programs and summer school programs—for children in failing schools.

Source: U.S. Department of Education

The No Child Left Behind Act also requires teachers to be qualified to teach in their subject matter within four years, and calls for staff changes for schools that show no improvement over a six-year period.

However, what the bill does not offer, and something President Bush and Republicans support, is school choice and funding for vouchers that can be used to pay for private or parochial schools. In addition, three other initiatives not covered in the bill but that could have an enormous impact in providing many more children with the proper tools to succeed include: preschool education, lower student-teacher ratio, and technology instruction.

Give Me School Choice

Parents in the United States are given control over most everything in their children's lives except in the freedom to choose how their children are educated. Since K–12 education is really an extension of the home, why be restrictive on a parent's ability to choose? School choice means having the opportunity to send your child to the best school that meets his or her needs, which is not necessarily your neighborhood public school. Further, school choice offers parents the means to send their children to public, private, or religious schools, or to home school, and comes in different forms including vouchers or scholarships, education tax credits, and education savings accounts and deductions.

Patrick Wolf, who performs ongoing research at the Washington Scholarship Fund, an organization that provides over thirteen hundred children with scholarship money for schools of their choosing, states two truisms about school choice: Parents love it and children excel. Parents are much more satisfied when they are able to pick their kids' schools, especially the low-income families that the Washington Scholarship Fund provides for. According to Mr. Wolf, these parents may make less money than the average family, but they are not mindless of their kids' education. Many of these parents make great sacrifices so that their children can have a better education. Low-income, urban, African-American children are closing the learning gap between black and white children when enrolled in schools of their choice. In Washington, D.C., Ohio, and New York, school choice children have closed the learning gap one-third to 6.3 percentage points versus the national average of about 18 percentage points.

What the Washington Scholarship Fund experts suspect to be true about school choice is that:

1. Parents tend to make responsible decisions. Poor parents are poor, not dumb, and they are looking for high achievement, discipline, and equity among schools just as children of wealthier neighborhoods are;

2. Private schools do little skimming in picking voucher students, and no parents in the Washington Scholarship Fund program have complained about not getting their kids into the school of their choice;

3. There is a cost savings to the American taxpayer in society. The average per pupil expenditure in public school is about $7,000, and the average cost of a parochial school is $3,000,

4. School vouchers put pressure on public schools to do better and enforce pressure on change and reform; and

5. Empirical research suggests that children of school choice are more likely to get involved in civic participation such as volunteering, and are often more tolerant of children of varying ethnic and religious backgrounds.

School choice works a lot like our university system—the envy of the world. Essentially, school choice is based on free market principles and competition, thus forcing schools to compete to maintain their student base. The voucher system, for example, simply reflects the way the rest of American society operates. The most notable case of vouchers started as an experiment in Milwaukee, Wisconsin, in 1990.

A Voucher Case Study: Milwaukee

Polly Williams, inspired by her experiences as a former welfare mother turned state representative, waged a massive battle against the Milwaukee public schools. At the time, with 100,000 students, the Milwaukee public school district was besieged with poverty, poor discipline, and violence problems. The dropout rate of Milwaukee schools was among the highest in the country, the average G.P.A. was a D-plus, and a majority of the students were suspended at least once during the year. Representative Williams proclaimed, "The system is the system. It doesn't care. It doesn't feel. If you're a parent, what do you do?"

The Parental Choice program was born and it answered state representative Williams pleas. Here's how the program works. It takes money directly from the public school budget and provides a voucher that pays for the tuition at eighty-one religious and thirty-one nonreligious schools in the area. About eight thousand schoolchildren are benefiting from the voucher plan, which provides each student up to $5,000 per year to the poorest Milwaukee families. And how did these kids fare? The kids in voucher schools scored 11 percent higher than the kids in public schools. According to *The Economist,* one school, Messmer High, "has eliminated the gap in test scores between blacks and whites." The program gained enormous momentum when, in 1998, the Wisconsin Supreme Court ruled that vouchers could go to parochial schools, and in 1999, local voters swept voucher opponents off Milwaukee's school board.

Ironically, the most fervent support for vouchers came from Milwaukee's large African-American community who got fed up with their kids being bused so that white neighborhoods could achieve racial balance. Activist Alveda King is convinced that school choice continues to "alleviate [education] inequalities [and] restore parents' and children's civil rights."

Today, Milwaukee's Parental Choice program serves as a national framework for other state legislatures considering voucher programs. Vouchers provide hope to level the playing field for so many children who never got a fair chance from the get-go. We need to reject the negative stigmatism Democrats seem to have about vouchers and give these children the equal opportunity they deserve.

PRESCHOOL EDUCATION

We would like to believe that all kids start kindergarten from the same place, but this is not the case. Mistakenly, in society, we assume that all children come from loving, two-parent households, where all children are immunized and go to bed at night in a secure environment after having a hot meal for dinner. Many young children who come to school devoid of a warm, loving home later grow into at-risk youths who join gangs and engage in violent and antisocial behaviors.

Equal opportunity for these children begins with quality prekindergarten education in hopes of providing a framework by which they develop the personal confidence necessary for academic success and effective interpersonal relationships. Early childhood studies validate that the first five years of a child's life provide the foundation on which all other experiences are based. Approximately 80 percent of a child's intellect, personality, and social skills are formed by the age of five. Without the appropriate verbal and intellectual experiences, a child's potential is stunted. In 1998, 64.5 percent of three- to five-year-olds enrolled in preschool programs and the research validates that:

- an estimated $7.16 for every dollar invested in preschool education is returned to the public;

- at-risk children who attend preschool spend 1.3 years less in special education classes, than those who do not;

- at-risk children who attend early childhood education are 25 percent less likely to be held back a grade in school than those who do not attend;

- at-risk children considered to fail in school who attend a preschool program are 33 percent more likely to graduate from high school than those who do not; and

- people who attend early childhood programs are three times as likely to be homeowners by age 27 as those who do not attend.

While school systems are allowed to use Title I funds to provide for preschool experiences, it takes money away from other rewarding programs, and leaves a significant number of nonserved four-year-olds. Local school district officials can now take advantage of the No Child Left Behind Act and start a preschool education program in their school district.

Lower Student-Teacher Ratio

Ever get tired of hearing about the overcrowding of classrooms? The size of today's classroom with thirty-five, forty, sometimes fifty children, is different from past eras and makes teaching and learning—especially in those critical early learning years—that much more distracting. Imagine how much easier it would be for a teacher to teach fifteen students instead of thirty-five and think about the benefits children would receive.

Educational research has shown that reducing the class size in schools with significant numbers of at-risk (kids who qualify for free or reduced lunches) children has demonstrated higher levels of student achievement in the K–3 grades. Research also supports early intervention as more effective than remediation. You can work with your school board officials to reduce the class size in kindergarten through grade three. One suggestion to reduce class size is to use the percent of students eligible for receiving free or reduced lunches and base the student teacher ratio to reflect the following:

At-risk Students Eligible for Free Lunch K–3 School Ratio

20 to 40 percent (kids who receive free lunch)	20 kids to 1 teacher
40 to 60 percent	18 kids to 1 teacher
60 percent or more	15 kids to 1 teacher

Technology Instruction

It flashes with color. It talks. It offers moving targets. The Internet is here and it could be the single greatest learning engager in education. Where television opened up the baby boomers' eyes to the global village, the Internet does one better. It serves as today's version of earlier generations' encyclopedia, only more substantial and fun. It operates twenty-four hours a day, and it doesn't just offer a window on the world, but a way of playing a part wherever you are. Plus, the Internet provides today's students with welcome change to the traditional style of learning—an "outside the box" way of thinking—and independence in critical thinking. The Internet also allows students to become more passionate, inquisitive, and challenging in learning. We're living in a remarkable period of innovation, and one thing is for sure: We need more from our education system than we did just ten years ago.

Critics have said that the era of the Internet can interfere with traditional methods of teaching, but it is time to cease the oscillation of a failing education system and embrace the triumphant advancement of technology. Since 1994, the percentage of public schools with Internet access has increased dramatically: 94 and 98 percent of elementary and secondary schools, respectively. So, let's use it!

On a state and local level, make sure your public officials have in place a technology plan, where minimum targets and expectations for what teachers need to teach and students need to learn in computer technology are set. Make sure there is an assessment component that will hold teachers, students, and school districts accountable for the mastery of these skills.

A Change of Attitude Wouldn't Hurt

Today's youth as well as every generation could benefit enormously if we set examples to glorify education and scholastic achievement. For whatever reason, American society places a disproportionate amount of grandeur on athletic talents over scholastic achievement. The perception is that smart kids are still dubbed "nerdy" and football quarterbacks and cheerleaders are viewed as "popular." Why are there ample opportunities for young athletes to compete yet few academic competitions for kids to strut their stuff? I once sat in on tryouts for the *Jeopardy!* show for high school students, and thought how unfortunate it was that kids today do not have more frequent occasions to compete beyond the annual spelling bee, science fair, and history competition.

While state and local governments can play a significant role in education reform, we need local school districts to seek innovative approaches to beat to the tune of a fast-moving drum. Parents, too, deserve to have choices over their child's education. We can change the state of education one child at a time, by getting proactive in our child's curriculum and speaking out at a school board meeting when we want to see change. The development of the Internet has certainly made it more inspiring, not to mention cool, to learn, but we have a long way to go before we place the appropriate value on education that it deserves. After all, education is the one thing that no one can take away from you.

RESOURCES FOR THE RIGHT

MILTON & ROSE D. FRIEDMAN FOUNDATION ON EDUCATIONAL CHOICE

This organization "strives to educate parents, public policy makers, and organizations about the desperate need for a shift of power to the disenfranchised parents of America who have limited choices and voices in the education of their children."
One American Square
Suite 1750
Box 82078
Indianapolis, IN 46282

317-681-0745
www.friedmanfoundation.org

EMPOWER AMERICA

This organization devotes a new framework for reform of century-old public systems in K–12 education.
1701 Pennsylvania Avenue, NW
Suite 900
Washington, DC 20006
202-452-8200
www.empower.org

CENTER FOR EDUCATION REFORM

This organization provides support and guidance to parents and teachers, community and civic groups, policymakers and grassroots leaders, and all who are working to bring fundamental reforms to their schools.
1001 Connecticut Avenue, NW
Suite 204
Washington, DC 20001
202-842-0200
www.edreform.com

INSTITUTE FOR JUSTICE

This organization is a civil liberties law firm specializing in school choice litigation throughout the country.
1717 Pennsylvania Avenue, NW
Suite 200
Washington, DC 20006
202-955-1300
www.ij.org

JULIANNE MALVEAUX

*What the best and wisest parent wants for his own child, that must
be what the community wants for all of its children. Any other ideal
for our schools is narrow and unlovely; acted on, it destroys our democracy.*
JOHN DEWEY
THE SCHOOL AND SOCIETY

*I believe that children are the future, teach them well and let them
lead the way
Show them all the beauty they possess inside
Give them a sense of pride and make it easy
To let the children's laughter remind us how it used to be*
MICHAEL MASSER AND LINDA CREED
"THE GREATEST LOVE OF ALL"

In both the 1996 and the 2000 elections, voters said that education was
a top issue for them. Because they are the primary caretakers of children,
and because mothers are more likely to have direct involvement with
schools than fathers, women were especially interested in the provision of
quality education for their children. The focus on public education goes
back as far as the eighteenth century, when laws mandating compulsory
education were passed. Access to public education is one of the ways our
society provides a chance for every child since, theoretically, both the child
of a janitor or the child of a CEO can benefit from public education. Indeed, across class lines, about 95 percent of African-American children and
90 percent of white kids go to public schools. Access to education has been
important in the women's rights struggle as well. The NOW Legal Defense
and Education Fund had a slogan: "Equal education for girls is poverty
prevention for women."

Historically, public schools have been a bridge to employment, achievement, and development for all of our nation's children, especially our nation's poorest children (though there were Southern exceptions to the way that black children were treated until a generation or so ago). Reformers struggled for compulsory education to move children out of factories, mines, and fields, and allow them the opportunity to become educated members of our society. Education was considered a public good, to be paid for by general taxpayer revenue, because an educated citizenry is an informed and productive citizenry.

The African-American struggle for equal rights and justice partly revolved around access to education. Rejecting the "separate but equal" doctrine spelled out by the 1896 Supreme Court, African Americans like Ernie Green and Melba Pattillo fought for the right to attend segregated public schools that often had better resources (though far less caring and genuine people) than their own schools. Their fight was for access to public schools, to the public education that their tax dollars paid for. While there is an array of educational issues that concern women on the left, I want to focus especially on issues of funding and school infrastructure, school choice, and new education legislation.

FUNDING

Widespread dissatisfaction with public schools is higher in high-cost urban areas with high concentrations of African-American and Latino students. Why? These schools tend to be segregated, underfunded, understaffed, dilapidated, and overcrowded. Additionally, election or selection to these school boards seems to be highly politicized, with many of those who say they seek to serve children also seeking to advance their own political careers, often to children's detriment. When these politicized school boards make headlines over internecine squabbling, they reduce confidence in public education. At the same time, the move toward appointed school boards is seen as eroding the voting rights of citizens who, as taxpayers, want their voices heard on educational matters.

The mechanism for funding public education is at least part of the reason why certain urban public schools are so underfunded, understaffed, and dilapidated. When property tax dollars are used to funds schools, those jurisdictions with more poor people (or declining population, another urban challenge) will have fewer dollars than surrounding areas to fund their school. There has been a gap between the funding available for inner city schools and suburban schools, as well as a difference in the quality of the physical plant in inner city and suburban schools. Some of the problems with inner city education would be solved were there more dollars to spend on education.

Conservatives bristle when they hear "more dollars." "We've put enough money into the public schools," they say. Yet more than 60 percent of the public schools in every state need some repairs. In the District of Columbia and twenty-five states, at least 85 percent of all public schools needed some repairs. One of every three public schools needs major repairs or total replacement. Eleven million students, one of every four who attends a public school, goes to a school that is in less than adequate condition, while 3.5 million attended schools that could be describe as in "poor" condition. We may we believe that children are the future, but our future is attending schools where the roof leaks, the ceiling crumbles, and the heating system doesn't work properly. In 2000, 60 percent of the classrooms in inner city schools were wired for Internet connection, and a nation that has promised to leave no child behind has left millions in classrooms where learning is a challenge solely because of the physical condition of their schools.

It is perhaps redundant to offer research in place of common sense, but because some conservatives think "buildings don't matter," (One actually told me that Abraham Lincoln learned in a log cabin, so why can't the homies in the hood. Answer: We're not in nineteenth-century Illinois anymore.) I'll close this section with informative research:

- A 1996 study by Virginia Polytechnic Institute and State University found that students in above-standard school buildings had higher test scores than students in substandard buildings. (In all honesty, the higher scores could be a reflection of a financial advantage as opposed to a physical disadvantage).

- More than 94 percent of U.S. educators believe computer technology improves teaching and learning in the schools, according to an April 1997 poll by the American Association of School Administrators.

SCHOOL INFRASTRUCTURE

Rebuilding infrastructure is something we have to "throw money" at. The National Education Association's School Modernization Needs Assessments has determined that $321.9 billion is needed for school modernization across America. They are among the groups attempting to move federal dollars to the school modernization effort, but their attempts have been resisted as Congress seeks to provide dollars, instead, for voucher and choice programs that further undermine the public schools.

Meanwhile, public schools need to both catch up from the deferred maintenance that has not been done and prepare for the enrollment boom that is expected to continue through 2008, when it is projected that more than forty-eight million youngsters will attend public schools. The Department of Education estimates that six thousand new schools need to be built to handle new enrollment.

Are there alternatives to public education to take up the slack? Vouchers, charter schools, and private schools are often mentioned. But charter schools are simply autonomous public schools run by teachers, parents, and community groups, usually with some oversight from the school board or other group charged with supervising public education. In September 1999, the authors of *Charter Schools in Action: Renewing Public Education,* said there were seven hundred charter schools serving 350,000 students in thirty-two states and the District of Columbia. Charter schools may provide some educational flexibility for public school students, and many say they can be the site of educational experiments that may well improve the entire school system. But some educational researchers say that the innovations and improvements implemented by charter school proponents have not yet had measurable improvements on educational quality.

SCHOOL CHOICE

The "school choice" movement has gained momentum from dissatisfaction with the quality of public education. Proponents would privatize public education with a universal voucher program available in every school district for every student, and usable in public, private, and religious schools. While "choice" sounds good, it's only been tested in two cities on a limited basis and it is not clear if it will pass judicial muster. (In February 2002, the Supreme Court heard oral arguments on whether public money can be used to fund community schools.) Instead of funding public schools, voucher programs would provide parents with a voucher that could be used toward tuition in a private or parochial school. Then a parent could choose the right school for her child, supplementing the sum of the voucher with personal funds if tuition exceeded the amount of the voucher. Few voucher proponents have dealt with issues of allocation and choice: What happens when more people want to go to a "good" school than there are spaces for? Which schools will educate students with physical or learning disabilities who require more resources than average? How will students with indifferent parents gain access to quality education?

There is little evidence that charter schools or voucher-supported "community schools" improve the quality of education. According to the data so far, there is no clear difference in scores or achievement in charter schools than in public schools. Some jurisdictions offer vouchers to parents to use toward tuition at private and alternative schools. Vouchers do not buy parents better quality education when the value of the voucher accounts for a fraction of the tuition in a private school (though vouchers often cover most of the cost of Catholic schools). There are issues, with vouchers, about which students schools are obligated to take, how students are governed, and what curricula must look like. While limited experiments with vouchers may provide us with more information about this form of educational access, it is unlikely that voucher programs will ever be a substitute for an institution that deals with 90 percent of the nation's children.

To be sure, public schools are not perfect. They could benefit from smaller class sizes, improved teacher education, increased parental involvement, and better technology. The class size matter is especially important, and research shows the increased effectiveness of education when class size drops. According to the National Education Association's Student Teacher Achievement Ratio or Project STAR Report (1990):

- Tennessee's STAR Project shows that children in small classes from kindergarten through third grade get better grades through high school, are less likely to drop out, and are more likely to graduate on time than their peers who were in larger K–3 classes.

- California's statewide class-size reduction program, launched in 1997, found that third-grade students in smaller classes outscored their peers on achievement tests in both third and fourth grades.

- Students in Wisconsin's Student Achievement Guarantee in Education (SAGE) program, which reduces the student-teacher ratio to fifteen to one in kindergarten through third grade in high-poverty schools, show similar dramatic improvements.

- Students in states with the smallest class sizes in early grades scored higher on the National Assessment of Educational Progress (NAEP) than students in states with larger classes (taking income level into account), according to a Rand Corporation study.

Inner city schools, where most of our public school "problems" are centered could also benefit from the recognition that young people in some communities do not come to school ready to learn; they come from such poverty that their needs are not only educational, but also nutritional, medical, and social. It burdens the public school to say that those trained in education must also be sensitive to an array of other needs, but the fact is that inner city schools are in crisis because inner cities are also in crisis, often operating with a diminished tax base, high crime, and significant challenges and barriers to development.

It seems cynical to take the challenges of urban public schools, project them onto the national stage, and use those challenges as the basis for attacking all public schools, but that seems to be what has happened in the last decade as public-school bashing (and teacher-union bashing) has become a favored public sport. Members of the National Education Association and the American Federation of Teachers are also mindful of needs for reform and have, absent the bashing, formed organizations to improve both the quality of public schools and the quality of teaching they provide. One example is TURN, or Teachers Union Reform Network, a group of presidents of large AFT and NEA locals, organized to "take on educational quality as its chief responsibility and [to] become a full partner with administrators, school boards, and parents in reforming public education." All reforms are not wrongheaded. Indeed, because children have such different learning styles, the notion that we should have "one-size-fits-all" educators makes little sense. A number of models of school-based reform that focus on staff collaboration and innovation have been developed over the past decade, but these models focus on improving, not replacing, public schools.

Charter schools, which can best be described (generally) as private schools operating under public school supervision, or "independent public schools of choice, freed from rules but responsible to results." These schools offer the opportunity for innovation and variation, providing possibilities for students who are overwhelmed by the very size of some public schools. But it is interesting to note that charter schools, like many private schools, rely heavily on parental involvement. There are students whose parents are poor, disengaged, or otherwise challenged, and will not be involved in their child's education. This does not suggest there should be no charter schools, but makes the case, yet again, for the continued viability of public schools.

I have antipathy for voucher programs and mixed feelings about charter schools, though I think that charter schools have the potential to expand educational options while preserving the integrity of public schools. Yet I must acknowledge that many on the left, and many African Americans, are excited about voucher and charter school options, mainly because they are so disgusted with low scores and poor performance in our nation's public schools that they are willing to try anything. In Milwaukee, Dr. Howard Fuller has written widely and argues passionately that charter schools focus on education first and politics second. From Atlanta, Professor Michael Owens describes vouchers as a "desperate remedy" made attractive by the political failure of the elected educational establishment. And a poll by the Joint Center for Political and Economic Studies says that 60 percent of African Americans favor vouchers. I say the negatives exceed the positives, especially when voucher programs providing a couple thousand dollars a year in tuition subsidies don't improve educational access for those whose parents can't afford the remaining tuition.

Whether you have children or not, you can be involved in improving the quality of education by supporting public and charter schools through your dollars and your volunteer time. Many public schools welcome volunteers, guest speakers, and participants in initiatives like Big Sister programs to provide mentoring to girls. Groups like Girl Scouts also provide girls with school-supplemental activities. We all say that we believe that children are the future, but our actions don't necessarily reflect our beliefs.

LEAVE NO CHILD BEHIND: TWENTY-FIRST CENTURY EDUCATION REFORM?

The all-out assault on our nation's public schools began in 1983 with the publication of the National Commission on Excellence in Education report, *A Nation at Risk.* This treatise made claims about the "failures" of American education, offering no proof but enough speculation to stigmatize all public education. From there, the nation's right wing has relentlessly pushed for the privatization of public schools, either through voucher schemes or through support of school administration firms like the Edison program. The coronation of George W. Bush to the presidency, along with his assertion that education reform is a top priority of his, turned his version of education reform into the No Child Left Behind Act of 2001. Described by some as "the most sweeping reform of the Elementary and Secondary Education Act since 1965," it offers possibilities and challenges to teachers, parents, children, and school systems. The act passed with bipartisan support in 2001 and was signed into law in 2002.

The legislation redefines the federal role in K–12 education and increases accountability, flexibility, and choice. Reading programs are emphasized, and the legislation has an articulated goal of having each child learn to read by the third grade. The legislation also provides school choice, especially for youngsters who are attending "failing" schools. It also provides for the regular testing of youngsters.

Although this legislation passed with bipartisan support, from my perspective it more clearly serves a conservative agenda than the education of youngsters. Indeed, it seems that the push for education reform is as much about politics as it is about anything. Conservatives have been attempting to reduce the size of government for years, and education and Social Security represent some of the largest institutions in government. If they can dismantle these bureaucracies, and eliminate the Department of Education (which many opposed establishing) they will have been successful in greatly reducing the size of government, but it is not clear that our nation's students benefit from these changes.

To hand education back to "state control" in the name of flexibility allows unacceptable variations in the quality and quantity of education that is offered state by state, possibly disenfranchising students at the bottom as they are tracked into vocational or compensatory education instead of having access to a full array of educational options. What if a late bloomer prefers the academic track to vocational education? Of course, tracking occurs now, but with federal oversight there are opportunities for individuals and groups to demand a certain quality of educational services and to use federal involvement as leverage for change. I've read enough history to get very nervous when words like "states' rights" come up, especially when they come up in provision of something as important as education.

I'm also not sure about the effectiveness of the regular testing that is part of the new legislation. Proponents of testing say regular testing of students establishes "standards" and "benchmarks" for achievement. Yet the frequency of the tests that Mr. Bush proposes suggests that teachers will be constrained to "teach to the test," not use their creativity to teach the material. The design of the Texas testing program also suggests a "scholastic Darwinism," wrote Teddi Beam-Conroy, a fifth-grade public-school bilingual teacher in San Antonio. Beam-Conroy says that testing, not teaching, is "king" in Texas, where teachers spend at least six instructional days a year doing rote testing. The No Child Left Behind Act of 2001 is based on the Bush experience in Texas, where students are tested in grades three through eight.

The Bush testing proposals remind me that while education is a service and a social transformation device, education is also an economic machine. Millions of dollars are spent on K–12 educational goods and services, including textbooks and testing materials, making it a major industry in our nation.

REAL EDUCATION REFORM

There is a case to be made for education reform, but it is a reform that would truly leave no child behind. Such education reform would require partnerships between federal, state, and local governments to change the way that education is financed, so that inner city children have access to some of the same amenities that suburban children have, such as computers, laboratories, libraries, and regular field trips. Such education reform would ensure that most schools are modern and attractive, and that the nation's stock of dilapidated inner city schools be replaced. Such educational reform would systematically focus on bringing out the best in every youngster (and every teacher) by effectively using testing tools, counseling, and intervention to place young people in academically appropriate settings. And such educational reform would develop low-cost (or free) postsecondary options so that youngsters (and others) would understand that with achievement they would have the opportunity to continue their education.

Technology has changed the way that people work, making our nation's human resources our most important resources. When we neglect our educational system, or turn it into a political scratch line, we neglect our future economic development. Our educational system ought to be designed not only to absorb every youngster and nurture her to the best of her ability, but also to become a haven for adults whose jobs have become obsolete as technology has changed. The American public has always supported increasing federal investment in public education, in school repair, and in modernization. When people understand that education reform affects their ability to maintain their skill level, it is likely that such support will increase. True education reform provides educational access for everyone, instead of limiting learning with unnecessary testing and weakening public schools with ill-conceived voucher programs.

What can you do to promote education reform? Get involved in the schools, and in after-school and supplemental education programs. Get involved in matters of school finance, advocating for more equality in the way education is funded. Get involved in developing partnerships between the private and public sectors around educational issues, getting your corporation or organization involved in "adopt-a-school" or internship programs. And remember that while education reform is a huge issue, each of us can touch a young person and help motivate her to make education a priority in her life. Each of us once had a teacher who lifted us up and motivated us. It helps to visualize that teacher when we think of the ways that we can help make education an inspiring experience for youngsters, especially young women and girls.

RESOURCES FOR THE LEFT

PUBLIC EDUCATION NETWORK
"The mission of the Public Education Network is to create systems of public education that result in high achievement for every child."
601 13th Street, NW
Suite 900 North
Washington, DC 20005
202-628-7460
www.publiceducation.org

ACORN
"The Association of Community Organizations for Reform Now (ACORN) is the nation's largest community organization of low- and moderate-income families. . . . Since 1970 ACORN has taken action and won victories, on issues of concern to our members. Our priorities include: better housing for first-time homebuyers and tenants, living wages for low-wage workers, more investment in our communities from banks and governments, and better public schools."
88 3rd Avenue, 3rd Floor
Brooklyn, NY 11217
718-246-7900
www.acorn.org

CROSS CITY CAMPAIGN FOR URBAN SCHOOL REFORM
"The Cross City Campaign promotes the systemic transformation of urban public schools, resulting in improved quality and equity, so that all urban youth are well prepared for postsecondary education, work, and citizenship."

407 South Dearborn Street
Suite 1500
Chicago, IL 60605
312-322-4880
www.crosscity.org

NATIONAL ASSOCIATION OF PARTNERS IN EDUCATION (NAPE)

NAPE works "to provide leadership in the formation and growth of effective partnerships that ensure success for all students."
901 North Pitt Street
Suite 320
Alexandria, VA 22314
703-836-4880
www.napehq.org

NATIONAL PARENT TEACHER ASSOCIATION

"National PTA is the largest volunteer child advocacy organization in the United States. A not-for-profit association of parents, educators, students, and other citizens active in their schools and communities, PTA is a leader in reminding our nation of its obligations to children."
330 North Wabash Avenue
Suite 2100
Chicago, IL 60611
312-670-6782
www.pta.org

PROJECT APPLESEED: THE NATIONAL CAMPAIGN FOR PUBLIC SCHOOLS IMPROVEMENT

"Project Appleseed has been working to increase parental involvement in all public schools for six years."
7209 Dorset at Midland Boulevard
St. Louis, MD 63130-3017
www.projectappleseed.org

Teachers Union Reform Network (TURN)

TURN is a union-led effort to restructure the nation's teachers unions to promote reforms that will ultimately lead to better learning and higher achievement for America's children. The primary goal of TURN is to create a new union model that can take the lead in building and sustaining high performing schools for all students in an increasingly complex and diverse world.

www.gseis.ucla.edu/hosted/turn/turn.html

COMMON GROUND

- **Modernization of school infrastructure and new construction** is needed for aging buildings, as the average school building is forty years old. While we agree on this point, we disagree on who should pay. Julianne believes that the federal government should take the lead role triggering and financing school construction, primarily because of disproportionate wealth of localities. Deborah believes that the federal contribution toward school construction becomes mired in bureaucracy, where money promised at the federal level never reaches the local level. Instead, funds through state, local, and private donations can be raised more effectively for school construction.

- We both feel adamant about **small class sizes** particularly in K–3 grades, as research has shown that children are better prepared for school in later grades as a result. Julianne believes that African-American children benefit greatly in smaller class sizes up to the sixth grade.

- We both support **preschool education** for three- and four-year-old children to level the playing field. Julianne would like to offer this to all children while Deborah supports this for children who would qualify for free or reduced lunch.

- **Charter schools** show promise and are an innovation within traditional public instruction. Julianne, however, feels strongly that charter schools should not undermine traditional public education.

- **Technology** can be the greatest learning tool of the twenty-first century. We agree that all schools should be state of the art and that teachers are capable of using technology to teach and inspire.

4

THE ECONOMY AND TAXES

JULIANNE MALVEAUX

When I tell people I'm an economist, they usually respond by telling me that they flunked economics in college. I'm not sure what I'm supposed to say after that. I'm sorry? Would you like a little make-up tutoring? Or, they take pleasure in telling me that they don't "understand" economics. Most amusingly, they push for stock tips, and sometimes jot them on the back of my business card, as if they are going to check up on how well my tips perform. I want to tell people that economists have no monopoly on financial good sense! If we did, a group of Nobel Prize–winning economists wouldn't have taken a bath with a scam organization called Long-Term Capital Management, an organization that was so heavily leveraged and so internationally involved that the Federal Reserve Bank had to lead a bailout for them! Economists have insights and analysis, but no crystal ball. And we certainly aren't infallible.

Our economy is a complex quilt of individuals and institutions that is partly managed by government, partly by individual corporations, and partly by individuals. Our gross domestic product, or the value of goods and services that are sold in our economy, was more than $9.3 trillion in the second quarter of 2001. Two-thirds of this money was money that people earned and spent. Despite all of the regulation and machination that exists, people make our economy go around. And though women are often portrayed as players at the periphery of the economy, in fact we make the majority of household purchasing decisions. We figure out what our families are going to eat and drink, wear and walk in, drive and fly.

Women on the left want both to be able to fully participate in our nation's economy and to make sure that neither the law nor public policy is biased against women. Historically, the law prevented us from being economic actors by restricting our wealth and access to money depending, among other things, on our marital status. Even today, a single woman who buys a home is designated "an unmarried woman" as if that status has anything to do with her ability to pay for housing. Women are discriminated against in economic arenas in terms of access to credit, access to capital, especially for business formation (more women finance their businesses with loans from friends than with bank loans), as well as in the labor market and in other markets.

More important than ending discrimination, though, most liberal women want policies developed to assist women in getting a toehold in the economy, either with programs that encourage our entrepreneurship or programs that allow us the opportunity to be awarded federal contracts that had only gone to men in the past. And, women want economic institutions to favor our lives, communities, and family circumstances, to deal with issues like child care, housing and community development, and human development.

Women on the left don't mind paying taxes as long as taxation is fair. Some get caught up in discussions of the "marriage penalty" but others understand that when we attack a "marriage penalty," single people, including single parents, shoulder a burden. Here's how the so-called marriage penalty works. If I earn $30,000 as a single person, and I have no special deductions, I have a personal exemption of $7,450 and pay $3,454 in taxes. If I marry someone who also makes $30,000 a year, and we decide to file our taxes jointly, we have a joint exemption of $13,400, and we end up paying $7,172 in taxes. We pay $504 more together than we would have paid individually, and some describe that as our "marriage tax." At the same time, a single person who earned $60,000 a year paid $11,338 in taxes, more than $4,000 more than the married family with a $60,000 income. Why? Our tax system is progressive, which means that people who earn more pay a higher percentage of their income in taxes. Our goal is also to treat "similarly situated" people in the same way. A household headed by a single person with an income of $60,000 has more disposable income than a household headed by a married couple with that income. Married couple taxation goes down even more, incidentally, if children are involved.

The main distortion comes when the two people earning $30,000 marry. They may consider themselves penalized because their combined taxes are more than their individual taxes, but what about their combined benefits? Our tax system is a progressive system, though, which means that in those rare cases where people of similar incomes marry they may shoulder a larger tax burden. At the same time, when a high-income individual marries one of lower (or no) income, taxes go down. For example, when the $60,000 earner marries someone without earnings, that couple only pays the same amount of tax as the family with two $30,000 earners.

A whole category of family has gone unmentioned in this discussion, and that's the family with children. According to Max Sawicky of the Economic Policy Institute, "In families of equal size and income, the single parent will pay more tax." So, what to do? Critics of marriage tax reform need a better tax cut of their own. The salient financial implication of marriage is not the union of adults but the result—dependent children. Since the ability to pay taxes depends on the number of children in a family, the logical remedy is to expand existing tax benefits for children. Much of the claptrap about the "marriage penalty" is an effort to make the tax system seem unfair to married couples, and to portray those on the left as anti-marriage. In fact, while our tax system can always be tweaked, current reform efforts favor the wealthy, not the poor.

The estate tax is another target of people on the right, who like to describe that tax as a "death tax." It is more accurately described as a "wealth tax" that redistributes income from the wealthy to others. Levied on an estate at the time of death, the tax has a large ($600,000) exemption. It, perhaps, imposes a hardship on family farmers and small business owners whose affairs are organized as sole proprietorships, not corporations. Women on the left tend to believe that the estate tax shouldn't be described as a "death tax." Instead, they feel the wealthy should pay more for the privileges they enjoy in our society, and that income should be redistributed so that people on the bottom can get a leg up and have more opportunities to participate in our economy.

Women on the left aren't crazy about tax cuts. After all, we are clear that a lot of our tax dollars—35 percent—go to support Social Security and Medicare programs, the very programs we'd like to see help support us in our old age. Nine percent of the budget goes to pay old debt, much of which was run up in the militaristic Reagan years. Nineteen percent of our tax dollars go to support education, job training, the environment, federal housing programs, government operations, highway maintenance, and other nonmilitary operations. Seventeen percent of our tax dollars go to support our military. While women on the left might quibble about the exact allocation of federal dollars, we understand that the federal government plays an essential role and we don't think that tax cuts are the answer, especially when tax cuts mean reductions in other essential government programs. We didn't get excited about the $300 tax rebate that Mr. Bush advocated in early 2001, preferring to see money go to services and education. Women on the left join women on the right and in the center in understanding some of the drawbacks of our tax system, but understand that taxes are the price we pay for community and public goods in our society, and are prepared to pay those taxes to support a progressive vision of our world.

Of course, defense monies are part of that progressive vision. However, we aren't always prepared to support the heavy increase in defense spending, even as the realities of September 11, 2001, increase our defense spending. Progressive women like those in WAND (Women's Action for New Directions) have been especially vocal in opposing the increased militarization of our federal budget, raising debate about the true nature of security, and supporting nuclear nonproliferation.

When budgets are discussed, liberal women aren't inclined to dismiss government programs as "pork." Instead, we believe that government intervention in markets can make them work to the appropriate social ends. Enforcing the Community Reinvestment Act may provide more home and business loans for women and low-income people. Developing programs to train women in construction jobs may open up nontraditional opportunities for women and their daughters. Further, programs should be targeted to women who may have been previously excluded as economic actors.

Women on the left don't get excited about deficits or balanced budgets, believing that countercyclical measures can be used to stabilize an economy, and that human investments can yield major dividends in the long run. They would fund education, Social Security, Medicare, and universal health care, believing that a strong social safety net will provide long-term benefits for our economy and our society.

It's also important to look at the growing gap between the wealthy and the poor. When we learn that the top 5 percent of the population has 20.3 percent of our nation's income, up from 17.9 percent a decade ago, we are alarmed. When we realize that more than ten million people (mostly women) earn the minimum wage, we are concerned for their economic well-being. When we reflect on the boom years 1991–2001, we realize that the benefits didn't trickle down and too many women were bypassed by the boom.

Women should be concerned with economic justice issues. I concur with the National Conference of Catholic Bishops whose 1986 Pastoral Letter on Economic Justice says, "The economy should exist to serve the human person, not the other way around." The bishops captured many of the paradoxes of our economic reality. Our country has one of the most technologically advanced health care systems in the world, but forty-two million people do not have access to health care. Profits and productivity grew during the boom years, while many workers say their income and sense of security declined. In the wake of September 11, the term "homeland security" has been frequently bandied about, yet millions live in the midst of economic insecurity, homelessness, hunger, and joblessness.

REGULATION AND THE ECONOMY

How does our economy generate such disparate results and distribute resources in such an unequal fashion? Neoclassical economists have lots of faith in markets, in the forces of supply and demand. They believe that markets are efficient when prices allocate, and that market forces can set a price so that goods and services are distributed fairly. Through a bidding process a fair price is agreed on. A transaction takes place and the market clears. Depending on where you are ideologically, you may or may not welcome market interference. Libertarians believe that markets ought to be allowed to work, simply work, without government intervention and let the chips fall where they may. Liberals favor market interventions, especially when they can be justified on distribution grounds. The minimum wage, for example, is a market intervention. It makes it illegal for someone to pay less than $5.15 an hour for a worker's time, even though the market may say that the worker is only worth $5. Why? There is a social benefit involved in paying people a fair wage. Conservatives tend not to want market interference in some markets (though they tolerate it in others). They tend to allow markets to work when individuals are involved, but they can make compelling cases for market intervention when corporations are lining up for handouts.

Dozens of federal regulatory agencies have their hands in the nation's economic Kool-Aid. The Securities and Exchange Commission, for example, regulates the workings of the stock market. They turned a blind eye to the conflict of interest between Arthur Andersen's consulting and accounting role for Enron, and as a result twenty-one thousand people have lost their pensions. Now, Congress is trying to decide how to regulate pensions. That's a market intervention that some would not have welcomed before the Enron debacle.

The Interstate Commerce Commission regulates sales across state lines and can introduce regulations that will slow sales and, thus, put brakes on the economy. The National Labor Relations Board is charged with making sure that workers are able to bargain collectively, but in recent years the NLRB has been beleaguered and often ineffective. Their actions have an impact on the setting of wages and on the defining of "bargaining units."

All these regulatory bodies exist because unfettered and unregulated capitalism is, in a word, predatory. The impulses of capitalism are to exploit people's "surplus value" or the value of their wages. Unregulated, capitalism's tendency is to push profits up and factor prices down. If you liken capitalism to a wolf, and regulation to a dentist, then the dentist's job is to cap the wolf's teeth. Now, the wolf will be allowed to eat, or to make some profit, because our society has not developed an alternative incentive system to our capitalist system. But the wolf won't be allowed to ravage consumers, not unless the antiregulatory forces get going, sharpening the wolf's teeth instead of capping them. Attacks on regulation and returns to "free markets" tend to exacerbate the effects of predatory capitalism.

Women are too often the victims of predatory capitalism. We are the majority of minimum wage workers (and some work in sweatshops earning less than the minimum wage). We are too often the folks who can't get access to credit. If we live in inner cities, we are paid low wages and endure high prices because supermarkets haven't located in our neighborhoods. Women shouldn't take "market forces" arguments as a given if we understand that those who rely on market forces to make a profit want regulation when it benefits their bottom line.

For about ten years our economy had been an expanding one, with growth rates so high that a whole range of social policy issues seemed to recede into the background. In the late 1990s, Federal Reserve Board Chairman Alan Greenspan said the economy was experiencing "irrational exuberance," which seemed strange to me since there were many who experienced poverty and unemployment even as the economy expanded. Of course, Mr. Greenspan's approach is of necessity a macroeconomic approach. His job is to manage our nation's monetary policy, to manipulate the Fed's interest rate in a way consistent with sound economic principles (for example, in a recession, he may lower the interest rate so that people will borrow more, and pump more money into the economy). His macroeconomic approach, however, ignores a range of microeconomic inequities.

Mr. Greenspan has not been able to speak of exuberance in the past two years, speaking instead about caution, the possibility of recession, and the need for consumers to remain confident. Consumers are a key part of any exploration of the economy because as long as consumers keep pumping money into the economy, growth rates will be shored up. And though more and more consumers are filing bankruptcy, our nation's buying spree hasn't slowed in the decade. Indeed, in his book *Credit Card Nation*, Robert Manning discusses the growing numbers of *teenagers* who declare bankruptcy!

Can we do anything about issues of bifurcation? Is the goal of economic justice too elusive for women to attain? I think if we embrace the tenet of the Catholic bishops, that the economy exists to serve people, then we encourage government to intervene in markets to help them distribute goods and services more fairly.

WOMAN AS CONSUMER

Whether women identify themselves as "left" or not, we have economic power in our role as consumers. We live in a consumer culture, with goods and services being shoved down our throats at an alarming rate. Technology has developed so rapidly that products are instantly obsolete. You may not be able to get replacement parts tomorrow for the computer you purchased today. If you need a computer to do your work, then you are supposed to buy a new one. Thumb through any women's magazine and you get a sense of what America's retailers think of women. We are barraged with products that will make us smell better, look nicer, and smile brighter. Everything is "new" and "better" and some things may wear out before you get them home. In a consumer culture, it is important to note that women can have a tremendous influence in our economy. We can stop buying products that are offensive. We can change our values (easier said than done) so that we shop out of necessity, not out of sport. We can decide that we can wear the same thing more than once, that we can empower ourselves to save and invest, that we can be actors in our nation's economy.

But patriarchy has manipulated women into being our nation's consumers. We earn less, but we spend more, our spending fueled by the notion that there is a consumer product somewhere that will so transform our lives that we will either be empowered or reach nirvana! When women begin to unpack the connection between our irrational spending, our unequal income, and patriarchy, we may begin to behave as true economic actors.

Instead too many women behave as if economics has nothing to do with them, yet various aspects of our nation's economy affect everything we deal with, from the water we drink, to the clothes we buy, to the trees we sit under on any given day. As long as our economy is a capitalist economy that allocates goods and services using prices, those with fewer dollars will be pushed to the periphery of the economy unless they find markets where they have particular influence. Women can influence consumer markets by spending or withholding their dollars, and can signal approval or disapproval of international hiring policies with their dollars. The economic boycott muscle is one that women have rarely flexed, yet it is an option if women want to influence aspects of our economy.

TOWARD A FEMINIST ECONOMY?

On its web page, WAND (Women's Action for New Directions) says, "Women are the majority in the United States. We start most of the new businesses, make most consumer decisions, and are the majority of Social Security and Medicare beneficiaries. Women have the most at stake in federal budget priorities, yet traditionally our voices have been absent or dismissed in debates on budget priorities and national security policies." Their statement is challenging and provocative.

One of my greatest frustrations as an economist is that I can't really visualize a feminist economy. Nancy Folbre noted in her book *The Invisible Heart* that a feminist economy will take matters of the heart into as much consideration as matters of the head. And I agree with economist Hazel Henderson's assertion that a feminist economy might use something other than price as a way of allocating goods and services. A feminist economy might give women credit for their unpaid or unwaged work, as groups like Wages for Housework have advocated for decades. It might also include the value of women's volunteer work in the GDP.

But if we do this for women, won't we do it for men, as well? Are fairness and feminism synonymous, since improving conditions for women means improving conditions for everyone? In June 2001, I attended a meeting of the International Association of Feminist Economists, held in Oslo, Norway, in the hopes that some of my colleagues would help me visualize an international economy from a feminist context. It was reassuring to know that we took any number of things as "given," including environmental sustainability and distributional fairness. But these issues aren't peculiar to women; they are peculiar to progressive voices that want to break the distributional stranglehold that the wealthy have on our world's resources. If a feminist economy is, indeed, a fair one, then it is something worth struggling for by working with groups like WAND to shift our nation's budget priorities, and to change the way we decide that the pie should be divided up at home and in the world.

RESOURCES FOR THE LEFT

ECONOMIC POLICY INSTITUTE
The mission of the Economic Policy Institute is to provide high-quality research and education in order to promote a prosperous, fair, and sustainable economy. The Institute stresses real world analysis and a concern for the living standards of working people, and it makes its findings accessible to the general public, the media, and policymakers. 1660 L Street, NW

Suite 1200
Washington, DC 20036
202-775-8810
www.epinet.org

THE LEAGUE OF WOMEN VOTERS

"The League of Women Voters, a nonpartisan political organization, encourages the informed and active participation of citizens in government, works to increase understanding of major public policy issues, and influences public policy through education and advocacy."
1730 M Street, NW
Suite 1000
Washington, DC 20036-4508
202-429-1965
www.lwv.org.

PROJECT VOTE SMART

"Project Vote Smart is a national library of factual information on over thirteen thousand elected offices and candidates for public office—president, governors, congress, and state legislatures."
One Common Ground
Philipsburg, MT 59858
406-859-8683
www.vote-smart.org

WOMEN'S ACTION FOR NEW DIRECTIONS (WAND)

WAND's mission is to empower women to act politically to reduce violence and militarism, and redirect excessive military resources toward unmet human and environmental needs.
691 Massachusetts Avenue
Arlington, MA 02476
781-643-6740
www.wand.org

DEBORAH PERRY

If, from the more wretched parts of the old world, we look at those which are in an advanced stage of improvement, we still find the greedy hand of government thrusting itself into every corner and crevice of industry, and grasping the spoil of the multitude. Invention is continually exercised, to furnish new pretences for revenues and taxation. It watches prosperity as its prey and permits none to escape without tribute.

THOMAS PAINE, *RIGHTS OF MAN*

We all recognize Lady Godiva to be an integral player in world history. However, not many people know why she rode naked on her horse through the streets of Coventry, England, in the eleventh century. Well . . . why did she do this? Lady Godiva was protesting the taxes her husband, the earl of Mercia, imposed on the townspeople. Her husband agreed to revoke the taxes only if she rode naked through the streets of Coventry. To his surprise, she agreed, and all townspeople were directed to shut their windows and doors. Legend has it that all townspeople agreed, except for a curious gentleman who was instantaneously struck blind (the source of the term "Peeping Tom") for witnessing the valiant act of Lady Godiva.

Echoing Lady Godiva's reasons for action, the United States was a country built on tax revolt. While taxes may not be a contemporary issue of discussion when hanging out with your girlfriends, American women have been intrepid protestors against taxation since first stepping onto American soil. In the eighteenth century, taxes were thwarting people's ability to progress economically, and the common person was powerless to stop it. But a seemingly innocuous group of women patriots, known as the Daughters of Liberty, shed their demure mind-set and fought off British taxes on imported goods in the spring of 1769. The women colluded with cantankerous merchants and imposed sanctions against the procurement of anything British. In lieu of the foreign imports, the Daughters of Liberty used traditional skills to make their own clothes (by raising sheep), experimented with tea substitutes, and conceded to everything homemade. Most significant, the Daughters of Liberty convinced other females to observe the ban on imports and to help influence a decision made by the Continental Congress to boycott all British goods. Within a year, Britain repealed almost all of its export duties.

Unfortunately, throughout time, government grew enormously and federal programs expanded in every direction. The need to finance the expansion became apparent to political leaders. There were several steps in history that led to government taxation, starting with the War of 1812, which was financed by trade tariffs. The late eighteenth century experienced taxation on distilled spirits, carriages, housing, and land, although the American people rebelled, and therefore, taxes became difficult to collect. For the financing of the Civil War, President Abraham Lincoln, on July 1, 1862, approved the first income tax measure. Then came a succession of intense debates over the necessity of income taxes versus tariffs, and the income tax was repealed in 1872, at a time when government enjoyed large budget surpluses. But in 1894, the Democrats insisted on the reinstitution of the income tax in anticipation of reduced tariffs from the 1894 Tariff Act. In 1895, the U.S. Supreme Court ruled the income tax as unconstitutional because states had not ratified the tax as required by the Constitution. Finally, the decision led Congress to amend the Constitution and, in 1913, the Sixteenth Amendment was adopted, granting Congress the authority to impose a tax "from whatever source derived."

AN EXCESSIVELY TAXED SOCIETY TODAY

President Bill Clinton put us in the highest marginal tax rate since World War II, but thanks to President Bush's 2001 Economic Growth and Tax Relief Reconciliation Act, we are getting some reprieve, which leaves more money in our hands than in the government's. Did you know that for the average household, taxes now exceed the cost of food, clothing, shelter, and transportation combined? According to the Tax Foundation, the typical American family must work until early May each year before earning enough money to pay its combined federal, state, and local tax burden. If you incorporate regulations, which work just like a tax, then July 6 is the date when the average American has paid off their tax burden and begins to earn income for their own family.

Taxes today have permeated our daily lives. Republican pollster Dr. Frank Luntz very cleverly delineates this point: "When you wake up in the morning and drink that first cup of coffee, you pay a sales tax. When you start your car, you pay an automobile tax. Drive to work, you pay a gas tax. At work, you pay an income tax—and a payroll tax. You get home at night, you pay a property tax. Flip on the light, you pay an electricity tax. Turn on the TV you pay a cable tax. Call a friend, you pay a communications tax. Brush your teeth, you pay a water tax. Even when you die, you pay a death tax."

Although taxes are a mystery to most people, as to many tax professionals, we get hit with taxes through individual income tax, employer and employee payroll taxes, estate and gift taxes, corporate taxes, sales taxes on goods and services, excise taxes, customs taxes, property taxes, contributions for social insurance, and more. Taxes are plastered in our paychecks and are hidden in regulations. Taxes are even buried in the sales price of that loaf of bread we purchase at the grocery store, carried down to us by the manufacturer.

What's more maddening? Through various layers of government, we can be taxed three and sometimes four times on the same money. For example, let's say you gross $3,500 a month. When you first earn this money, you pay a personal income tax, a payroll tax including Social Security and Medicare (otherwise known as FICA), and unemployment taxes on that same money. Then, you decide to invest your money in the stock market so you can eventually put a down payment on a home. After your investment increases in the market, you decide to sell the stock in preparation for a down payment, and you are slapped with a capital gains tax. Then you purchase a home, and have to pay property taxes. You have now been taxed three times on the same $3,500 you earned for the month.

Even worse for women is how the tax code treats us differently. I deliberately chose the opening quote from Thomas Paine's *Rights of Man* because it is men whom the present tax system is designed for. Since modern taxes were crafted between the 1930s to the 1950s, men were the ones in the workforce and women were the ones who stayed home and did "housework." When women permeated the workforce and drove household income into higher tax brackets, gender tax biases in marriage, alimony, Social Security, and estate taxes went unheard, as calls for wage equality took center stage. In fact, while conducting research for this chapter, I discovered little information concerning the gender bias of the tax code. Women today are discriminated against in taxes, and if we are to reverse this inequity, we must first be made aware of taxes' hidden favoritism.

MARRIAGE PENALTY TAX

As more married women have entered the workforce, working couples have been penalized in the most peculiar fashion in the tax code. The tax code is clearly biased against married couples, but holds most women—as secondary earners—hostage to their husbands' salaries as described below. The marriage penalty tax imposes higher tax rates on two-income couples than on two single wage earners who live together and file separately. Make sense? I don't think so. U.S. Representative Dave McIntosh (R-IN) shared a true story about an engaged couple from his congressional district who had to postpone their marriage vows because of the marriage penalty tax. Prior to their wedding, Sharon Mallory and Darryl Pierce visited with her accountant about their current and future financial status, and realized that they could not afford the taxes after marriage. As a single filer, Sharon received a $900 tax refund, but if she were to marry holding the same salary, she and her future husband, Darryl, would owe the IRS a check for $2,800, because Sharon's salary is too comparable to Darryl's.

As most women are secondary earners under a joint-filing system, working women enter a tax bracket dictated by their husbands' income, and may actually lose money for the household by working. If Sharon made much less money she would not be so penalized. In fact, the married couple would actually receive the reverse of a marriage penalty and enjoy a "marriage bonus." This occurs when a couple pays less federal income tax filing jointly than they would if they were unmarried and filed as a single or head of household. So the only way to avoid a marriage penalty is to marry someone who makes much more or much less money than you.

The bottom line is that the tax system is set up against two-earner marriages, and is biased against marriage itself whenever economic conditions oblige both partners to have to work. President Bush's 2001 tax bill provides a temporary relief by reducing the marriage penalty tax beginning in 2004, and continues to phase it out until 2009. But, the marriage penalty tax reduction returns to its current rate in 2011, unless President Bush or other future presidents can encourage Congress to make these changes permanent.

ALIMONY

If a woman with children gets divorced, she must literally pass the buck—to Uncle Sam. Even though alimony is considered a "personal" expense, it is treated differently in the tax code where the payor—typically a man—receives a "no limit" deduction (as long as it is in line with a person's income). The alimony recipient—usually a woman—must pay tax on the alimony money on what is already considered reduced income. For example, if a woman receives $50,000 a year in alimony, the man lands a $50,000 deduction worth $18,000 in savings (in a 36 percent tax bracket) whereas the woman will owe $7,500 in income tax. Yet, the child support she receives is not taxable. So, why is the system set up so that child support is nontaxable, but alimony is? Women unable to afford the tax bill of alimony often negotiate to minimize their alimony and increase the child support, but this strategy can backfire when child support ends.

Social Security Tax

Social Security payments discriminate against divorcées. There is a strange loophole in the law that states a divorced spouse must be married at least ten years in order to claim up to 50 percent of an ex-spouse's Social Security earnings. This puts women at risk who opt to stay at home, making it difficult to achieve long-term financial security in their later years if they divorce. The law does not even allow courts to compensate divorced people for the spouse's greater Social Security entitlement by offering them a greater share of some other asset. With more than half of marriages ending in divorce, many stay-at-home women may not be entitled to the Social Security benefits of their former spouses. We discuss Social Security at length in chapter five, "The Economic Safety Net."

Estate or "Death" Tax

Widowed women and men face the estate tax, otherwise known as the "death" tax, but women are more at risk because they tend to outlive their spouses on average by seven years. At first glance, the $1-million-plus figure that this tax currently applies to seems like a large sum. However, when you add up your family's net worth, including your home, cash, personal savings, collectibles, investments, personal property, vehicles, jewelry, life insurance proceeds, retirement benefits, pensions and savings plans, and in many cases the family business or farm equipment, a million dollars accumulates quickly over a lifetime of work. Many families face this steep and debilitating tax.

Few family businesses—only 30 percent—remain afloat after the death of a spouse. When the surviving spouse or children inherit a family business after death, the family business is smacked a life-altering tax due to the IRS nine months after it is levied. That's what happened to the *Chicago Daily Defender*, one of the oldest and most influential African American–owned daily newspapers in the country. It was forced into bankruptcy after the death of its publisher, John Sengstacke, and the surviving family was slapped with a three-million-dollar estate tax bill. It was cost-prohibitive for the family to continue to do business, so the Sengstacke family was forced to retire the paper. For the few family businesses that temporarily survive, 77 percent of them eventually end up in bankruptcy after being imposed by the estate tax.

Again, President Bush's 2001 tax plan provides temporary relief as the death tax rate will continue to spiral down until it is completely eliminated in the year 2010. However, in 2011, the estate tax is scheduled to reappear at the original tax rate of 55 percent unless further legislative action is taken. The Democrats' defense of the death tax is that the rich have accumulated "too much." What? Parents should not be able to pass on to their children any good fortune? It is best described by the National Black Chamber of Commerce as a "legacy killer" for the African-American business community and it is for the rest of us as well.

THE NEED FOR TAX CODE REFORM

We need a tax code that fosters fair, simplistic, uniform, and consistent principles that support pro-growth policies. Most taxpayers do not get the benefit of loopholes, and therefore, we treat the Martha Stewarts of America as if they were superior to the Sally Homemakers of America.

Fairness in the tax code will only happen when the family in the opulent house pays their fair share in taxes with no improper tax breaks or loopholes. One way to achieve fairness, simplicity, uniformity, and consistency is to advocate for a flat tax, where everyone pays the same rate, suggested at around 20 percent. A flat tax would also cultivate stronger economic growth by reducing the bias against savings and investment.

According to the Heritage Foundation, the flat tax would reduce complexity and compliance problems. Taxpayers would no longer have to reveal all their assets to the government. No one would have to pay a double tax on capital gains, investments for their children's education, their own re-

tircment, or any other return on investment for their future financial security. Taxpayers would not have to calculate their tax bill twice and pay
the government the higher of the two amounts. No one would have to
calculate depreciation or track itemized deductions. No one would pay taxes
on dividend income already taxed at the business level or interest income
already taxed at the financial institution level. Families would not need to
sell the family farm or business to pay the death taxes on a dead relative.
Finally, a flat tax would help the poor, as it has been proposed in Congress
that families would not pay taxes on annual income up to $35,400.

THE ECONOMY

American women have made an enormous contribution to the stabilization
and reinvigoration of the U.S. economy through our strong participation in
the workforce. Author Ralph Peters writes, "When the stock market soars,
thank Elizabeth Cady Stanton and the suffragettes, not just their beneficiary, Alan Greenspan. After a century and a half struggle by English and
American women, the U.S. economy now operates at a wartime level of
human-resource commitment on a routine basis."

So, in addition to working towards a pro-growth tax policy, Citizens for
a Sound Economy suggests Congress pass legislative initiatives that will
restore economic growth and vitality, such as energy security, trade promotion authority, and controlled congressional spending. In doing so, we
need to remove regulatory barriers to economic prosperity, which are designed to protect particular industries or industry subsets.

Energy Security

For far too long, the United States has been reliant on foreign energy supply. In fact, the United States imports nearly 60 percent of its crude oil,
an all-time high in history. Oil prices also rose dramatically from $12.00 to
$34.40 a barrel in November 2000, the highest price since October 1990.

This reliance on oil imports gives foreign governments the ability to have undue influence in America's economy. For more on oil drilling, see chapter ten, "The Environment."

Trade Promotion Authority

One of the most effective ways to keep our economy afloat is through increased trade relations with other countries. Particularly in times of crises, according to Citizens for a Sound Economy, "free trade agreements can enrich the lives of people in underdeveloped nations, expand the virtues of civilized society to all corners of the globe, and benefit American consumers and entrepreneurs in the process."

By supporting trade promotion authority, President Bush will be able to react quickly to eliminate trade barriers between the United States and its trading partners. The American consumer will benefit from lower prices and better quality products from countries that hold an economic production advantage in a particular item rather than being forced to purchase a lesser quality product from an inefficient domestic industry. Hence, other countries can benefit from American manufactured goods where we hold an advantage. For more detail on trade, see chapter nine, "Foreign Policy and Globalization."

Controlled Congressional Spending

Particularly in times of economic trouble or war, Congress must show restraint in spending in pork barrel projects. After the September 11 attacks, Congress appropriated $15 billion to the airline industry to help bail it out of financial ruin. Several other industries quickly jumped on the bandwagon, and lobbied for financial assistance programs as well. These legislative fixes sent Congress down a slippery slope of endless spending and government intrusion into some of America's most profitable industries.

* * *

So, how can women be a proactive force against the existing discriminating tax practices, and for economic policies that foster growth? First of all, we can support members of Congress such as Representative Jennifer Dunn, a Republican from Washington, who has championed the permanent elimination of the marriage penalty tax. Other members of Congress such as Senator Richard Shelby, a Republican from Alabama, have been long-term advocates of the flat tax.

Second, we can monitor the tax and economic legislative initiatives of two committees in Congress—Senate Finance and House Ways and Means—by looking at their websites (addresses below). Other congressional committees occasionally get involved in tax and economic measures, but these two committees have predominate jurisdiction over these matters. If you see something you like or don't like, write—via snail mail or e-mail—or call your member of Congress and let them know how you feel about it. You would be amazed to know how often members of Congress are swayed one way or the other based on the amount of mail or phone calls that come into their office.

Third, we can be just as proactive on the state and local level, by monitoring the tax and economic initiatives of your governor, state representatives, and local county/city commissioners. If you do not have access to the Internet, most legislators send out a newsletter (usually every quarter) highlighting their legislative initiatives, usually with some emphasis on taxes and the economy. So, quit griping about how high our taxes are, and know that you have the power to do something about it—available to you right at your fingertips.

RESOURCES FOR THE RIGHT

SENATE COMMITTEE ON FINANCE
U.S. Senate
Washington, DC 20510

202-224-4515

www.senate.gov/finance/

HOUSE WAYS AND MEANS COMMITTEE

U.S. House of Representatives

Washington, DC 20515

202-225-3625

www.house.gov/ways_means/

THE HERITAGE FOUNDATION

This organization is a think tank whose mission "is to formulate and promote conservative public policies based on the principles of free enterprise, limited government, individual freedom, traditional American values, and a strong national defense."

214 Massachusetts Avenue, NW

Washington, DC 20002

202-546-4400

www.heritage.org

AMERICANS FOR TAX REFORM

This organization opposes all tax increases, and believes in a system in which taxes are simpler, fairer, flatter, more visible, and lower than they are today.

1920 L Street, NW

Suite 200

Washington, DC 20036

202-785-0266

www.atr.org

CITIZENS FOR A SOUND ECONOMY

This organization supports free enterprise and limited government.

1250 H Street, NW

Suite 700

Washington, DC 20005-3908
202-783-3870
www.cse.org

COMMON GROUND

Our common ground regarding the economy, as it is in the Equal Pay section, is weak. We both admit that **the tax system is complex and unfair,** but differ in the ways that it is so. While Deborah would support a flat tax, Julianne believes that such a tax is regressive and as unfair as the policies currently comprising the tax code.

5

THE ECONOMIC
SAFETY NET

DEBORAH PERRY

RETIREMENT PROGRAMS

How many times have you heard people say, "I can't wait until I can retire so I can just kick back and enjoy a leisurely life of golf, tennis, and canasta card games," as if big government will provide for all of your expenses for the remaining years of your life? Yeah, right! There is no national retirement security or health care program in my version of the Bill of Rights. We don't live in one of those European countries where you pay about 70 percent of your life's income in taxes to the socialist government, and you and all your aging buddies receive a comprehensive retirement.

The Democrats in America act as if we do live in one of those European countries, and speak about an expected social contract in exchange for working. They have made promises to the American people that—frankly— they can't keep. The Democrats say, "Don't worry about tomorrow, because you are entitled to various government funds at the expense of the American taxpayer." This may sound idyllic, in a communist sort of way, but it definitely does not work. In fact, it only provides people with a false sense of security. Here's why.

First of all, programs like Social Security were never designed to be permanent, and can be changed or eliminated by Congress at any time. Second, we have a rapidly growing aging population. In just nine years, the oldest members of the baby boomers will be sixty-five years old. Couple this with low infertility rates and increasing life expectancies, and we get a formula of fewer workers to support older retirees. The number of workers to support retirees will plummet over the next twenty-five years, from 3.3 to 2.1—a 36 percent drop! It is the Democrats who have set up this nanny state in which we now live, and even the federal government has a responsibility to limit the largesse it promises to senior citizens.

We Republicans have more faith in your ability to care for you and your family in retirement. Of course, the best way we can all prepare for retirement is through planning and personal savings, and to be mildly reliant on government. We all need to save for today and tomorrow. Instead, we like to make excuses for why we can't save, period, as we have grown into the "spend culture" where American cupidity for designer goods far exceeds the value of retirement security. And who suffers the most in retirement from this mentality? Women.

The fact is we live longer than men, and widowed women constitute the largest percentage of the elderly poor. Social Security is the sole source of income for nearly one in five elderly women, and provides at least 90 percent of income for almost one-third of elderly women. How is a woman supposed to afford to live when she loses 50 to 64 percent of the only money she and her husband were living off of—his Social Security? And, divorced women and women who never marry also tend to end up ill-fated in retirement, because the system largely ignores inequities in how the system treats families and single people. Is this how we want to end up?

If we can plan for tomorrow, then we will be assured of a less stressful future. Think of retirement income as a "three-legged stool," where each leg serves as the principal sources of income in old age: Social Security, pensions from employers, and private savings, such as a 401(k) or individual retirement account (IRA). But for the many seniors who did not plan for retirement and can't afford to live off Social Security alone, these people reentered into the workforce, and created a fourth alternative for income.

SOCIAL SECURITY

When President Franklin Roosevelt launched Social Security in 1935, he expected retired workers to rely heavily on personal savings and private pensions. Unfortunately, today, less than half of American workers have personal savings and about 30 percent of women as compared with 46 percent of men are covered by a private pension. Social Security, which was designed to be a small slice of the pie, is now relied on as our primary source of retirement money.

Just what is Social Security? It is an entitlement program, meaning something you are "entitled" to and not guaranteed. The Supreme Court has ruled, in the case of *Flemming v. Nestor* (1960), that workers have no contract or inherent rights to their Social Security funds or benefits, and where Congress can change, reduce, or cut off benefits to anyone and everyone at any time. For example, Congress not only increased the age of retirement from sixty-five to sixty-seven (starting in 2003) for those individuals born after 1938, but also reduced Social Security benefits to individuals who are below the age of 70 and reenter into the workforce. Congress also decided that for working seniors a portion of benefits may be subject to income tax.

As younger workers, we pay a tax rate of 7.65 percent for the Federal Insurance Contributions Act (FICA), of which 6.2 percent covers Social Security and 1.45 percent covers Medicare. Our employer matches the Social Security tax by also paying 6.2 percent. If you don't think that is a big chunk of change out of your paycheck, think again. The average family spends the same amount on Social Security taxes as they do on housing, and almost three times as much for health care expenses. In 1971, Social Security taxes were levied on the first $7,800 of income, but in the year 2002, the taxes were collected on the first $84,900, adjusted each year, of course, based on inflation and average real wage growth. These taxes go into something like a "trust fund." However, our money really does not go into a fund, rather it is used to pay retirement benefits to folks of retirement age. Any excess money is spent and exchanged for special-issue U.S. treasury bonds. This so-called "trust fund" is just something on the books and is merely a promise to pay future benefits.

Social Security Discriminates

The original Social Security Act benefited women by providing coverage for dependent wives and mothers with young children. This was a monumental victory for women advocates such as Florence Kelley, Mary Anderson, and Mary Elizabeth Dreier, who had worked on behalf of protective legislation for women and children. It also fostered support for dependent widows and children, and the educational benefits these children gained access to. In the 1970s, the government expanded Social Security benefits for home-makers who had spent time raising children and maintaining a home, with retirement protection when involved in divorce.

While Social Security did help women in an era when women were homemakers, it now discriminates against most women in the workforce, and here's why. Simply put, a wife's Social Security benefits are measured against her husband's income. It does not matter how much she has con-tributed, a wife automatically receives Social Security benefits equal to at least half of her husband's benefits. Even if a wife has worked a lifetime, she will only receive full benefit if she has earned more than 50 percent of the value of her husband's income, as exhibited in the chart below.

	FAMILY A	FAMILY B
Husband Annual Income	$34,200	$17,100
Wife Annual Income	$0	$17,100
Annual Social Security Tax	$2,120	$2,120
Total benefit at retirement	$1,632/ month	$1,348/ month
Total benefit to survivor	$1,082/ month	$674/ month

Source: Independent Women's Forum

Does the current system seem illogical? Hold on . . . it gets worse when a woman loses her spouse or divorces from her husband. In a death, the sur-viving wife's Social Security benefits are reduced anywhere between 50 to 64 percent of a couple's joint retirement contribution. And, in a divorce, the courts do not honor a husband's Social Security benefits to the wife in settlement unless a couple has been married for at least ten years (for more detail, see chapter four, "The Economy and Taxes"). If you divorce after nine years, eleven months, and twenty-seven days of marriage, you get nothing from Social Security in auxiliary benefits and are entitled to no share of your spouse's benefit. If you are married more than ten years, the government pays you less than if you were to stay married. Years ago, men whose working wives passed away actually had to sue for retirement benefits for minor children, whereas widowed women received it automatically, but at a reduced rate.

Social Security has become an enormous burden where few receive back what they have put into the system. This is particularly certain for younger workers, as they will get back less money from Social Security than they would have earned in a U.S. savings bond. The average rate of return for today's younger workers between their twenties and forties, drifts somewhere between 0 percent and less than zero.

GIVE ME MY PERSONAL RETIREMENT ACCOUNT

President Bush's proposal to privatize a portion of Social Security and unroll personal retirement accounts—also referred to as personal savings or Social Security accounts—is one of the most precocious ideas on the national agenda today. It would allow for workers to have the opportunity to take a partial portion of payroll taxes they are already paying into Social Security and instead invest it into an account that he or she would be in control of and legally own. These accounts would offer a safe investment fund with a limited number of options, such as a stock market index mutual fund similar to Standard & Poor's 500 Index mutual fund; a high-grade corporate bond fund; or a super-safe government bond fund that invests in the new Series I savings bonds (these bonds are designed specifically for retirement savings and pay an inflation-adjusted rate of return that is guaranteed for the thirty-year life of the investment).

Here's a comparison of returns between the current Social Security program versus the innovative idea of privatization. According to the Heritage Foundation, if a thirty year-old couple, for example, each made about $29,000 a year, their combined contribution into Social Security taxes would be about $320,000 (including employer shares). In the current system, at a 1.23 percent return on their money (which is generous), they can expect about $450,000 in total retirement benefits if they stayed married. If this same couple volunteers into a personal retirement account in a conservative portfolio of 50 percent full-proof U.S. treasury bonds and 50 percent stock index funds, they could expect to have $975,000 at the time of retirement—$525,000 more than they would get from the current Social Security system.

These accounts are designed to augment the Social Security net, and to give workers, especially younger workers, greater control over their own money. In addition, there are two key principles of privatization of Social Security: First, make it entirely voluntary, as no one should be forced into a personal account; second, provide a built-in "safety net" into the investment aspect of these accounts so that no one fears retirement poverty.

It is no wonder that 75 percent of working women and 48 percent of unemployed women prefer some investment opportunity with investment accounts. In part because private investment accounts would continue to earn interest regardless of whether a woman was employed, taking time out to raise children, or deciding to continue her education.

Privatization is not a novel idea as we've been witnessing the colossal successes in Chile, Australia, Mexico, Colombia, Peru, and Great Britain (Britain's privatization has become so successful it has surpassed the country's annual economic output and is larger than the pension funds of all other European countries combined). China and Sweden are moving toward privatization. Even in recent years former communist countries such as Hungary and Poland have built huge pensions through privatization.

EMPLOYER-SPONSORED PROGRAMS

A paramount government-private partnership is the provision in the tax code that grants special tax status to profit-sharing and employer-sponsored pension plans, such as a 401(k)-type plan. Most 401(k) plans offer a variety of investment vehicles, from individual stocks or mutual funds to money market accounts. And, the money you invest does not count as income when you complete your annual tax return. For example, if you earn $35,000 but put $5,000 into a 401(k), your taxable income for the year would be only $30,000. Although earnings are taxed when you withdraw after the age of 59½, there is a stiff 10 percent penalty should you withdraw money prior to the allowable age.

Women should know that President Bush's 2001 tax cut law offers women over age fifty a "catch-up" contribution to their savings plans—for the many women who leave the workforce to raise children or care for an ailing parent. In concert, the law also reduces the vesting period for employer contributions to retirement plans from five to three years. For women who enter and depart from the workforce more frequently, this component helps accumulate greater retirement benefits.

Opportunely, with regard to the IRA or Roth IRAs, the law raised the contribution limits without additional penalties: $3,000 in 2002, $4,000 in 2005, $5,000 in 2008 with limits indexed in future years. IRA catch-up provisions will increase those limits for those 50 and older by $500 in 2002 and by $1,000 starting in 2006. Over five years, the new law allows for increases from $10,500 to $15,000 the amount that an individual can contribute to a 401(k) plan.

These plans are expected to account for a growing share of retirement income, but government can help to enlarge the employer-sponsored programs especially to small businesses. Also, government can better inform employers, big and small, of their responsibility to employees under the law, and increase assistance to employers, plan sponsors, and service providers.

Individual Savings

We like to consume goods in America . . . lots of goods. We are in the *got .o have, got to have, got to have more* era. It is a style of living beyond our means where we *live for today, buy now . . . and say the heck with tomorrow.* Americans' personal savings rate (personal savings as a percentage of disposable income) has been steadily declining since 1975, and is at its lowest rate (below 1 percent) since World War II. For comparison, Japan's savings rate is above 25 percent. This means we spend more than we save. We need to think about whether we want to give up some of our luxuries today to have a more secure financial future.

Private retirement saving opportunities for women can always be enhanced by augmenting private pensions. And, government can also encourage personal savings by giving us more tax breaks that promote increased savings. For example, why not create tax incentives for a medical savings account for people who wish to save in anticipation of large medical expenses related to old age, because Medicare and Medicaid are also in deep financial trouble.

A Medicare Nightmare

There is a common myth among many women that Medicare will cover all of their health care needs during retirement. When President Lyndon Johnson signed the Medicare Act in 1965, older Americans were promised never to be denied "the healing miracle of modern medicine," nor to have illness "crush and destroy the savings they had so carefully put away." That was then and this is now. Today, medicare is carved into three parts: Part A finances hospital insurance (HI); Part B finances supplemental medical insurance, which covers outpatient services and physicians' fees; Part C or the Medicare+Choice program creates a highly regulated market of private, mostly managed care plans for those seniors interested in enrolling (this was the cornerstone of President Bill Clinton's 1997 Balanced Budget Act).

Presently, the government is struggling to keep the second-largest entitlement program afloat, as Medicare has two major problems: financial health and quality health care in the face of exploding costs, regulations, and growing gaps in coverage. Financially, the federal government paid the costs of whatever health insurers demanded, causing the system to practically become defunct. First-year benefits in 1967 paid out $3.2 billion to Medicare recipients. In 1999, Medicare expenditures grew to an estimated cost of $216 billion. That figure, according to the Congressional Budget Office, is expected to be an astounding $428 billion in 2007. What's going to happen when 77 million baby boomers start to retire in 2011 and need coverage? In the face of exploding costs, Medicare regulations have increased, according to the Mayo Foundation, to a total of 110,758 pages (of the 132,729 pages of federal health care regulations). This bureaucratic nightmare directs money to paperwork and staff time and away from in suring the elderly and the poor.

Because many women wrongly thought that Medicare would cover all of their health needs, many are forced to dip into retirement funds to pay for basic health care costs, such as prescription drugs. For the 40 percent of seniors without prescription drug coverage, out-of-pocket expenses can be anywhere between $500 and $2,000 annually. While most private insurance companies offer some form of coverage for prescription drugs, this component of the Medicare debate got mired in political infighting and left off the bargaining table. Even though over 60 percent of seniors have some form of prescription drugs through employer-based insurance programs, Medigap plans, Medicaid, or state pharmaceutical drug coverage, there is budding concern for prescription drug coverage for seniors under Medicare. Another enormous problem with Medicare is that the rising costs of health care forces many recipients on average to spend an out-of-pocket $3,100 per year.

CHANGE MEDICARE NOW!

President Bush proposed an option for Medicare recipients afforded to members of Congress and the millions of federal workers, retirees, and dependents, who share a unique health care system based on free-market principles of consumer choice and competition—known as the Federal Employees Health Benefits Program (FEHBP). The way this program works is .or hundreds of insurance providers across the country to compete for the personal business of federal workers, and once a year, these consumers have the opportunity to pick from a dozen or two providers at the coverage level and cost they wished to pay. It is unparalleled coverage and virtually a one-of-its-kind in the country, inclusive of most prescription drugs (with a small co-payment), and enormously satisfactory to the consumer (I know as I was a recipient of this health plan). Senators John Breaux (D-LA) and Bill Frist (R-TN) have also offered a proposal in Congress that works within the FEHB framework.

Meeting the challenges of a rapidly growing aging population is new for the United States. What this means is that younger workers need to take greater responsibility and foster a self-reliant approach to our retirement. Supporting President Bush in his initiatives of personal savings accounts, expansion of employer-related programs like the 401(k), and increasing personal savings through tax incentives will help all of us into a stronger financial future. It will not only be good for us as individuals, it will help ensure a prosperous future for later generations.

Resources for the Right

The 60 Plus Association
This organization is a seniors advocacy group promoting an agenda of a free enterprise, less government, less taxes approach to seniors' issues. 60 Plus has set ending the federal estate tax and saving Social Security for the young as its top priorities.
1655 North Fort Myer Drive
Suite 355
Arlington, VA 22209
703-807-2070
www.60Plus.org

CATO INSTITUTE

This organization is a research foundation that focuses on traditional American principles of limited government, individual liberty, free markets, and peace, and has done extensive research on Social Security reform.

1000 Massachusetts Avenue, NW
Washington, DC 20001
202-842-0200
www.socialsecurity.org

THE CENTER FOR THE STUDY OF WOMEN IN THE ECONOMY
NATIONAL CENTER FOR POLICY ANALYSIS

This organization fosters pragmatic conversations about women in the economy, and focuses on employment, Social Security reform, taxes, and health care.

12655 North Central Expressway
Suite 720
Dallas, TX 75243
972-386-6272; Fax: 972-386-0924
www.womenintheeconomy.org

JULIANNE MALVEAUX

We the People of the United States, in Order to form a more perfect Union, establish Justice, insure domestic Tranquility, provide for the common defense, promote the general Welfare, and secure the Blessings of Liberty to ourselves and our Posterity, do ordain and establish this Constitution for the United States of America.
PREAMBLE, UNITED STATES CONSTITUTION (1787–1788)

Inevitably, when one deals with issues of government programs and public benefits, rich folks always get their pants in a bunch. It's "my money" they say and on go the complaints about being taxed to Timbuktu and how it's not fair that they don't even reap the benefits of what they sow. That's a silly notion because the United States will spend at least $330 billion on defense next year, far more than we will on social spending—and I would say having a strong defense is a benefit for all citizens, just as is social spending. Furthermore, let's not even talk about corporate welfare—billion-dollar industry bailouts for every sector from military aviation to commercial airlines, savings and loan corporations to information technology (for example, in the form of $1.4 billion allocated for IBM in the fall of 2001). This discrepancy between what we give to our country's fat cats in the form of corporate welfare and what we give our country's poorest families in the form of public assistance is unfortunate at best and absolutely reprehensible at worst.

Ultimately, the necessity of an economic safety net, of public assistance, social security, publicly funded parks and libraries, and other programs, is predicated upon what one believes should be the purpose of government. I believe that the role of government is, as stipulated in the preamble to the U.S. Constitution, to promote the general welfare of its people. Strict constructionists would suggest that the founders of this nation never meant for families to receive entitlement benefits in the form of Aid for Families with Dependent Children (the pre-1996 welfare program) pay ments from the Depression through the years leading up to welfare deform; I would suggest that the founders of this nation never meant for families to even witness the Depression that wrecked the homes and lives of thousands. It was precisely because FDR believed in government's role as the provider of an economic safety net for its citizens that this nation re covered and prospered. However, the Depression had an especially devas tating impact on black Americans. Already poor, less than seventy-five years out of legally sanctioned slavery but still toiling away on southern farms and plantations in the name of "sharecropping" (which is an interesting term since "sharing" is not what comes to my mind when I think of the way former slaves were treated during the process of ending slavery), many black folks had nowhere to go and little infrastructure to support them. Conven iently enough, the Social Security Act of 1935, which was meant to guar antee pensions for all individuals who worked until sixty-five years of age, did not even apply to farm workers or domestics—jobs held predominantly by women and African Americans. Coverage was broadened in 1954, when the self-employed, including farmers and domestics, received Social Secu rity coverage.

Poverty in America existed well before the Depression raged in the 1930s. It did, though, simply plunge more deeply into poverty those who were already poor and stripped livelihoods away from others; in sum, the Depression only served to make poverty more visible. With the visibility of poverty returned the Pilgrimesque notion of the worthy versus the unworthy poor. Widows and unemployed men were worthy of "pensions" or "insur ance;" single moms and divorcées were deemed less worthy and were of fered "aid" and "public assistance." It is important to truly think critically and rationally about issues surrounding the societal safety net. Many Amer icans believe that we should offer assistance to individuals who may find themselves in precarious economic situations; we also believe that we should make everyone work. This brings us to Temporary Assistance for Needy Families program, which replaced AFDC in 1996 when the Personal

Responsibility and Opportunity to Work Reconciliation Act (PROWRA) was passed.

TEMPORARY ASSISTANCE FOR NEEDY FAMILIES

In 1996, Congress passed and President Bill Clinton signed into law a piece of landmark legislation that ended "welfare as we know it." PROWRA, the Personal Responsibility and Opportunity to Work Reconciliation Act, came to be known as welfare reform (though those of us in the progressive community foresaw some of the damage that would be caused by ending AFDC), providing public benefits through block grants to the states and de-emphasizing education as a tool for economic improvement, all of which happened as a direct result of the PROWRA legislation. However, the legislation has been touted for encouraging (or forcing, as the case may be) public assistance recipients to work, and providing them with assistance to make the successful transition from welfare to work (although some education and job training is not covered as transition assistance).

PROWRA is faulty for many reasons, because the entire piece of legislation is predicated on the belief that (1) marriage is the foundation of a successful society; (2) marriage is an essential institution of a successful society that promotes the interest of children; and (3) promotion of responsible fatherhood and motherhood is integral to successful child rearing and the well-being of children. The legislation featured components authorizing abstinence-only education, even though this type of sex education has not been proven to either lower teenage sexual activity nor does it provide teenagers with the tools with which to approach sex wisely and with discretion. Not that I find fault with marriage in and of itself, mind you.

My major concern is the arrogance exhibited by privileged white men in making the decision that if I am one-half of a poor couple, I should stay home, raise my babies, and let my husband work his minimum wage job to support us all. From where I sit, this is part of the right-wing agenda to favor one form of family over other forms, and also to provide less assistance to poor women. To be sure, the majority of kids will turn out to be stable and productive members of society if they are raised in stable, productive homes. Children will not turn out to be model citizens just because they grew up with two parents—those two parents must be quality caregivers and providers, which is why it makes sense that House Republicans mentioned the "promotion of responsible fatherhood and motherhood" in PRO-WRA legislation. Maybe I'm out of the loop, but while I've seen fatherhood programs cropping up all over the country, I haven't seen many programs geared toward improving Mom's parenting skills.

TANF, long story short, is predicated upon the ideas that work and marriage are essential to a stable society. Gone is the idea that education is the best way to prevent poverty—a concept for which the Washington, D.C.–based Center for Women Policy Studies has been advocating for decades. Despite analyses completed by organizations as varied as the Center for Women Policy Studies, Jerome Levy Economics Institute at Bard College, and the Institute for Women's Policy Research, which suggest that women receiving postsecondary education not only stay off of welfare longer but also have kids who are more likely to go to college and who will make money and thus pay taxes, our government is still elitist enough to think that education is for the rich and that poor women aren't "worthy." If we really want to help vulnerable populations get out and stay out of poverty, we will improve K–12 education and make postsecondary education available for all who wish to pursue it.

Further, the abolition of AFDC and the creation of TANF, a block grant program administered by each state and operated based on each state's own TANF plan, put stringent work requirements on welfare recipients, which I do not necessarily oppose. I do oppose the practice of sticking welfare recipients in job clubs and job readiness activities whose effect on their economic viability is tenuous at best. I do oppose the practice of making any work better than no work and am hard-pressed to believe that working minimum wage for Wackenhut Corporation (which operates prisons as well as provides security for private clients) for however many hours a day, keeping one away from one's family, could somehow be better than being able to receive general assistance while attending college during the day while your children are also in school, being home to help them with their homework, and being home to make them dinner. We have our priorities screwed up—and our current welfare policy is the perfect example of what happens when the question of who we should help rather than why and how we should dominates public discussion.

While the Clinton administration tackled welfare reform during an economic expansion, the Bush administration is attempting to tighten welfare requirements in a shaky economy. They favor raising the number of hours that women on welfare should work, and on using funds that might be otherwise used for job training to "promote marriage."

THE DANGERS OF SOCIAL SECURITY PRIVATIZATION

Because the nation's population is aging, the issue of Social Security solvency is a major one. President Bush appointed a commission to consider privatization options, and had the nation's seventh largest company, Enron, not declared bankruptcy in late 2001, the privatization issue might have been resolved by now. But with more than twenty thousand people having lost their pensions, many have suggested that the privatization issue be approached cautiously. After all, allowing people to make their contributions to private funds, not government-guaranteed ones, is scary in light of the Enron debacle. Still, some feel that privatizing Social Security will give people larger rates of return and help keep the system solvent. I disagree. Social Security is more than a retirement system. Privatizing will leave too many people out in the cold.

While Social Security originally did not benefit a large number of African-American and women workers, the case is quite the opposite today. Social Security protects workers by insuring them against loss of income due to retirement, death, or disability, and women, children, and African Americans are the major beneficiaries. According to the Economic Policy Institute, African Americans make up just 12 percent of the population, and constitute 18 percent of disability beneficiaries. Women make up 52 percent of the population but are 72.3 percent of all survivorship benefits. Sadly, children under the age of eighteen, who make up just 6 percent of the population, make up 26.9 percent of survivorship beneficiaries and 22.1 percent of disability beneficiaries. Quite simply, Social Security is just a good deal for the average worker and the lowest wage workers, who may not have the means to save funds for retirement if they didn't have Social Security. The Economic Policy Institute reports that the average rate of return from Social Security for workers between 1956 and 1964 is 2.7 percent versus the 2 percent that is expected to be the rate under privatization. With the knowledge that women, children, African Americans, and low-wage earners are the most vulnerable to changes in Social Security structure, I approach this issue with caution.

Privatization is such a misguided idea. Women, African Americans, children, and low-wage workers will be disproportionately (and negatively) affected when the fool's gold that is privatization doesn't pan out—and I am especially concerned. If we partially privatize Social Security and move a portion of Social Security revenue into individual accounts, this means that there will be less income available to Social Security itself; it then follows that benefits will have to be cut as a result. Some estimates suggest that a diversion of 2 percentage points of payroll (out of a total of 12.4 percent) will require a cut in all benefits of 41 percent for anyone who is younger than fifty-five in 2002. In addition, Social Security currently redistributes funds toward low-wage earners, which yields them a higher rate of return on their contributions, and which makes perfect sense. With individual accounts, low-wage workers could be left out in the cold as higher-income individuals leave the system. And, quite frankly, we cannot let the livelihoods of individuals who have worked throughout their life become dependent on something as precarious and unpredictable as the stock market.

Ultimately there are some serious issues to consider when debating Social Security privatization. For one, have we considered the costs of transitioning from a pay-as-you-go system to a pre-funded system, which is what would happen with privatization? Some of us have, and this group includes the Institute for Women's Policy Research, which notes that 90 percent of current payroll taxes are used to pay current retirees, survivors, and disabled workers. If individual accounts became policy and practice, the generations living through the transition would be financially responsible for the retirement of both their parents and their grandparents. Secondly, what about the cost of removing the disability and life insurance components of Social Security? Do we really think that low-wage workers can afford to purchase said options on the free market? It's not likely, and putting low wage workers in that position is careless and not a sound idea. Those conservatives who would suggest that retirement preparation works best by combining Social Security, private savings, and pensions from employment overlook the fact that many jobs, especially low-wage jobs, do not offer pensions and also do not offer the kind of pay necessary to put money away for the future.

The future is something we all worry about—and Social Security disproportionately makes it more stable for women, children, African Americans, and low-wage workers—and it would be myopic and fruitless to restructure the system to their detriment. While we all worry about the future, the present—especially knowing where your next meal is coming from and how healthy it will be—invades the lives of more Americans than many people care to recognize.

DOMESTIC HUNGER

Too many Americans experience hunger, and this is a fact that did not change much despite a decade of economic expansion from 1991 to 2001. While the poverty rate dropped and the welfare rolls shrunk, millions had more month than money, running out of food and funds by the twenty-fifth or twenty-sixth of each month. The National Conference of Mayors annually reports increased unmet food and shelter needs. And while many of the hungry are recent immigrants and their children, the recession has left suburban families experiencing hunger, as well. The technology bust left people in California's Silicon Valley hungry, despite the veneer of affluence.

In September of 2001, Rachel Smith (her name has been changed, but she is not Latina) walked up to her local county Department of Social Services office in a southern state intending to apply for food stamps in Spanish. She had a tough time, and she relayed it to progressive people in her state. I'm sure it seemed a bit strange to the workers behind the counter. Nonetheless, this situation—of an applicant wishing to apply for food stamps in Spanish—is entirely possible if not extremely frequent, given the precipitous rise in the Hispanic population in the South. Somehow a local news outlet got wind of what went down at the DSS office and she had herself a story. The only reason this sequence of events even made the news was because the director of a low income legal services office had asked Ms. Smith to apply for food stamps in Spanish and see where it got her. Had this been Hector, Juan, or Concepcion, who truly could not speak a word of English, the circumstances might have been different; we may have never known the difficulties of applying for food stamps or any other public benefit when one doesn't speak English. Where this incident took place, they now know, and they are making strides to correct deficiencies in their system. The most telling repercussion of Ms. Smith's, and thus hundreds of Spanish speakers' experiences, is that these people are least likely to get adequate public benefits in a reasonable amount of time. Events such as these, coupled with the ridiculous length of some state food stamps applications (California's, for example, can take hours and hours to complete and is twenty-one pages long) and the irrelevant and difficult questions asked on these food stamps applications, make it clear that food stamps are not always getting to the most vulnerable populations. It is certainly true that the answer to the hunger problem cannot be solved by food alone, but food is certainly part of the solution.

Each year, approximately 8 percent of children under twelve are hungry, according to America's Second Harvest, the United States' national network of food banks. According to the Food Research and Action Center (FRAC), 26.8 million children eat school lunches each year. Of this number, 15.2 percent of them receive free or reduced-price lunches. This is disconcerting (that we have hungry children, not that we manage to feed them through federal programs) because the fact remains that we are, indeed, the world's richest nation and yet some of the pesky problems that keep food in Zimbabwe from getting from the farm to the market and to the consumer are the same problems that keep food in the States from getting to the consumer: Prices, access, transportation, and rurality all confluence to make it difficult for poor people to afford healthful foods and difficult for them to get to an adequate grocery store. Our answer to the hunger problem could easily be to pump more funds into TEFAP (The Emergency Food Assistance Program) or food stamps or school lunch and school breakfast programs (if there's one thing we should be able to do it is at least feed children). The problem with that solution is that it is terribly myopic. Hunger cannot be solved in a vacuum. If we feed the stomach of a child who is hungry, chances are her mind and soul are still suffering from starvation. The only true way to end hunger is to tackle the root causes of poverty: circumstances such as joblessness, racism, unaffordable housing, poor educational opportunities, and, yes, ineptitude (I know a positively brilliant young man whose friends think he is going to end up homeless because he's so absentminded he'll forget to pay his rent).

This being said, how can anyone honestly believe that our current safety net is adequate while anywhere between 700,000 and 2 million people go inadequately housed each year, nearly 11 percent of households go inadequately fed, and unreal numbers of people are in the intenable position of having to make $33.60 per hour to afford a two-bedroom apartment in metropolitan areas like San Francisco and San Diego? I have conceded that solving the hunger problem in the long term will take much more than food. In the meantime, however, there are several ways our government can provide less systemic but nonetheless effective solutions to hunger and food insecurity. This is what we should work toward:

- Refrain from devolving the food stamp program so that it is not distributed via block grants;

- Fully fund food stamps and WIC (Women, Infants, and Children) so that families can purchase healthful foods as opposed to just what is least expensive;

- Increase the number of schools offering school breakfast and lunch programs;

- Publicize opportunities for children and the elderly to be eligible for summer and year-round (only one in five of the 15.2 million children who received reduced or free school lunch or breakfast received meals from two federal summer nutrition programs according to the Food Research and Action Center);

- Provide universal multilingual forms for public benefits applications.

These are just a few of the ways we can tackle but one of the myriad problems associated with poverty. There is still a great deal left to do—and we still need an economic safety net, for those who have trouble making ends meet, for those who never make ends meet, and for the children and the elderly.

WHY WE STILL NEED AN ECONOMIC SAFETY NET

I had a long talk with one of my assistants about the economic safety net, in preparation for writing this piece. She had spent a year as a Mickey Leland–Bill Emerson Hunger Fellow of the Congressional Hunger Center. By the time she was done she had more information and data on hunger and poverty in America at her fingertips than she could shake a stick at. As part of the fellowship, Reginna spent time at the Hawaii Foodbank in Honolulu. At first, she told me, it was really tough explaining to the average Jane why she was going to the land of paradise to fight hunger because everyone had this vision that Hawaii was devoid of hunger and poverty. Truth be known, Hawaii has some astounding levels of food insecurity, an economy heavily buttressed by tourism and travel, and pervasive race issues, all of which lend themselves to a fragile economy. What I gleaned from her was that even in paradise, times are tough. Reginna reported that more than half of the food pantries on Oahu noticed an increase in the number of clients from 1999 to 2000. If the milk and honey have dried up in paradise, we are all in jeopardy—and we must never renege on our commitment to promote the general welfare of the people of the United States.

Washington politicos and savvy pundits can sit around tables pontificating about corporate welfare, privatization of Social Security, taxes, TANF, food stamps, and Section 8 housing for as many hours a day as voters and viewers can stand. The fact remains that many Americans don't have the time to have an opinion on these issues because they're too busy working two jobs, neither of which offer any health insurance. Ultimately, the need for an economic safety net is not so much a need for subsidies and cash payments as it is a need for choices. This means being equipped with the ability to make sound choices regarding retirement and healthful choices among quality foods as much as it means possessing the tools necessary to make a livable wage and live in housing that meets standards of livability. Choice, I always thought, was the American way. Our fellow citizens who find themselves malnourished or hungry, ill-housed or homeless, uneducated, or in the words of Lauryn Hill, miseducated, find themselves restricted by enclosures that have not been erected by themselves. We must continue to provide those less fortunate with a safety net because until we succeed at providing unrestricted access to level playing fields regardless of race, national origin, or sex, there will be individuals trapped in ghettos, enclosed by poverty, and, most assuredly, seeking some semblance of the promise stated in the Preamble to the U.S. Constitution.

RESOURCES FOR THE LEFT

NATIONAL COMMITTEE TO PRESERVE SOCIAL SECURITY AND MEDICARE (NCPSSM)

"The National Committee to Preserve Social Security and Medicare was founded in 1982 to serve as an advocate for the landmark federal

programs of Social Security and Medicare and for all Americans who seek a healthy, productive, and secure retirement."
10 G Street, NE
#600
Washington, DC 20002
202-216-0420
www.ncpssm.org.

CENTER ON BUDGET AND POLICY PRIORITIES
The Center on Budget and Policy Priorities is a nonpartisan research organization and policy institute that conducts research and analysis on a range of government policies and programs, particularly those that affect low- and moderate-income people.
820 1st Street, NE
Suite 510
Washington, DC 20002
202-408-1080
www.cbpp.org

CENTER FOR COMMUNITY CHANGE
The Center for Community Change helps low-income people build powerful, effective organizations through which they can change their communities and public policies for the better.
1000 Wisconsin Avenue
Washington, DC 20007
202-342-0567
www.communitychange.org

FOOD RESEARCH AND ACTION CENTER
FRAC works to improve policies to eradicate hunger and malnutrition in the United States.
1875 Connecticut Avenue, NW
Suite 540

Washington, DC 20005
202-986-2200
www.frac.org

AMERICAN ASSOCIATION OF RETIRED PERSONS (AARP)
Membership organization for persons fifty and older.
601 E Street, NW
Washington, DC 20049
800-424-3410
www.aarp.org.

COMMON GROUND

- We agree that there is a **need for an economic safety net,** but we disagree on the extent to which it should be utilized.

- Further, we disagree on what the role of government should be in retirement savings, but we agree on the fact that **women need to be more engaged in their financial futures** since women tend to live longer than men, thus requiring more savings.

6

CRIME AND VIOLENCE

JULIANNE MALVEAUX

CRIME AND "JUST-US"

It was one of those crisp fall nights, and I had a big old chip on my shoulder. I was carrying $200 in cash to buy a sweater I didn't really want from a friend who was broke enough to need a break but prideful enough to insist on knitting me a sweater instead of borrowing money. And she didn't want a check! I was doing her a favor, but she had the nerve to insist that I bring cash for the sweater, and to come by after my squash game, not before. Grousing, I schlepped over to a cash machine, got some money, then trudged through one of those crosstown paths in Central Park, going to play some squash. I had on sweats and a cap and felt as frumpy as I looked, with my spirit almost too funky to enjoy the changing leaves.

I hadn't noticed the footsteps echoing mine as I trudged across the park, but I heard a voice.

"Hey, lady," the young man said. I turned to look at him. First mistake. He is African American, about my height, lean, scowling.

"Yeah," I say. I'm not intimidated. I figure he's going to ask me for the time or something.

"Give me the bag, give me your money," he says. I am not giving up this bag. It is a leather bag, specially cut for a squash racket. And I have money! I'm twenty-eight, an assistant professor at the New School in New York. I'm not broke, but I'm not rolling in dough, either. I'm not giving anything up. I size the kid up and say, "No."

"What do you mean, no?" he says.

"No. I'm not giving you spit (or a word like that). Do you have a knife or a gun? Why should I give you my bag?"

"This is a robbery," he says. I am looking at this boy whose face has as many sharp angles as a rich, dark piece of Shona sculpture, looking at him and thinking that I am just not going to give him my bag. Not today.

"Do you have a knife or a gun?" I ask.

"No," he says.

Then I laugh. "Look," I tell him, "I'm five-foot-six on a good day and you are about the same. I weigh about 160 pounds, and so do you. I'm not just going to hand you my money. You have to have some persuadiator" (which is not a real word, but he got my drift).

Now I'm off on what some of my friends call Malveaux lecture mode.

"What kind of robber are you, anyway? You don't even carry the tools of your trade. You just expect me to *give* you my money. That's not a robbery, that's a social service program, and I'm not playing social worker today."

I am rattling, a mile a minute, telling this young man about himself.

"Look, you are no good at this. Why don't you go to school or something? You are attractive. Probably you are smart. You can't make a living trying to rob people when you don't even have a knife or a gun."

The guy shouts, "You're a crazy bitch."

"Yeah," I say, "but you aren't getting my money."

He mumbles some threat, then turns and walks in the opposite direction.

I turn and walk toward the East Side. All the way to the squash club I'm paranoid as all get out, and by the time I get there I am literally shaking. Sometimes my mouth makes deals that my butt can't cash, and after the fact, I am full of "what ifs." What if he shot me? What if he jumped me and beat me down? What if he showed me a gun, put it up to my head or in my mouth like they do in the movies? I guess, then, I would have given him my money.

My squash game is more pitiful than usual, but I play on. When I call a friend that night, I sob and talk about the fear that has come hours after the fact. He urges me to call the cops, to give up a description. I tell him there was no harm done; the guy was really just a kid. I'm not about to have some young brother locked up for a botched robbery. We talk into the night about law and order, crime and punishment, race and rage. I confess then, as I do now, that I often consider the criminal justice system the "just-us" system, with "just us" being those in power, usually white folks. I don't think it reasonable or fair. Of course we need law and order, but I'd like to see it meted out evenly.

Racial profiling, as in the murder of Amadou Diallo by overzealous police officers who didn't know the difference between a wallet and a gun, seems to suggest that it is much harder for an African-American person to get a fair shake from the criminal "just-us" system. The horrible assault on Abner Louima, who was sodomized with a plunger by police officer Justin Volpe with the concurrence of dozens who were on duty in his station house, is harrowing. The fact that our president may have a criminal record about which we will never know precisely because of who he is (a Bush) and what the crime may involve (cocaine) suggests a justice system dominated by privilege and patriarchy. Sometimes I feel nearly strangled with mixed feelings that really aren't that mixed. I want law and order, but I want it to be both compassionate and fair.

I think most women want it to be fair, but I think that race and class affect women's perspectives on crime, since women's experiences with criminal "just-us" are shaped by our position on the race/class hierarchy. To be sure, almost every woman shudders at the thought of any kind of violence—street violence, domestic violence, sexual violence. But we know that those who are victims of violence have their victimhood calibrated by their social position. You need only look at different reactions to the rapes or disappearances of different "kinds" of women. Thousands of police hours were spent looking for government intern Chandra Levy during the summer of 2001, but dozens of African-American women were missing in Washington around the same time Chandra was missing and only a fraction of the police hours (or media attention) was focused on them. To be sure, Chandra's disappearance was linked to a member of Congress, so it made sense that her story would garner headlines. But as we learned about her humanity and foibles, I shuddered to think of the number of disappearing women who were anonymous Jane Does and whose uniqueness was never acknowledged or celebrated by the media.

As women, we rally together around issues of gun safety, but often we forget that "Saturday night specials" flood some communities and profit others. As women, we eschew the violence we see on television directed toward women, the virulent violence that spews out of the mouths of babes (also known as rap music). As women of color, we also understand that some of these babes have grown up in immersed in violence and know little else. Many women are concerned with the death penalty, especially because it is such a final remedy. And, as men of color are increasingly incarcerated, this has an impact on the women in their families—their mothers, sisters, wives, and daughters. Prison reform is an issue for every woman who has a loved one connected to the prison system, and it should also be an issue for all women because of the increased incarceration of women in our society.

Mixed feelings course through the minds of black women. I have zero tolerance toward domestic violence, but I listen to sisters and friends who have crazy husbands or boyfriends—men who will just show up without an invitation. They'll get loud and ignorant, and get to throwing things, slapping folks. The law offers them a remedy, but they tell me, and I identify with this, that they don't want to lock a black man up and subject him to more violence and brutality. One friend told me a poignant story of a man she just wanted to shrug out of her life after their two-month hot-and-heavy affair had fizzled. He wasn't having it. So, he nearly stalked her, coming around at all hours of the day and night, parking outside her home, sitting on the porch. Never threatening, but menacing.

Exasperated, she told the man and everyone who knew him that if he kept it up she would be forced to report it to the police. Mind you, she didn't want him beaten or even incarcerated. She just wanted to be left alone. Her nemesis was emboldened by her statement and used old keys to let himself into her home. Frightened, she followed up on her promise to call the police. But she says that when the police came, her former lover did not resist arrest. Still, they hit him with a billy club three or four times, and hog-tied him. She sobbed as she told me the story. She said, "All I wanted them to do was warn him. If this was a white woman getting her butt beat in the suburbs, do you think the cops would have hog-tied her preppy and powerful husband?" The ambiguity of unequal treatment is always there.

Does this mean I'm soft on crime? Not at all. I just want law and order, and punishment to be fair. And, as I said, I want it to be compassionate. I don't want thirteen-year-olds getting life in prison for a murder. I want them to be looked at as warped and distorted children who need help, not doing time with really hardened criminals. And I see the inequality. When white boys get their guns out and go shooting up a school, commentators talk about the sociology of the matter: What might have gone wrong? When black boys are involved in crimes with a fraction of the impact, we are ready to lock them up and throw away the key. A six-year-old black boy shot his white female classmate at Buell Elementary School in Flint, Michigan, about a year ago. The powers that be opined that this child was depraved. Some even called him O. J., Junior. They didn't deal with the real dimensions of his tragedy. His mother was forced into a work program by welfare deform and was away from home twelve hours a day traveling back and forth from her job. She had also been evicted and had no choice but to leave her son with his adolescent brother for makeshift care. The child got one of his uncle's guns, took it to school, and shot his classmate. Wrong, wrong, wrong. But there is culpability on the part of our society, as well as on the part of this child and his family. Notably, the uncle was sent to prison for his part in the tragedy. But the father of our latest school shooter who opened fire at southern California's Santana High School, who had one of his dad's guns, will face no such penalty. Am I getting redundant when I say that the Flint man was black, the California man white? And I'd simply like to ask the reader to search her memory and compare how one family's circumstances was treated with compassion, while the other was treated as a depraved criminal.

GUN CONTROL

Why are guns so available in our society? We have almost a handgun per person in our country and yet some folks chafe at the notion of gun control, reading the Second Amendment as their personal right to bear arms, not the societal right the amendment speaks to. We regulate automobile use, but we don't regulate gun use. More than 3.5 million brand-new guns have been manufactured since 1990, at the pace of about a gun every twenty seconds. Give me a break! We don't need all those guns. I've heard Charlton Heston and those National Rifle Association folks assert that "guns don't kill, people do." But people without guns can't use them, and all those folks who say they are "shooting" haven't specified their prey. If we could put a lock on guns, we could lower our crime rates.

Think about all the accidents that take place because someone got their hands on the wrong gun. If we simply restricted the public's access to guns, we'd reduce loss of life. I get tired of hearing stories about the kids who find a parent's gun and then let loose with it, not to mention all the Columbine-type stories of frustrated and angry children boiling over in a schoolyard with a gun they weren't supposed to get their hands on. How many accidents like this will we have to have before we draw the line?

The National Rifle Association buys politicians like some folks buy peanuts and have so skewed the debate that it is unlikely that our nation can have a conversation about stopping the easy availability of guns in our society. They donated over $3 million for the 2000 election cycle, have twenty-two million members, and have skewed some of their recruitment material. While the Million Moms March brought hundreds of thousands of women to Washington to fight the gun lobby in May 2000, they might have been more effective at their state capitals. According to Salon website correspondent Bruce Shapiro, "No license or registration is required to own a gun in thirty-five states; forty-three states require no permit for assault weapons; and in eighteen states, kids can buy rifles and shotguns before they can drive or vote."

Contrast us with Great Britain, where individual citizens can't own handguns and the police hardly even carry them. No wonder children in the United States are twelve times more likely to die from guns than children in other industrialized nations! We occupy absolutely no moral high ground here. Indeed, the proliferation of handguns in this country is the shame of the world, especially when trick-or-treating exchange students are shot and killed because a trigger-happy person thought them an intruder!

PRISON REFORM

The subject of prison reform contains many layers. What many of us may not realize is the increase in how many women are being incarcerated. Since 1980, the prison population of women has more than tripled. Among African-American women, it has increased eightfold. And, too often the women who are locked up for drug offenses are locked up because they have bad judgment in men! They aren't using drugs, just hanging out with men who use drugs. Take the case of Kemba Smith, the Hampton University student who was sentenced to more than twenty-four years in jail at age twenty-four because her boyfriend, Peter Hall, was a drug dealer. He was shot in the middle of an investigation of his drug dealing, and Kemba was left holding the bag, getting a longer sentence than if she had been guilty of second-degree murder. She was pardoned by then-President Bill Clinton after serving more than five years of her sentence. If every woman who had bad judgment in men had to serve five years of time, our jails would be overflowing!

Women in prison face worse conditions than men do, even though more than half of the women who are incarcerated are mothers. They go into lockdown where many are raped and brutalized. Their children see them behind bars and are scarred by that experience. Medical care for all prisoners is poor; the situation is far worse for women prisoners. According to the National Women's Law Center, "Because prison health care systems were created for men, routine gynecological care, such as pap smears, breast exams, and mammograms, is extremely rare in prisons. Care is frequently only administered once the situation becomes an emergency." Women in prison also don't get the education and support they need to come out of jail and build lives for themselves.

Mandatory sentencing is often the reason judges can't use discretion in dealing with women who are accused of crimes, especially drug-related crimes. In 1970, 16.3 percent of those incarcerated in federal prisons were there for drug offenses. By 1994, a high of 61.3 percent of those incarcerated were found guilty of drug offenses. The proportion had dropped slightly by 2001, when an estimated 64,900 people, 56.3 percent of those jailed, were jailed for drug offenses. So many people are locked up by mandatory sentencing, incarcerated for their involvement with drugs, that there has been an explosion in the number of prisons that have been built in our nation in the last decade.

If mandatory sentencing is unfair, let's look at the death penalty. Too many have been declared guilty, unjustly. The death penalty does not make sense to me, especially given the number of mistakes we keep finding, the DNA evidence that exculpates people who have served ten and even twenty years for crimes they didn't commit. According to the National Coalition to Abolish the Death Penalty, we know of twenty-three innocent people who were mistakenly executed this century. Further, over seventy people have been released since 1972 as a result of being wrongly convicted. Why? The issue of eyewitness testimony is a red flag, and research shows it is extremely unreliable. Class also makes a difference. O. J. Simpson could afford to hire the best, but most people who are charged with murder can't. Only recently some states have declared death penalty moratoriums because of the possibility of mistakes. This change has only taken place because dedicated volunteers, like the people at Death Penalty Focus, have fought against the death penalty and gotten involved in specific cases.

Y   Y   ⚹

The increase in male incarceration has skyrocketed also. According to the Sentencing Project, a watchdog of the American criminal justice system, the United States now is the world leader in the rate of incarceration (including jails and prisons). We incarcerate 699 people per 100,000 while Russia, who led in this category for years, dropped to an incarceration rate of 644 people per 100,000.

Who benefits from the proliferation of the prison population? I can tell you it's not the communities who have been raped of mothers, fathers, and wage earners. Instead, corporations like the Nashville, Tennessee-based Corrections Corporation of America (CCA) or Florida's Wackenhut Corporation have had amazing success: CCA alone currently corners more than half of the United States private prison market. In 2001, Wackenhut posted revenues of $2.8 billion—a 12.1 percent increase over its 2000 revenues. Draconian three-strikes laws (like the one in California that has increased the number and severity of sentences for nonviolent offenders who, according to the Sentencing Project, now make up a full two-thirds of the state's second- and third-strike sentences) and a financial interest in imprisonment have made the "just-us" system presciently profitable.

Even if I were to accept our nation's crazy quilt pattern of incarceration, I wonder if we have thought through its purposes. One, supposedly, is to rehabilitate, so that after someone has served his sentence he can return to productive life. Right. We've cut back on the number of classes and degree opportunities that are offered in prison and cut back on recreational opportunities. Instead we make them work, for little or nothing providing them with "skills" they may or not be able to parlay into pay once they are released. Oregon, for example, voted in 1994 to pass a constitutional amendment that mandated that Oregon prisoners work forty hours per week and require the state to actively market them to private employers. It's not enough that criminals are being punished with a prison sentence, a criminal record, and separation from their families. We extend the punishment beyond their prison terms and make it difficult to live even upon release by failing to prepare inmates for a return to mainstream society. Instead of sending better people back out into society, we send people out who are often mean, angry, and embittered. This approach is myopic, racist, and destructive and I'm glad that groups are organizing against the prison industrial complex from California to Texas—often ground zeros for the malfeasance of justice.

It is easy to get angry about the unfairness of the prison system. At the same time, I understand why so many people have "zero tolerance" for crime. We ought to be able to see the connection, though, between the proliferation of guns and the spread of crime. We should be able to see the connection between heavy prison spending and reduced educational spending. We all get upset about street crime, muggings, and burglaries, but white-collar crime cost ten times as much as street crime does. These are women's issues just like the federal budget is a women's issue, since money spent in one area often crowds out more socially responsible spending.

I don't know how typical I am of the left, because I think our mixed concerns about law and order cut across ideological lines. On the left, people believe in prisoner's rights, rehabilitation, and compassion. Many of us support gun control, oppose the death penalty, and think that mandatory sentencing makes no sense. Some of us think the drug war is a boondoggle that ought to be stopped. If we provided people with more alternatives to drug use, then put more money into rehabilitation, not incarceration, we might rid our society of drugs. Many of us look askance at the police, possibly because of our own collisions with them during '60s and '70s protests. But there's an adage about the left that I am mindful of—"A liberal is a conservative who hasn't been mugged yet." The criminal justice issue is a hot button, one that plays upon our basest fears. I say step back, assess, and make sure the system is both compassionate and fair.

RESOURCES FOR THE LEFT

COALITION TO STOP GUN VIOLENCE
"The Coalition to Stop Gun Violence is composed of forty-four civic, professional, and religious organizations and 100,000 individual mem-

bers that advocate for a ban on the sale and possession of handguns and assault weapons."
1000 16th Street, NW
#603
Washington, DC 20036
202-530-0340
www.gunfree.org

NATIONAL COALITION TO ABOLISH THE DEATH PENALTY (NCADP)

"NCADP provides information, advocates for public policy, and mobilizes and supports individuals and institutions that share our unconditional rejection of capital punishment."
1436 U Street, NW
#104
Washington, DC 20009
202-387-3890
www.ncadp.org

THE SENTENCING PROJECT

The Sentencing Project is a national nonprofit organization engaged in research and advocacy on criminal justice issues.
514 10th Street, NW
Suite 1000
Washington, DC 20004
202-628-0871
www.sentencingproject.org

CALIFORNIA COALITION FOR WOMEN PRISONERS (CCWP)

CCWP raises the public consciousness about the cruel and inhumane conditions under which women in prison live and advocates for positive changes. They promote the leadership of and give voice to women prisoners, former prisoners, and their families.

100 McAllister Street
Suite 200
San Francisco, CA 94102
415-255-7036
http://womenprisoners.org

DEBORAH PERRY

In the aftermath of the Columbine High School shooting in 1999, I pitched a story to *Ladies' Home Journal* on school violence. My editor and I agreed to focus on the legislative initiatives in Congress since the outbreak of school violence willed Congress into addressing the gun issue. The majority of members of Congress knew that there would be a contentious debate on violence in schools and rectifying measures, as the very mention of the issue brings out competing interests. On the one hand, there was an immediate cry for more gun control laws as Columbine and the string of school shootings in Mississippi, Arkansas, Pennsylvania, Oregon, and Kentucky bewildered people throughout the nation. On the other hand, we are a nation that is reverent for our body of laws and the Second Amendment of our Constitution, which states, "A well regulated Militia, being necessary to the security of a free State, the right of the people to keep and bear Arms, shall not be infringed," is sacred to the democracy of this country.

For my story, I chose to interview the one member of Congress whose tragic encounter with violence forever changed her life. U.S. Representative Carolyn McCarthy, a Democrat from New York, came close to losing her entire family in one horrifying act of violence. You may remember that in 1993 a gunman randomly sprayed bullets on a Long Island commuter train. Just one stop before their departure point, Representative McCarthy's husband and only child, their son, became victims of this random shooting. Her husband died and her son became partially paralyzed. Rather than allow this tragedy to defeat her, then-nurse McCarthy took up a public campaign against violence and ran for Congress in 1994 and won on a single issue— gun control.

During my interview, Representative McCarthy, her press secretary, and I sat in a room adjacent to the House Committee on Education and Workforce of the U.S. House of Representatives, of which she is a committee member. Of all of the interviews I've conducted, this is the one that gets to me the most, as I can't even fathom what it is like to walk in her shoes. As I maintained my composure as best I could, I felt Representative McCarthy's agony when she specified, "Deborah, when people think of my tragedy, they think of it as one horrific day. People don't realize that I live with this for the rest of my life . . . Would you like for me to tell you what the physical or the emotional trauma is day in and day out for my son? I can describe what it is like six days, six months, or six years after the accident. The emotional scars he endures compete with his physical damages . . . People don't understand that tragedy is dealt with on many levels."

While Representative McCarthy is one of the millions of Americans who have been affected by crime and violence in America, crime overall has declined in the United States 27 percent between 1990 and 1999. In 1999, the United States averaged 426.7 crimes per 10,000 residents, in comparison to 1980 when total crime rates were 595 per 10,000 people. Even drug use fell dramatically. Why this has happened for sure is anyone's guess, and since so many factors—social, demographic, economic, and political—affect crime rates, it is difficult for even the Federal Bureau of Investigation (FBI) to suggest a definitive answer. But here's what the experts surmise. One explanation is that "zero tolerance" policies—which refuse to tolerate even tiny infractions of the law such as spray-painting walls or jaywalkers—have caught on like fire throughout the country since former New York City Mayor Rudy Giuliani heralded unparalleled success in lowering crime rates. It is believed that when you go after quality of life crimes and provide people with a more livable environment, then violent crimes tend to drop as well. Another reason for falling crime rates may be that imprisonment rates have soared and have kept repeat offenders off the streets, and out of harm's way of law-abiding citizens.

Yet, irrespective of any decline in crime and violence statistics, life-changing victimization is an issue that will always weigh heavily on the minds of women who fear for the safety of themselves and their families. This is why I have chosen to focus on some of the issues revolving around violent crime that have taken center stage in recent years in the political landscape, including gun control, victims' rights, and the death penalty. That being said, let's take a look at these issues, and dissect their effectiveness.

GUN CONTROL

Gun control is an emotional issue where the competing parties of the debate—for and against—have intensified their advocacy through the halls of Congress and state legislatures throughout the country. I don't know anyone who is against gun safety. The fact of the matter is that there are proven gun control laws on the books but are only effective when they are properly carried out through our judicial system. In Richmond, Virginia, for example, the Project Exile program relegates illegal offenders to stiff mandatory federal prison terms. The result is that homicide rates in Richmond have been cut dramatically by aggressively and consistently enforcing existing gun laws.

Additional gun control laws are not going to prevent people from shooting one another, it will only limit the circulation of guns to law-abiding citizens who use them for legitimate purposes such as protection, hunting, or other sporting activities. The implementation of the Brady Law in 1994 introduced seven-day background checks of potential purchasers of guns. The Center to Prevent Handgun Violence claims that gun violence has curtailed significantly because of these background checks. However, their claim holds little or no value, because if you really want to shoot someone, you will find a gun whether you borrow it, get it on the streets, or hire somebody else to do it. The *Journal of the American Medical Association* disputes the Center's claims, and published a study that found that the introduction of background checks had not worked to reduce homicide rates or the overall suicide rate. More gun control laws are a Band-Aid approach and ignore the deeper societal ills of contemporary life.

Keep in mind that the problems do not lie with guns and the people who legally own them are not the conduit to gun violence. In fact, gun violence is perpetrated by how guns are distributed throughout society and for what purpose those guns are to be used. Second Amendment advocates commonly speak that guns do not kill people, but people kill people. This is true when you think about it. Just because everyone owns steak knives does not give us the right to use them to stab and kill other people. The government does not place any restrictions on how and when we can buy a steak knife, because we think of it as a tool for food. But, if we pick it up to inflict serious harm, even death, to someone, then it becomes a weapon of choice. We don't place restrictions on common household products or sporting goods such as a baseball bat, just because these items could inflict harm. The bottom line is that people who legally own guns predominantly use it for recreational sports such as skeet shooting, hunting, or target practice, and not to kill people.

So, we have to be cautious not to advocate for simple solutions, such as more gun control laws, to very complex problems. A commonly employed strategy in American politics is to play on people's emotions to get policymakers to act. For example, one often referred to, but skewed, statistic used by many nonprofit gun control advocacy groups is that a child dies every thirteen seconds because of a handgun. Here's the problem with this statistic. Their definition of children is inclusive of young adults such as an eighteen-year-old or anyone less than twenty years old. "Using a more usual definition of children—aged fourteen or below—1.7 children die daily from gun violence, and the numbers drops to 1.3 when teen suicides are excluded," states Iain Murray in "The U.S. Gun-Control Debate: A Critical Look" in *Encyclopaedia Britannica*. In fact, many more children die of neglect and child abuse.

In Congress, there are innovative approaches to gun safety that appropriately strike the balance between Second Amendment defenders and gun safety advocates. Representative Bob Barr, a Republican from Georgia, crafted legislation called the Firearms Research and Development Safety Act to enhance the "research and development tax credits permitted to firearms businesses to accelerate and explore further what has been termed as Smart Gun Technology." If there is enough support from the public for this bill, then the chances of it being heard before Congress are very real. If the public remains silent, advanced gun safety technology falls upon deaf ears.

VICTIMS' RIGHTS

More often than not, the civil liberties of violent crime offenders are disproportionately protected over the rights of victims. It makes absolutely no sense that we take greater care in the regard for a murderer or a rapist than we do for the civil rights of an innocent victim. However we got here, we have to put an end to a victim's rights getting lost in the shuffle in the judicial system. A National Institute of Justice study found that "large numbers of victims are being denied their legal rights," and even in the thirty-two states that have passed victims' rights laws, less than 60 percent of victims were notified when defendants were sentenced and less than 40 percent were notified of a defendant's pretrial release. University of Utah law professor Paul Cassell says that "victims' rights provisions have too often failed in the face of bureaucratic habit, or the mere mention of a defendant's rights." According to Mr. Cassell, a study found that racial minority victims are the least likely to be afforded their rights.

Just ask Frances Davis, a middle-aged, African-American woman living in Brooklyn, New York, who knows what it is like to be a victim and have the criminal justice system fail her. Her three sons, Raleak, Andrew, and Frankie, were all murdered by gunfire over a six-year period and all died within one block of one another. Then, her nephews, Dwayne and Glennis, were shot and killed. Raleak's murderer plea-bargained and spent only three and a half years in jail, and just one of the three men involved in the shooting of Frankie was arrested and convicted. The murderers of her nephews were never found.

U.S. Senators Jon Kyl, a Republican from Arizona, and Dianne Feinstein, a Democrat from California, are trying to change that. These senators believe in permanent, fundamental rights for crime victims and are pushing to add the Crime Victims' Rights Amendment to the U.S. Constitution. Essentially, the amendment reads as follows:

> The rights of victims of violent crime being vital to a system of
> ordered liberty and being capable of protection without abridging
> the rights of those accused or convicted of victimizing them, the

rights of any such victim to full consideration and fair treatment
in the protection and punishment of crime shall not be abridged
by any State or the United States. Victims of violent crimes shall
have the rights of timely notice of any release, escape, and public
proceeding involving the crime; not to be excluded from such
proceedings; to be heard at release, plea, sentencing, commuta-
tion, and pardon proceedings; and not to be subjected to undue
delay, or to decisions that disregard their safety or their just
claims to restitution; nor shall these rights be restricted, except
when, and to the degree that, compelling necessity dictates.

We live in the greatest democracy in the world, but we have flaws in
our criminal justice system that deny crime victims their most fundamental
rights to be treated with dignity, fairness, and respect.

DEATH PENALTY

Many people around the world find it draconian. Religious leaders worry
for our immortal souls because we believe that an "eye for an eye" is just.
Policymakers, most notably governors, toss and turn when faced with this
almighty decision. It is the death penalty—otherwise known as capital punishment—and it has been a part of our judicial system since the birth of
this country except during a brief moratorium between 1972 and 1976. We
may not be quartering or hanging people like we did two hundred years
ago; however, lethal injection puts modern-day violent criminals to death.

Even though public opinion has consistently held a two-to-one ratio in
support of the death penalty, national anxiety in recent years has heightened
over the constitutionality of the death penalty and making sure that innocent defendants are not being sentenced to death. The U.S. Supreme Court
continues to address whether death sentences for mentally retarded offenders and juveniles younger than sixteen is "cruel and unusual punishment" prohibited by the Eighth Amendment. Governors, such as Governor

George Ryan, a Republican of Illinois, has put a moratorium on death penalties—after thirteen death row inmates were wrongly convicted—until better methods ensure justice, fairness, and due process in the death sentence conviction. Even the House Judiciary Committee of the U.S. Congress has held hearings and introduced a bill to re-evaluate the imposition of the death penalty at the federal level until a commission on the federal death penalty studies its use. While we want to follow the rule of law, the issue now being raised is do we require DNA identification evidence or another technology to make a determination about an individuals' guilt or innocence. In other words, can twenty-first century science convict a person beyond a shadow of a doubt?

While DNA testing sounds like proof beyond a reasonable doubt, consider some of the challenges policymakers face in the following example. A woman hugs a male colleague whose hair gets caught in her jacket and strands of his hair are now embedded in her clothes. One hour later, she is murdered by another man who leaves no DNA evidence on her body. An autopsy identifies the hair of her male colleague, an innocent man who will now be a likely suspect if he is unable to provide a reliable alibi. It is a tough predicament for policymakers. However, irrespective of the reliability factor of DNA evidence or other twenty-first century sciences such as bite mark technology, I think modern day sciences should be a requirement in helping to reach a conviction toward an individual's guilt or innocence.

Another problem lies with the fact that the death penalty is not enforced in an effective manner, and costs the taxpayers of the thirty-eight states that have instituted capital punishment statutes an enormous amount of money and time because of the endless appeals and protestations of innocence even when someone is absolutely guilty. Take the case of Ted Bundy, for example, who confessed to killing twenty-eight women, but is believed to be responsible for raping and killing more than fifty women. After three separate trials, he was finally convicted for the killing and brutal murder of a twelve-year-old girl and the deaths of two Florida State University sorority sisters. He spent ten years on death row, involving numerous appeals and excessive imprisonment fees, eventually costing the Florida state taxpayers more than six million dollars.

If we enforce the death penalty effectively, the law could actually reduce the number of violent murders by eliminating some of the repeat offenders. Research conducted by Emory University economists Hashem Dezhbakhsh, Paul Rubin, and Joanna Mehlhop, suggest that the death penalty deters other murders to the extent of saving between eight and twenty-eight innocent lives, with a best-estimate average of eighteen lives saved per execution.

While only fifty-four women are currently on death row, the issue is of grave concern to us, because we want to know that violent killers are eradicated off the face to the earth. We want to know that there is closure to the murderers of children, like five-year-old Adam Walsh (the son of *America's Most Wanted* host, John Walsh). We want to know that terrorists like Timothy McVeigh are no longer roaming our streets. We want to believe in the proportionality of murder met with an "eye for an eye." Murderers need to understand that crimes carry consequences. Lastly, there should be moral affirmation to those who have lost their lives that the criminal justice system does not fail those left behind.

Women interested in ensuring that the law does the most thorough job regarding a death penalty conviction can write their members of Congress about supporting a bill such as the Federal Death Penalty Moratorium Act, a bill which institutes a moratorium on death penalties at the Federal level "until a Commission on the Federal Death Penalty studies its use and policies ensuring justice, fairness, and due process are implemented." While no bill in Congress has been introduced to require DNA or other technologies in death penalty convictions, you can certainly suggest this idea to your member of Congress or governor.

TOUGH ON CRIME . . . PERIOD

If we want to live in a safer environment, we have to be tough on crime. If we want to restore people's faith in our criminal justice system, our judges have to carry out penalties that correspond with the saying "if you do the crime, you pay the time." End of story! We have to stop making excuses for the people who had it rough growing up, or lost a job, or got ticked off by road rage; there is no justification for crime or violence in our society. We need to be tough on those who are not law-abiding citizens and infringe on the rights of the innocent.

My dear friend and communication coach, Steven Gaffney, always says, "Blaming others gives you no power to deal. For when you blame others, you give up control." Whether you, someone you know, or someone you read about was victimized in a life-altering way, do something about it. Start or get involved in your neighborhood watch program, suggest violence prevention legislation to your local, state, or national policymakers, or run for Congress as Representative Carolyn McCarthy did. In the words of Representative McCarthy, "You have to personalize it. That's what gives you the energy to keep fighting."

RESOURCES FOR THE RIGHT

NATIONAL RIFLE ASSOCIATION (NRA)
This organization protects our Second Amendment rights granting "the right of the people to keep and bear arms shall not be infringed."
11250 Waples Mill Road
Farifax, VA 22030-7400
703-267-1000
www.nra.org

NATIONAL VICTIMS' CONSTITUTIONAL AMENDMENT NETWORK
This organization supports the adoption of an amendment to the U.S. Constitution recognizing the fundamental rights of crime victims to be treated with dignity, fairness, and respect by the criminal justice system.
789 Sherman Street
Suite 670

Denver, CO 80203

303-832-1522 or 800-529-8226; Fax: 303-861-1265

www.nvcan.org

STATISTICAL ASSESSMENT SERVICE (STATS)

This organization "is devoted to the accurate use of scientific and social research in public policy debate," and focuses on the death penalty.

2100 L Street, NW

Suite 300

Washington, DC 20037

202-223-3193

www.stats.org

RACE MATTERS

DEBORAH PERRY

James Byrd's life ended in a tragic assassination one spring evening in 1998. Perhaps you remember hearing or reading about him. He was the forty-nine-year-old African-American man who accepted a lift home from three white boys in Texas. Mr. Byrd was chained, jettisoned, and dragged behind the boys' truck for 2.5 miles. The reason? Sheer bigotry over the color of his skin.

Shaken up over this unimaginable act, I wrote an op-ed for a newspaper and in the piece, I encapsulated an episode of religious and racial discrimination I, myself, experienced. It included my former boss in the first Bush administration, Jerry (in respect for his privacy, I've changed his name), who is African American. Never have I met a more gregarious, "take-charge kind of guy," and we bonded immediately, in part because we both felt dislodged amidst the massive officialdom at our place of employment—an agency in the Department of State.

One day, Jerry and I went to the Embassy of Saudi Arabia for a business meeting. A fellow who we met at the embassy, named Tarik, later called Jerry to question him about my background and marital status. Tarik, being a part of the royal family of Saudi Arabia, had to be cautious in who he went out with, and had no interest in dating someone outside of his Muslim religion. Jerry shared with Tarik that I was definitely not of his faith.

I jokingly thanked Jerry for making me feel so discriminated against and realized that I hit a nerve. Jerry instantaneously shot back, "How do you think I feel every day of my life?" I reacted with a blank stare. I had no idea what he was talking about, because I honestly had always seen people for who they are and never classified people because of what they look like or what religion they practiced. I asked him what he meant and he responded by telling me that he is discriminated against every day of his life. I was baffled, for I had tremendous respect for him and never really paid attention to the color of his skin. To me, he was just "Jerry."

It took me several days to get over Jerry's view of being black in contemporary America. I know that I felt categorized for the religion I was born into, and came to the realization that our society likes to prejudge people. How can anyone make a condemnation against someone else because of one's religion or the color of skin?

Racial and religious discrimination will always remain ingrained in American society in one fashion or another due to precipitous ignorance. No one is born prejudiced against skin color or religion. It is a learned behavior. Even though racial stereotyping is not a fixture in the human mind, it has become such a prevalent habit or pastime that it has characteristics of an incurable disease. Many of my ethnic friends say that the "institutional" discrimination that covertly exists throughout American society is dreadfully agonizing.

IT'S NOT JUST BLACK AND WHITE

Mostly when we think of discrimination, we almost always think of white equality and black inequality. Nearly every ethnic group of people in American society has been discriminated against at one time or another. The Chinese who practically built the transcontinental railroad were considered such a threat to the white man's job that in the 1870s they were socially segregated and denied political rights. Native Americans lost their land and were forced to eclipse most of their traditions, and by 1885, were a people without rights, privileges, or freedoms. In the late 1800s and early 1900s, "No Irish Need Apply" signs could be found in storefronts across America. During World War II, many Japanese Americans were removed from their homes and detained in camps solely because of their ancestry.

Flash forward to the twenty-first century, and America is thriving with multiculturalism. We boast a vigorously multicultural population, which no other country throughout the world can claim. And according to *The Economist,* younger Americans say that they do not experience the past racial stereotypes and injustices that, regrettably, earlier generations have endured. The table below represents the latest snapshot of our peoples:

ACCORDING TO THE 2000 CENSUS

Caucasian	69.1
Hispanic	12.5
African American	12.1
Asian American	3.6
Native American and Alaskan	.7
Native Hawaiian and other Pacific Islanders	.1
Two or more groups	1.6

Source: U.S. Census Bureau

Irrespective of my own sensitivities over discrimination and race relations, we have to ask ourselves whether government can mandate racial harmony. Certainly, the Civil Rights Acts of 1957 and 1964 outlawed public discrimination, inequality in employment based on either race or sex, and created federally assisted programs. The Acts took moral fervor and political skill to give all Americans full civil and legal rights. The 1957 law also empowered the Department of Justice to take action against bigoted voter registrars, and created the Commission on Civil Rights to investigate complaints of discrimination. In 1969, President Richard Nixon mandated the policy of affirmative action, which allowed minorities to have special preferences in college enrollment and employment.

While these programs had an important place in history, we do not need to assume that someone is or is not qualified to do something because of the color of their skin or religious background. So, we need to ask the tough questions such as whether programs like affirmative action or minority business set-asides had their time and place in history, but are no longer needed. And, what about racial privacy? Does the government really need to know who we are in order to do its business, or does race classification in America further set a divisive tone?

END AFFIRMATIVE ACTION/MINORITY BUSINESS SET-ASIDES

Even former President Bill Clinton, the most pro-quota president in history, initiated a review of affirmative action, and asked, "Does it work? Is it fair? Does it achieve the desired objectives?" According to the Code of Federal Regulations, "Individuals who certify that they are members of named groups (African American, Hispanic, Native American, Asian Pacific, Subcontinental Asian) are to be considered socially and economically disadvantaged." Huh? Is the government in the business of judging someone's ability to perform based on their skin color or ethnicity? The government even thinks that under some programs women are "socially and economically disadvantaged, too."

Programs such as affirmative action and minority business set-asides had their place in history when deep-seated divisions between blacks and whites equated to palpable inequality. Blacks had been profoundly held back in American society first by slavery, then by Jim Crow laws, and finally by informal restrictions on where they could live, and even whom they could or could not date. It was a crusade between a white population whose ancestors held varying degrees of culpability during the dark history of our slave trade, versus the children, grandchildren, and great grandchildren of former slaves, who were trying to get ahead in society, and provide for a better future for their children. We needed to heal deep-seated wounds, and minorities in this country deserved an opportunity of special preferences in order to level the playing field.

However, that was then, and this is now. Affirmative action now discriminates against the very people it was originally designed to help, and we should end it. To assume that minorities do not have the ability to succeed on their own without special treatment is outright discriminating. And, in light of the latest census, how do you even determine who should get special preference? Is it all minorities or the group who considers themselves a combination of two or more minority groups? As far as I am aware, Asian Americans are not having fundamental problems in getting ahead in American society. Do we really need laws to force us into a multicultural workplace and into higher education?

Much of big business has embraced multiculturalism, both to have a workforce that reflects the demography of its customer base and to avoid discrimination lawsuits from minority employees. American employers are also smarter than we give them credit for, and recognize that a multiethnic workforce unites to winning marketing strategies, not to mention how it adds to a company's profitability.

Affirmative action in higher education is also discriminating, not to mention unconstitutional, and should be abolished. According to Lewis A. Randolph, in "Black Neoconservatives in the United States: Responding with Progressive Coalitions," U.S. Supreme Court Justice Clarence Thomas resented affirmative action. It made Justice Thomas feel stigmatized and set him apart from his classmates all throughout his education.

A federal judge in Michigan upheld the right of the University of Michigan to use affirmative action when admitting students, and here's how incredibly unfair it is. The university does give points to applicants for qualification such as good grades and high test scores. But, it gives African-

American, Hispanic, and Native American applicants twenty extra points, which is the equivalent of raising their high school grade point average by one full point (from a C average to a B average, for example). Applicants also get bonuses for being poor (twenty extra points), excelling in athletics (twenty points), a Michigan resident (ten points), or the child of an alumnus (four points). Is this fair to the child who has worked exceptionally hard in academics, but whose bonus points do not equate to an African American, Hispanic, or Native American who has not worked as hard? Absolutely not!

Rather, government can encourage every student to work hard, and reward those who excel academically. This is what President Bush did when he was governor of Texas, and introduced a policy of affirmative access in response to the 1996 case of Cheryl Hopwood, a white student who had been refused admission to the University of Texas law school while minorities with lower test scores were admitted. Then-Governor Bush backed a new law that aims to achieve racial diversity in the university by granting automatic admission to every Texas public high school graduate in the top 10 percent of his or her class.

Affirmative action is similar to another evil in our society called racial profiling, where you are identified by your group and not by your character. If there should be any special preferences at all, it should be based on income level and not on one's skin color, ethnicity, or religion. California, the most ethnically diverse state in the country, was the first to scrap affirmative action, and now an advocacy group in California called the American Civil Rights Coalition is working on a Racial Privacy Initiative to cease the categorizing of people all together.

END CATEGORIZING PEOPLE AT ALL

Do you realize that every time you fill out some government form, you have to identify your race? What are you, it wants to know. The Racial Privacy Initiative demands to find out why it should matter to the government at all. Race, after all, is a private matter, and the government does not need to be identifying individuals by race, ethnicity, color, or national origin in the operation of public education, contracting, or employment.

According to the Racial Privacy Initiative, in the past thirty-one years, government race classifications have ballooned from 5 categories to 63, and 126 if you include ethnicity. Surely, government does not believe that so many new races suddenly emerged. Why in the world would the government think that a person's skin color or ethnicity determines how much money they make, whether they are literate, or how hard they work? When programs are designed by race to deal with poverty and illiteracy, they are makeshift approaches and do not work to help people become productive members of the workforce.

We are all Americans, and it should not matter to anyone, most especially the government, what someone's heritage is or is not. Besides, race categorizing, in the history of the world, is often used to violate people's fundamental human rights. From the slave trade to the Holocaust, from the Japanese-American detention to South African apartheid, race classification cultivates hate. We ought to be true to our founding principles that "all men are created equal," and strive for a color-blind society.

WOMEN AND RACE RELATIONS

Women played a monumental role in the abolitionist movement at a time when they were not allowed to have much of a voice outside of the home. In 1833, Lucretia Mott, a devout Quaker and fierce abolitionist, created the Female Anti-Slavery Society of Philadelphia modeled after the American Anti-Slavery Society, which women were not allowed to be part of. Also, in 1833, Lydia Maria Child embodied the evils of slavery in a first antislavery book entitled *Appeal in Favor of that Class of Americans Called Africans*. By 1837, over half of the 150,000 members of the 1,006 antislavery groups were women. It is the women who played a crucial role in changing the tide of public opinion about slavery and made it the foremost public issue in the 1840s and 1850s.

Ida B. Wells-Barnett, an African-American teacher and journalist, documented the lynchings of blacks that took place at a rate of two per week in the South between 1890 and 1899. She wrote, "In the past ten years over a thousand black men and women and children have met this violent death at the hands of the white mob. And the rest of America has remained silent." In 1909, a white settlement worker, Mary White Ovington, W.E.B. DuBois, and fifty other founders established the National Association for the Advancement of Colored People (NAACP) to end racial discrimination, segregation, and achieve full civil and legal rights. Women have always cared about social injustices of the world and have historically made an impact when they banded together to take action.

Race relations remains a fundamental issue on moral grounds. It requires a change of attitude in the way we think of others. Government mandates that categorize people and make them feel less than equal in society only propagate the feelings of ennui, defeat, and humiliation. There is no reason that any government program should make any person feel as if they are less of a human being. Rather, we should have another look at the Booker T. Washington approach to uplifting all people. Washington's vision was to foster the embodiment of racial harmony through education, greater responsibility, and less remorse of past ills. In other words, we need to move forward, and not linger on the past.

We should want to reach out to people of different cultural backgrounds because it enriches life. I know for me racial harmony grants the purview to see life through a kaleidoscope in contradiction to limiting my social interaction with people who look like me. I so value my cultural friendships, as life would be monotonous and characterless if it were not for the diversity of my friends.

RESOURCES FOR THE RIGHT

CENTER FOR EQUAL OPPORTUNITY
This organization concentrates on the elimination of affirmative action.
815 15th Street, NW

Suite 928
Washington, DC 20005
202-639-0803
www.ceousa.org

CENTER FOR NEW BLACK LEADERSHIP

This organization is a public policy research and advocacy organization
that believes "enduring racial equality presupposes a parity of economic
and skilled development between the races."
202 G Street, NE
Washington, DC 20002
202-546-9505
www.cnbl.org

COALITION ON URBAN RENEWAL AND EDUCATION

This organization provides national dialogue on how social policies impact America's inner cities and the poor, and promotes faith-based and
free market solutions on issues of race and poverty.
6033 West Century Boulevard
Suite 950
Los Angeles, CA, 90045
310-410-9981
www.urbancure.org

RACIAL PRIVACY INITIATIVE

This organization is dedicated to ending the categorization of all people.
Sponsored by the American Civil Rights Coalition.
P.O. Box 189113
Sacramento, CA 95818-9113
916-444-2278; Fax: 916-444-2279
www.acrc1.org

JULIANNE MALVEAUX

"The problem of the twentieth century is the problem of the color line."

W.E.B. DUBOIS

There are many ways that race matters have special implications for women. The issue of public assistance is dealt with elsewhere in this book, but what racial lens must white women view the world through to not embrace public assistance as a feminist issue? Women qualify for public assistance because of their motherhood status, yet many women see welfare as a "black" program (it isn't—the majority of those receiving public assistance were white when so-called welfare reform was implemented in 1997). When policy toward women, especially poor black women, is discussed in our country, I often want to echo Sojourner Truth and holler, "Ain't I a Woman?"

When South Carolinian Regina McKnight, who repeatedly sought drug treatment during her pregnancy, gave birth to a stillborn child, she was sentenced to twelve years in jail with no chance of parole. There were no women's groups to rally around her, no headlines to stir up sympathy for her. In contrast, when Andrea Yates drowned all five of her children, Katie Couric used her *Today* show platform to direct viewers to the Yates legal defense fund and raise awareness about postpartum depression. While postpartum depression is certainly an important issue about which there is insufficient awareness, one might argue that the criminalization of motherhood is an equally important issue.

Thousands of cases, and much public policy, are filtered through a racial lens. The perception that welfare is a "black" program makes it acceptable for members of Congress to give speeches on the House floor vilifying those on welfare as "people you would not leave your cat with." The perception that women who take drugs are irresponsible (not ill) allowed for the legal railroading of Regina McKnight. The fact that poor, black women are more likely than white women to be seen in public health clinics where their addiction can be noted, but not treated, gives them more exposure to criminal prosecution than, say, the upper-class white woman who, though alcoholic or drug addicted, gets treatment in a private hospital. While former Spelman College president Dr. Johnetta Cole has written convincingly that the elimination of racism should be a women's issue, there is little evidence that women have made greater strides on this issue than men have. That women who can articulate their gender oppression are insensitive to the oppression of women of color is often a thorn in the side of activists who work to eliminate racism.

Further, it makes it difficult for African-American women and other women of color to deal with gender issues. Too often we are asked to choose between making race or making gender a priority. This was never more poignant than in the Clarence Thomas Supreme Court confirmation hearings, when Anita Hill's riveting testimony about Mr. Thomas's sexual harassment caused dissent among African Americans. At least three collections of essays were produced to deal with the matter, which was, of course, complicated by the fact that Thomas played the "race card" when he said that he was being "lynched" electronically. The irony that Thomas seemed to eschew race in judicial matters but could invoke it when it served him seemed to be lost on the Senate Judiciary Committee, as well as on those many African Americans who felt some solidarity with Thomas because of his race, though Anita Hill was no less black.

At the same time, it is important to note the oppression of African-American men, and the fact that the relationship between black men and women is very different from the relationship between white men and women. As I wrote in the chapter on crime and violence, while African-American women do not want to be victims of anybody's violence, we understand the way the criminal justice system treats black men, and so don't always see that system as an ally. Black men don't have the power, the wealth, or the income that white men do, so they can't be cast as oppressor, even if they can be criticized for sexist attitudes. When women describe men, generally, as oppressor, that's a turnoff to those African-American women who struggle shoulder to shoulder with African-American men on civil rights and racial justice issues.

When I write about race matters, I feel mixed affinity with the left, and almost none with the right. The state of race matters in the United States leaves me frustrated and angry because race places a wedge between me and folks I'd like to work with, folks with whom I share an affinity about economic issues, gender issues, taxes, and politics. Still, when their racial insensitivity bubbles up, I find myself viewing potential allies with antipathy.

I've been described as one of the "angry" people, and it is a label I both embrace and look askance at. In my own work, I describe myself as a "mad" economist, reminding people that "mad" can mean "angry," "crazy" or some combination thereof. You'd have to be mad, angry, and crazy to be black in an America that constantly puts you in an outside position. You'd have to be either mad or myopic to meander through life without noticing the many ways white America reinforces its hegemony and challenges you to assimilate. It surprises me that there are those who find my anger remarkable. I know other African Americans who are as angry, but more contained about their feelings. I think it would be remarkable if I were not "mad."

Still, as I read drafts of this essay, and seek feedback from colleagues and readers across the racial spectrum, I am stunned at how put off they are by my anger. Do they read history differently than I do? Do they see progress as so major that it should stifle my anger? Part of me wants to tone down so as not to turn off. Black folks aren't the only ones for whom race matters in our society, but I write from my experience and from a history that says that when our society addresses the problems that plague African Americans, other people of color also benefit. So, I'd ask other readers of color to understand the Afrocentric focus of this chapter. Further, I'd ask white readers, on the left and on the right, just to read through this essay like I've lived through your oppression. The pen may be mightier than the sword, but it never stopped a rope. Indulge me. Hear me. Help me shape next steps and solutions, especially solutions that empower women.

Neither the left nor the right quite understand race matters. On the left, there is the nod to diversity, though new resistance to affirmative action. How long, some ask, must we continue these policies, especially when white kids are denied educational opportunities at elite universities? There is concern about racial profiling, and some support for minority business set-asides. But along with the acknowledgment that all is not well, there is a weariness at still having to tackle racial problems, and a readiness to see reverse discrimination where African Americans and other people of color simply see new doors opening for them.

On the right, there is often the acknowledgment that, no, life wasn't fair. Discrimination existed once upon a time in a fairy-tale land, far, far away, but it's over now. And even if it isn't fair, this is America where everybody comes and rolls their sleeves up and works hard to get ahead. So, black folks need to just "get over" slavery, stop whining about apologies, pull themselves up by their bootstraps, and get with the program and the American dream. To do anything less, says the right, including a vocal group of right-wing African Americans, is to embrace victim status. The only victims in the race debate, in my opinion, are those who are so historically deprived that they can only experience life in the here and now (unless they are touting historical figures to make their own points).

Both sides suffer from denial about the institutional and cultural hold that racism has on American society and on the many ways slavery has shaped our nation's culture. As long as both liberals and conservatives are in denial, they won't acknowledge slavery, or spend the kind of capital we've spent on so many other monuments and museums (think Holocaust Museum, think upcoming World War II monument) to commemorate slavery on Washington's national mall. Indeed, there may be a moratorium on building on the mall because it is becoming too "cluttered." This is a metaphor for a national consciousness too cluttered and avoidance-seeking to deal with our nation's "original sin."

For some African Americans, the national nostalgia for the "good old days" is especially painful. In the name of national nostalgia, for example, people have rediscovered our nation's second president John Adams. I read about Adams with a tinge of bitterness, realizing how blithely black rights had been bartered away "for the good of the union." Our nation's founding fathers simply postponed the reckoning that was the Civil War, and it is unlikely that the descendants of slaves can ever be made whole from the economic, cultural, and social losses we sustained from slavery (reparations may help, but only a little bit).

Slavery's legacy can be seen in the racial economic gaps that persist. African Americans had median earnings that were less than 60 percent of white earnings in 1999. Historically, African-American unemployment rates are more than double white rates. In the year 2001, for example, the nation experienced a low unemployment rate of 4 percent; the rate was 3.5 percent for whites and 7.6 for African Americans. While 71 percent of whites own their homes, just 46 percent of African-American and Latino populations own their homes. Why the gap? Some of the reasons include redlining and banking discrimination. Further, we can go back into our nation's history and find official government policy that discouraged African Americans from purchasing housing in certain neighborhoods. From infant mortality to life expectancy, statistics tell a story of differences.

Some of the differences are blurring with time. And certainly, the issue of race matters is not simply black and white, what with the Latino population's size now approximating that of African Americans, and the Asian-American population growing. Our nation's increasing multiculturalism may blunt some of the sharpness of black-white race matters, but they are likely to remain a source of conflict until they are dealt with. The potential for conflict among people of color exists as well. I watched a television program where the conservative columnist George Will nearly salivated with glee that African Americans were no longer the nation's largest racial minority. He said that if Latinos and Asians worked together they could silence the African-American population. Not. The issues that African-American people focus on won't go away because our relative size is supposedly decreasing. It's about the history and the justice, not the contemporary demographics.

It is interesting to note that gaps between women are proportionately smaller than gaps between men. With median annual earnings of $24,229 in 1999, African-American women earned more than 91 percent of white women's earnings (Hispanic women earn 72 percent of what white women earn). In contrast African-American men earned 80 percent of what white men earned, while Hispanic men earned 61 percent of white men's earnings. This does not mean that race matters less among women, but that gender bias plays a strong role in the size of women's earnings. Regardless of race and ethnicity, women are more likely to work in "typically female" jobs with lower pay, which partly explains the closeness of their wages.

Women's work histories illustrate the differences between black and white women, and the extent to which these differences sometimes make it difficult for us to work together. Black women were born with brooms in our hands, with the historical expectation that work would always be part of our lives. As early as 1910, black women's labor force participation rates were more than double those of white women. One in five black girls worked in 1910, twice the number of white girls who did. Despite faulty stereotypes of black women as lazy welfare recipients, work has always been a part of black women's lives. That's why the women's workplace revolution was business as usual for some of us.

The percentage of white women who work jumped from 42.6 percent in 1960 to 60 percent in 2000. Black women's labor force participation rates didn't rise as sharply, but they increased from 49.5 percent in 1960 to 63.5 percent in 2000. The complications of the workplace seem to baffle some white women, who write (in books like Ann Crittenden's *The Price of Motherhood,* or in Elizabeth Perle McKenna's *When Work Doesn't Work Anymore*) that they were somehow hoodwinked into thinking that they could have it all, and now bemoan the fact that the workplace isn't fair.

African-American women have "been there, done that." We juggled family and the workplace without the fancy academic jargon of "intersection." Our legacy, in the words of Dr. Dorothy Height, the legendary president emerita of the National Council of Negro Women, is to "make a way out of no way," which meant that we worked at home and in the paid workplace, at our churches and in civil rights organizations. Where did we find the time? We made time from the corners of our lives. The moments that might have been spent over a cup of tea were spent, instead, organizing a fundraiser. The sisterly phone call quickly shifted affection to a call for action.

When white women reveled in the new world of work in the late '60s and early '70s, black women who had always known work rolled our eyes. Our work facilitated white women's labor market participation and their leisure. We were the maids and child care workers, the home health workers and caterers, who made parts of white women's domestic lives come together. That white women speak of a workplace revolution without acknowledging the presence of the working women around them, those who facilitated their employment, is galling.

Although I've written dozens of academic papers on African-American women in the workplace, this is a personal issue for me. I come from a long line of working black women, many who worked in jobs they were overqualified for to get their families by. My grandmother graduated from Tuskegee University, but worked as a domestic because that was the only job she could find. My mother, while a college student, worked as a maid because it was the only way her tuition payments could be paid. I don't invoke my family history to be served punch at a pity party, but because the differential workplace status of African-American women is a persistent reality. African-American women have yet to reach the corporate heights of their white colleagues in corporate America. While 647,000 white women, about 1.4 percent of those with income, earn more than $100,000 a year, just 62,000 African-American women, 0.8 percent of black female earners, have six-figure salaries.

I write in a room lined with pictures of working women. My favorite visuals include an Annie Lee print of black women picking cotton, a photograph of my mentor, Dr. Phyllis Wallace (author of the seminal book *Black Women in the Labor Force*), and a photograph of my great grandmother, Addie Hawkins, sitting grandly on a bench in Cedar Rapids, Iowa, sometime in the 1940s. She was visiting a daughter, Louise, who worked with her husband as maid and chauffeur to a Cedar Rapids family.

Addie Hawkins was a maid, cook, and restaurant owner in Biloxi, Mississippi. She gave birth to seven children; four of the five who survived infancy attended college. Three graduated, and one earned an advanced degree. Annie Mae and Rose, my great-aunt and grandmother, worked as teachers, but also as maids. Louise, another great-aunt, was a nurse and maid. When I look at Addie's picture, I contrast her workplace reality with my own, and realize that she scrubbed floors and sent her children to college so that descendents like me would have more options.

Much of our jargon about women and work ignores Addie Hawkins' reality. She worked on her knees because she had no choice. Today, many working-class women work at minimum wage jobs because they, too, lack choices and opportunities. Our working women's revolution is much richer if we recognize our differences by race and class, and acknowledge that some folks have come a long way because others have not yet made major strides.

Our nation will have unfinished business around race matters as long as racial economic gaps remain. Dealing with them means more than lip service, or efforts like President Clinton's "One America" set of national conversations that promised much and yielded nothing. (For the record, Republicans have promised nothing and delivered less, so this is not a partisan slam against Mr. Clinton.) It means acknowledging those structural factors that continue to generate racial differences in access and treatment in our society. It means enforcing the antidiscrimination legislation already on the books. (Currently, those who sue for discrimination have a difficult time finding lawyers and bringing cases to court and the civil rights enforcement agencies are often hampered by low budgets and limited authority.) It means working vigorously to close racial economic gaps using whatever means necessary—affirmative action, business set-asides, wealth transfers, or other tools. Racial gaps are evidence of our deficiencies, of both historical and contemporary biases. Working vigorously to eliminate them signals a willingness to have everyone participate in our society.

Still, in an era that many would describe as a post–civil rights era, thousands of Americans still file racial discrimination lawsuits against our nation's largest corporations. Why? Joe R. Feagin, a Florida sociologist who happens to be white (and who I cite in this case because some would raise questions about the objectivity of an African-American sociologist's work on the existence of racism), has written about the persistence of "systemic racism" in his book *Racist America* (Rutledge, 2000). He writes, "Systemic racism is about everyday experience. People are born, live, and die within the racist system." Most African Americans have tales of racist minutiae, of being stopped by the wrong police officer at the wrong time, of being denied a job, a loan, or even just a place in line. Many whites, upon hearing these tales, go to elaborate lengths to attempt to suggest that it wasn't race, but some other factor, perhaps a myopic sales clerk, a coincidence, anything but racism.

Does this matter from a policy perspective? Dr. Martin Luther King said, "The law cannot make you love me but it can keep you from lynching me." The role race plays in our lives, even subtly, suggests that public policy and measurement are all the more important for moving us toward an antiracist (as opposed to nonracist) society. But Dr. King's quote also suggests that there are solutions to be formulated outside the policy arena. I am encouraged by the whites who spend time attempting to build an antiracist society, along with those like the writer Tim Wise who sees the matter of white-skin privilege as one that must be revealed and remedied. Unfortunately, though, too many white Americans are able to shrug off race matters as issues that rarely pertain to them.

AFFIRMATIVE ACTION AND MINORITY BUSINESS SET-ASIDES

"The civil rights movement was fundamentally a struggle for liberty, not equality," writes Stephen Steinberg in his 1998 essay, "Occupational Apartheid in America: Race, Labor Market Segmentation, and Affirmative Action." In other words, while the civil rights movement removed the barriers of segregation and secured citizenship rights for African Americans, it did little to redress the racial economic gaps that resulted from two centuries of slavery and another of Jim Crow. Though conservatives revel in using Dr. Martin Luther King's dream that people "will be judged by the content of their character, not the color of their skin," they have been less willing to view the economic aspects of his work and the fact that King implicitly dealt with affirmative action when he said:

> It is impossible to create a formula for the future, which does not take into account that our society has been doing something special against the Negro for hundreds of years. How then can he be absorbed into the mainstream of American life if we do not do something special for him now, in order to balance the equation and equip him to compete on a just and equal basis?

Further, King spoke explicitly of "the debt" that America owes black people, and exhorted our nation to honor broken promises to African Americans by "cashing the check" that had been marked "insufficient funds." In other words, affirmative action and minority business set-aside programs are imperfect ways to level a playing field that had been tilted for centuries. I support these programs because they are the best we can do, for now. But if our goal is, for example, closing the racial wealth gap, then it makes sense to consider reparations, not partial solutions like affirmative action.

It was Republican President Richard Nixon who implemented the Philadelphia Plan in 1969, which required all federal contractors, including colleges and universities, to implement affirmative action plans and hiring programs. Says Steinberg, "Affirmative action was unquestionably the most important policy initiative of the post–civil rights era. It drove a wedge into the structure of occupational segregation that had existed since slavery. And affirmative action achieved its principal policy objective, which was the rapid integration of blacks into occupational sectors where they had been excluded historically." While racial occupational segregation has lessened since 1969, the relative absence of African Americans in upper corporate management, in the sciences, and as university professors, and in other elite occupations makes the case for continued affirmative action. Affirmative action is not only effective for the educated, though. As the labor market changes structurally, there is increased competition for "good jobs," jobs with benefits and job security. Affirmative action ensures that African Americans and other minorities can get a foot in the door, from entry-level jobs to middle management.

There have been mixed judicial rulings on the use of affirmative action in higher education admissions, and some states have passed legislation outlawing affirmative action. The strong backlash against affirmative action seems unjustified when the numbers are considered, but those who oppose affirmative action speak of "race neutral" college admissions, as if tests like the SAT tests are some measure of neutrality. Actually, multiple-choice standardized tests are flawed measures of ability, so flawed that some universities choose to admit "legacy" students despite their scores. This is not seen as affirmative action, but some form of a historical entitlement, the modern-day version of the grandfather clauses that excluded blacks from voting in the post–civil rights era. (Historically, southern grandfather clauses allowed you to vote only if your grandfather had voted, disenfranchising the descendents of slaves even after the passage of the Thirteenth, Fourteenth, and Fifteenth Amendments.) In those states where affirmative action has been eliminated in higher education, African-American and Latino enrollment has plummeted. In California, after the passage of Proposition 209 in 1996 (a ballot initiative to eliminate affirmative action programs), black and brown enrollment dropped by as much as 45 percent in parts of the UC system. In Florida, Jeb Bush's One Florida plan reduced enrollment for African-American freshmen at the University of Florida by 43 percent in the fall of 2001.

Some may view the spoils from affirmative action policies as greater in the minority business contracting arena, which would explain why conservative legal foundations have spent millions of dollars attempting to eliminate minority business set-asides. Beginning with the 1989 case *Croson v. Richmond,* affirmative action opponents have been largely successful in limiting the scope of set-aside programs, or in forcing cities to commission elaborate studies to "prove" past discrimination. Some activist mayors, such as San Francisco's Willie Brown and Atlanta's Bill Campbell, have insisted on their right to include people of color in the contracting process. Their courage is not helped by weak agreements to "mend it, not end it," or by weak efforts like President Clinton's One America commission, charged with initiating "a national conversation on race." African Americans were supposed to be satisfied with a symbolic commission, soothed by the platitude that "at least he is doing something." Our confusion about race matters is such that well-meaning gestures are a substitute for policy. How do we move beyond the well-meaning? We take the concept of "diversity" seriously, implementing it in our clubs, our churches, our schools. Whites can get involved in organizations that focus on racial justice, including the NAACP. Many will be surprised to learn that the founding members of the NAACP were both black and white. Its first chair was a white woman, Mary Ovington.

Our solutions to racial matters up until now have been less than perfect. Our national ambivalence about race is such that the One America commission sparked conversation in several town hall meetings and in smaller efforts initiated in dozens of cities and towns. Conversations and efforts to get to know each other simply don't deal with issues of economic distribution, nor is it possible to reach consensus on race matters when people approach things from such different perspectives. Affirmative action and minority business set-asides are not the perfect ways to deal with distribution, but they should be supported until other policies are developed to replace them. Incidentally, white women benefit as much, if not more, from affirmative action and set-aside programs as people of color do because women are a protected class. But while women have been discriminated against, many African-American women have been discriminated against and disadvantaged. In some cases, it is easier to diversify a workplace with a white woman than with a person of color. Thus, white women's ambivalence about these programs and their unwillingness to support them more forcefully is often galling. Some groups, like the Fund for a Feminist Majority, were active in opposition to California Proposition 209. While many feminists have lobbied for "fair share" provisions that include them in areas where they are underrepresented, though, they are far less enthusiastic in promoting the inclusion of others. Thus, women who say they care about fairness have to take it past gender and include issues of racial economic justice as concerns.

RACIAL PROFILING

In 1999, the American Civil Liberties Union reported racial profiling by police in two dozen states. In New Jersey a black dentist was stopped by the police more than one hundred times over a four-year period as he commuted from his home to his office in an expensive car. In New York, when Mayor Giuliani spoke of "zero tolerance" for petty crime, people of color understood that they would be the ones stopped for jaywalking, loitering, or littering, while whites would not be. Many consider racial profiling an epidemic. Florida sociologist Joe Feagin says, "Such police actions across the nation today reveal important aspects of racism—the commonplace discriminatory practices of individual whites, the images of dangerous blacks dancing in white heads, the ideology legitimating antiblack images, and the white-dominated institutions allowing or encouraging such practices."

As with the affirmative action issue, the issue of racial profiling sparks anguished conversation about what is fair, what is right, and what is reasonable. Could a police officer reasonably have thought Amadou Diallo was firing a gun when he was raising his black leather wallet to provide identification to the police? Police lawyers shopped for a jury (and found one in Syracuse, New York) to give them the result they wanted, but millions of African Americans saw no justice in their verdict. Shouldn't a Cincinnati officer have tried to detain Timothy Thomas, who ran to escape apprehension and was shot in the back? Again, a jury affirmed the officer's action, while Cincinnati's black population seethed.

According to Cathy Harris, author of *Flying While Black,* African-American women may be special targets of racial profiling in public places.

As a customs officer, she observed the disproportionate search of African-American women, often in the most humiliating circumstances. Few whites either "get" the magnitude of humiliation and anxiety, or feel that policy action is necessary unless people can "prove" racial profiling. If we want to get past race matters, we must eliminate the scourge of racial profiling. There is no denying the enormous progress that has been made on the racial economic front, even as gaps exist. The black middle class has grown rapidly, with 15 percent of African-American families having incomes of more than $50,000 a year (compared to 25 percent of white families). Despite macroeconomic gaps, many of these families say they are living "good lives." Failures in affirmative action may annoy them, but the reality of racial profiling and racist minutiae stick in their craw and make it more difficult for people to "get over" racism.

What should women do about race matters? Those on the left that mouth the platitudes about their commitment to equality ought to take their blinders off and make sure they walk the walk that they talk. Are they interested in women of color as allies only when they are subordinate and needy? Do they accept women of color as equals? Are they willing to work as hard for racial and ethnic diversity as they are for gender diversity? I don't know how to advise women on the right, and, frankly I wouldn't presume to. So many of them walk around talking about how color-blind they are that I wonder if their blindness extends beyond color. The myth of color-blindness has no place in a multicultural society where race, gender, and ethnicity often shape our identities. A commitment to inclusion and to the acknowledgment of history, on the other hand, has a place in every sector of our society.

W.E.B. DuBois wrote that the problem of the twentieth century is the problem of the color line. We have taken twentieth-century problems into the twenty-first century, and race matters will continue to plague us until white folks take racism as seriously and personally as black folks do. One of my assistants had an experience, recently, that I'd like to see replicated a thousandfold. She went to pick up some supplies at an office supply store, and the clerk told her she could not accept a check. A young white woman, waiting, challenged the clerk. "You took my check," she asked. "Why not hers?" The clerk stumbled and said something about two forms of ID. Then she mumbled something about theft. The young white woman asked to see a manager, so the clerk backed down and accepted the check. My assistant was amazed that a stranger would go out of her way, and also that she "got it." More white folks need to "get it" and use their understanding to fight for racial justice.

RESOURCES FOR THE LEFT

NAACP
"The primary focus of the NAACP continues to be the protection and enhancement of the civil rights of African Americans and other minorities."
1025 Vermont Avenue, NW
#1120
Washington, DC 20005
202-638-2269
www.naacp.org

NATIONAL COUNCIL OF NEGRO WOMEN (NCNW)
NCNW works to improve the condition of women at the local, state, national, and international levels.
633 Pennsylvania Avenue, NW
Washington, DC 20004
202-737-0120
www.ncnw.org

LEADERSHIP CONFERENCE ON CIVIL RIGHTS
"The Leadership Conference on Civil Rights consists of more than 185 national organizations, representing persons of color, women, children, labor unions, individuals with disabilities, older Americans, major reli-

gious groups, gays and lesbians, and civil liberties and human rights groups."
1629 K Street, NW
#1010
Washington, DC 20006
202-466-3311
www.civilrights.org

League of United Latin American Citizens

"The Mission of the League of United Latin American Citizens is to advance the economic condition, educational attainment, political influence, health, and civil rights of the Hispanic population of the United States."
1133 20th Street, NW
#750
Washington, DC 20036
202-835-0491
www.lulac.org

The National Urban League

"The mission of the Urban League movement is to enable African Americans to secure economic self-reliance, parity, and power, and civil rights."
1111 14th Street, NW
#1001
Washington, DC 20005
202-898-1604
www.nul.org

COMMON GROUND

- We both would like to see an **end to racial profiling** and **strong enforcement of existing civil rights law.**

- We further agree that people of color's **access to mainstream America's opportunities** are changing for the better. Julianne would like to see the pace quickened, however.

8

REPRODUCTIVE RIGHTS

JULIANNE MALVEAUX

How did women's reproductive health get to be such a political football? After all, a woman's health, and her access to safe and legal abortion, ought to be a health matter between a woman and her doctor. All of the major medical associations, including the American Medical Association, the American College of Obstetricians and Gynecologists, and the American Medical Women's Association have opposed obstacles that impair women's access to safe and early abortion services. But politicians and ideologies have made this issue a political issue and drawn lines in the sand around a woman's right to choose, turning the matter into a political litmus test. As a result of this narrow view, the science around reproductive rights and freedom has been stalled in the United States. And for many, abortion is not a health matter, but a political one.

It tempts a long-term lefty to lean into Marx and wax indignant about men attempting to control "the means of production." After all, women's ability to produce economically, socially, and politically is limited by reproductive barriers. When politics trumps science and restricts the ability of women to control their reproductive rights, women's ability to fully participate in the world is limited. And when women's ability to fully participate in political and social life is marginalized, as is the effect of the politicization of abortion, women's voices are stifled.

It's the rare woman who chooses abortion easily or willingly or makes abortion the birth control method of choice. Still, many women need the flexibility to direct her reproductive choices, to take birth control, and when it fails, to terminate a pregnancy. To me it is the pinnacle of arrogance for one set of folks to tell others that they should have no control about what happens with their bodies or to circumvent a decision that a woman wants to make in consultation with her physician.

Abortion must be something that a woman chooses for her health, for her economic well-being, or for her social well-being. Too often, I want to tell those who oppose abortion that if they don't like abortions they shouldn't have any! But it is patriarchal and dictatorial for them to restrict the choices of others. Yet members of Congress, like Senator Rick Santorum (R-PA), flock to testify about how brutal certain abortion procedures are. They elevate little-used methods, coin provocative terminology (such as "partial-birth abortion"), and offer incendiary illustrations to suggest that the termination of any pregnancy is wrong. They make this a litmus test on decency, using language that is extreme and divisive, as a way of imposing their political agenda on others. Antiabortionists have turned the unborn into a political minority, but they often abandon these unborn people upon their birth.

In the case of child welfare agencies across the country, scores of children are mistreated, abused, and ignored because they were not welcome at the moment of conception and continue to be unwelcome after birth. Our treatment of children belies conservatives' staunch dedication to the fetus: Twelve million children are food insecure and approximately 39 percent of fourth-grade students read below basic grade level. This notion of protecting the fetus at all costs does not continue into childhood, which suggests that abortion is not really about the sanctity of human life but is instead more about the subjugation of women.

The expectation that every pregnancy should lead to a birth has introduced a criminal aspect to some pregnancies. Drug-addicted women who give birth to sick children have been increasingly prosecuted for endangering their fetuses, as if they aren't also people who are endangering themselves. The criminalization of motherhood is frightening, especially when it is juxtaposed with the deification of endangered motherhood. In other words, women who take drugs to induce pregnancy, who give dangerous birth to tiny multiples, are applauded. Women who take drugs for addiction, who give dangerous births to drug-addicted children are demonized. There is a horrible double standard here, one that applauds some motherhood at all costs, but punishes other motherhood because it was without any support. This is a standard that emerges from the flawed notion that fetuses are to be protected no matter what. Will a woman who loses a multiple be as sternly prosecuted as a woman like South Carolina's Regina McKnight, a drug addict who was convicted and jailed for child endangerment because she gave birth to a stillborn child?

To be sure, there are historical reasons why some women might look askance at abortion. The nineteenth-century eugenics movement targeted women of color and poor women as intellectually inferior mothers and attempted to discourage their motherhood. Echoes of that movement reverberate in the twentieth century with attempts at forced sterilization that took place into the 1970s. Attempts at abuse should not restrict choice, though. Women should neither be forced to bear children nor restricted from their ability to bear them. The choice should be one that women select, not one that is politically decided.

In 1971, a young woman in my freshman dormitory became pregnant. Illegitimate pregnancy held such a stigma, especially at my Catholic undergraduate school, that when my classmate attempted to abort herself with a wire coat hanger, I was sworn to secrecy and warned against calling any authority figure or member of the medical establishment. While my classmate nearly died, timely intervention allowed her to survive. Thousands of American women have not been so fortunate. I hardly have the words to describe blood-soaked sheets, a late-night ambulance, the stultifying atmosphere, and everyone's awareness that Anna's life was forever changed. Talk about birth control! That was enough to keep me from having sex for a while, but it was also enough to transform me into someone who is passionate about women's reproductive health.

When I tell young women Anna's story, they can hardly believe it. It cements me in their minds as a relic, a forty-something woman who came of age before women had full access. The young women that I spend time with are products of an age where the right to privacy has been invoked to protect a woman's right to control her reproductive capacity. They hardly believe my story, but when they listen, they are pained. They have heard the stories of back-alley abortions, butchers as doctors, and blindfolded procedures, but they think of it as something that happened way back when, in the dark ages, when want ads were still gender specific. Back-alley abortion has never been a reality in their lifetime. For this, they—and I—are thankful. Truthfully, however, it has only failed to be a reality for women of a more fortunate economic status. Those women misfortunate enough to be born poor, in a rural area, or of color still stand a higher chance of being in the same position as my freshman classmate. And for women aged below eighteen, often victims of rape or incest, the story is horrifically the same.

Whether we are sexually active or not, women need to have access to contraceptives. We need our health plans to provide us with contraceptive options. We need to know about our actions and their consequences. Budget or state of residence should not bar us from abortion or other contraceptive services.

The United States stands poised to return to an era where the rule of civil law will prevent women from exercising their human right to control their reproduction. True, there is always the possibility of abstention from sex, and the movements to teach girls how to say "no" deserve applause. But isn't there something inherently sexist about suggesting that girls have all the control in this situation? Shouldn't boys be taught to say "no," too? And shouldn't we be taught to address the basic patriarchy that exists in a society that when a girl "does it" she's a slut, while a boy is a "stud"? Too much of this "just say no" message puts an unfair burden on girls because it looks at just one part of the problem of adolescent sexuality.

Further, it is amazing that people who would ask that government come out of our pockets would insert government into our bedrooms. They want school "choice" but not reproductive "choice." They want to eliminate government's role, except when it comes to legislate morality. Women deserve the opportunity to control their reproductive lives. They don't need politicians telling them what to do.

Laws that restrict the ability of minor women to control their reproductive choices are repugnant to my value system. When do parents come to own the bodies of their daughters? Why can't young women make choices that are consistent with their values? Parental consent and notice laws, according to the American Medical Association, "appear to increase the health risks to the adolescent by delaying medical treatment or forcing the adolescent into unwanted childbirth." While youngsters should discuss their pregnancy with their parents, anyone who is old enough to have sex is also old enough to make a decision about the outcome of a pregnancy.

When the law renders young women incapable of making decisions without parental consent, it forces young women into motherhood or into potentially life-threatening situations, such as the one that plagued my freshman-year classmate. Similarly, laws that restrict the access of poor women to abortion services exhibit both a class and a patriarchal bias. If women with means can obtain abortions, why can't women who face economic challenges access them? These women, after all, are the women who will be most challenged to support their children, once born. Public funding of abortion services makes abortion available to the broadest population of women. To provide women with health care, absent access to abortion services, is to limit women's ability to put their reproductive needs in the context with other health services. It is patriarchal and makes no sense.

Yet many health plans provide for a comprehensive array of health services, except for reproductive health services. Organizations like NARAL (National Abortion Rights Action League) have fought a legal battle to ensure that contraceptives are provided under health care plans. Granted, the statistic that a quarter of all pregnancies in the United States are terminated by abortion is sobering (even though this number is smaller than the number in other parts of the world, especially Vietnam and central European countries). Might these procedures have been avoided? If our health care system dealt with reproductive choice in a more holistic way and if birth control were more readily available, fewer women might feel the need to have abortions.

Further, if women who were poor and pregnant felt they would receive more social support for their pregnancies, they might not feel forced to choose abortion. But there is a staggering hypocrisy on the part of those who oppose abortion. They would push women in a corner, forcing them to have children, and then they would invoke a Malthusian morality, limiting the social supports that poor women can count on.

This goes past politics to a frightening emotionalism that seeps into legislative activism. Mandatory waiting periods and other obstacles that delay abortion also increase health risks and the costs incurred and also make it more difficult for abortion providers to perform the procedure. Legislative interference is bad enough, but antiabortion forces indulge themselves in a sick emotionalism and extremism that has resulted in the bombing of abortion clinics and the massacre of physicians who perform abortion. Their attempt to intimidate those who seek abortions is frightening and intrusive. Yet, it is accepted by right-wing conservatives who reject women's right to choice. The battle over the introduction of Mifepristone is indicative. In 1982, a French pharmaceutical company announced it had developed a pill that would end a pregnancy if taken within weeks of contraception, which soon came to be known as RU-486. This was good news for those who supported women's reproductive freedom, because it expanded women's options. Many also felt that both the surgery and politics of abortion could be eliminated if a pregnancy could be terminated by taking a pill, even though this pill could be taken weeks into a pregnancy and needed to be administered with doctor's supervision.

Discussion of Mifepristone was clouded by confusion between it and emergency contraception, also known as the "morning after" pill, and suggests that the right has considerable control of the discourse around choice issues (even to describe someone as proabortion as opposed to pro-choice has connotations). To me, "morning after" suggests reckless irresponsibility even though the drug is taken in instances of true contraceptive failure and not just because someone knowingly and willingly had unprotected sex. Scientifically, "morning after" is an inaccurate description of the process.

While the drug Mifepristone became available in western Europe, abortion opponents blocked its introduction to the United States by threatening boycotts of any company that would introduce it in this country. It took nearly two decades for RU-486 to be introduced in the United States. For two decades, women's options for health care were limited by a politically motivated, narrow, and myopic group of people determined to shove their will down the throats of women who seek maximum reproductive flexibility. Also, they have attempted to limit reproductive education. Some so-called pro-lifers want to stop young girls from learning anything about reproductive choice, especially in public schools. They advocate teaching "just say no," and there is nothing wrong with abstinence education. Still, this education shouldn't be presented in a vacuum. Young women need to know about reproductive health, and a political lobby should not stifle that information.

The antichoice movement has tentacles that reach into legislative matters on health research. This group of people has opposed stem cell research, which would use test-tube embryos to investigate diseases like Parkinson's and Alzheimer's. In August 2001, President Bush attempted to seek a Solomonic solution to requests to undertake stem cell research by allowing such federally funded research but restricting the stem cells available for use. It is disturbing that politics restricts an array of exciting scientific developments. But patriarchal politics seem to have always restricted women's reproductive freedom, with western European countries always developing more reproductive options for women than scientists in the United States are willing to offer.

What About the Rights of Others?

When I think about women's reproductive health my focus is on a woman who should be entitled to the full spectrum of reproductive options. Yet it takes two to tango, and a woman doesn't conceive a child alone. Where are fathers in this picture? Some would say that their needs should also be considered, and that a woman shouldn't have the right to terminate a pregnancy without the father's input. While I am sympathetic to a father's concerns, I am more sympathetic to the fact that a woman should be able to control her body. All too often the "father's rights" movement seems to be a power play to intimidate women and to force them into doing someone else's will. Individual women certainly should consider a father's input, and accept or reject it as she sees fit. At the bottom line, her pregnancy should be her choice.

To be sure, women have reservations. We have abortions and then second thoughts. We are plagued with guilt about our choices. But people often have second thoughts about decisions that they make. The fact that they have second thoughts should not prevent them from the right to make decisions or to have options.

I'll begin to respect so-called pro-lifers when they really do support life in all of its manifestations. If they support the life of an unborn child, they should support the right of a living child to eat, to be educated, and to thrive. There's no evidence that their support of life goes past the womb. What hypocrisy! What tragedy!

RESOURCES FOR THE LEFT

PLANNED PARENTHOOD FEDERATION OF AMERICA
"Planned Parenthood believes in the fundamental right of each individual, throughout the world, to manage his or her fertility, regardless of the individual's income, marital status, race, ethnicity, sexual orientation, age, national origin, or residence."
810 7th Avenue
New York, NY 10019
212-541-7800
www.plannedparenthood.com

In addition to Planned Parenthood of America, the International

Planned Parenthood Federation (IPPF) "links national autonomous Family Planning Associations (FPAs) in over 180 countries worldwide." www.ippf.org

NATIONAL ADVOCATES FOR PREGNANT WOMEN (NAPW)

"NAPW is dedicated to protecting the rights of pregnant and parenting women and their children. NAPW seeks to ensure that women are not punished for pregnancy and addiction and that families are not needlessly separated based on medical and public health misinformation. Pregnancy and addiction should be treated as public health issues, not criminal justice issues."
45 West 10th Street
#3F
New York, NY 10011
917-921-7421
www.advocatesforpregnantwomen.org

NATIONAL ABORTION RIGHTS ACTION LEAGUE (NARAL)

"For over thirty years, NARAL has been the political arm of the pro-choice movement and a strong advocate of reproductive freedom and choice. NARAL's mission is to protect and preserve the right to choose while promoting policies and programs that improve women's health and make abortion less necessary."
1156 15th Street
Suite 700
Washington, DC 20005
202-973-3000
www.naral.org

DEBORAH PERRY

The historic 1973 *Roe v. Wade* Supreme Court decision should have solved the abortion debate, but it did not. Conversely, it created a dispute over ethical politics, where reasonable people on each side of the issue demonstrate equal intolerance of one another. Most of the abortion debate centers on when life begins and equates to personhood. Is it at conception? First trimester? Third trimester? When is it a fetus? Is a fetus a person? A fair—but rarely agreed to—question.

I want to be fair in this debate, for there is an emotionally charged argument here on both sides. For the purposes of this chapter, let me stake out the territory, the court overview, and the political battleground over choice, and address the health risks associated with abortion. And let me follow up by presenting the Republican view supporting both sides, and why I morally can't support abortion except in the case of rape, incest, or the physical health of the mother or baby.

In American politics, there is no other issue more polarized. The abortion controversy weighs heavily on policymakers for two main reasons: politicization and government interest. The politicization of abortion means that this one issue has turned into an overriding litmus test for politicians seeking your vote. "Pro-choice" and "pro-life" slogans were coined by advocacy groups and promoted by the media. During the 1970s, the National Organization for Women fashioned the slogan "I'm Pro-Choice and I Vote," and made a vital attempt to galvanize women across the country to support pro-choice candidates running for political office. The National Right to Life Committee advocates countered by displaying bloody fetuses on placards to remind you that abortion is murder. For many people across the nation, abortion is "single issue–style politics," meaning that they cast their vote on this issue alone. As a result of this, many scholars believe that the politicization of abortion affects the very principles of American democracy.

The government also has a legitimate interest in abortion. There has to be regard for the social order of American generations to ensure that populations carry on at a balanced pace so that younger workers can support retired folks. Americans are living longer than ever before. This trend of increased longevity coupled with declining rates in fertility means that we are faced with a disproportionate aging population. Today there are almost five working individuals for every retiree, but in 2030 this ratio will drop to less than three workers for every individual over sixty-five years of age. The bottom line is if government does not monitor the balance of American generations, then who will ensure that we have enough working people to support people in retirement?

No matter where you stand on the issue, abortion by its very definition is an "induced termination of pregnancy before the fetus is capable of survival as an individual." No one knows for sure how many abortions take place each year, but to the best of our knowledge, there are about 1.4 million. Of this figure, experts suspect that rape and incest account for about 16,000 abortions. What this figure does not account for are the many women who induce abortions with day-after contraceptives such as RU-486. A best approximation is that over forty million lives have been lost since the historic 1973 ruling of *Roe v. Wade*. To truly understand the deluge of controversy surrounding the abortion debate, it is important to reflect on the history and the players in support of and in opposition to abortion.

THE HISTORY OF THE ABORTION MOVEMENT

The fight over abortion has been a tumultuous battle. Let me summarize what the feminists say about the history of abortion because it runs counter to their principles today. In the mid-nineteenth century, it was the medical community that led the fight for the antiabortion movement. Believe it or not, early feminists and eugenics, and antivice crusaders joined the bandwagon of antiabortionists, and held individual viewpoints for not supporting abortion.

In 1857, Dr. Horatio Storer, a leading medical authority at the American Medical Association (AMA) publicly announced that married women used abortions as a means of birth control. Dr. Storer and the other anti-abortionists set out on a mission to do away with abortion as birth control by classifying abortion as a crime, and an immoral act against humanity.

The AMA's opposition to abortion redefined the debate in America as to the legality of abortion. In 1859, the AMA created the Committee on Criminal Abortion and released a report to denounce abortion as morally and socially reprehensible. The report, inclusive of a few resolutions, quoted the Bible and concluded that a woman who has an abortion "overlooks the duties imposed on her by her marriage contract." Physicians knew of the posed physical risks on women when having an abortion, yet their positions were not based on scientific reasoning. This report was sent to all legislatures and territories in 1860, and by 1880, forty states and territories passed laws against abortion.

Early feminists such as Susan B. Anthony, Elizabeth Cady Stanton, and Mary Wollstonecraft were part of the antiabortion movement because they wanted to stop men from abandoning their responsibilities in unwanted pregnancies. The antivice crusaders were morally against abortion and opposed all forms of birth control. They benefited greatly by the passing of 1873 Comstock Act, which prohibited public distribution of written materials on abortion and contraception. The eugenicists jumped on the bandwagon in the late nineteenth century because they were concerned about the declining birthrates of Anglo-Saxon women in a scare of race suicide. With the large numbers of Catholic immigrants and declining birthrates of native born, natives also feared a possible "race suicide." With regard to any religious opposition to abortion, it was not until 1869 that Pope Pius IX declared "the fetus, although not ensouled, is directed to the forming of a man. Therefore, its ejection is anticipated homicide." From that point on the Catholic Church vehemently denounced abortion at any stage of fetal development.

In 1821, Connecticut became the first state to enact a criminal abortion statute, and by 1910 every state had employed laws banning abortion, although wealthy women were granted a loophole in legislative acts as private doctors could provide abortions. By 1959, the winds began to shift as the

American Law Institute (ALI) proposed a model penal code for state abortion laws. It suggested legalizing abortion for pregnancy due to rape and incest, or the mental or physical health of the mother or baby.

In the ensuing years, Colorado, California, Oregon, and North Carolina passed ALI-model legislation. And, in 1970, New York further liberalized the movement to allow for abortions on demand for up to twenty-four weeks into pregnancy. Alaska, Hawaii, and Washington quickly followed suit. By the end of 1972, a total of thirteen states had ALI-type laws. Four states allowed abortion on demand. Thirty-one states allowed abortions to save the mother's life. Mississippi and Alabama had previously allowed abortion for rape and incest, and for the mother's health, respectively.

On January 22, 1973, the U.S. Supreme Court issued its ruling in *Roe v. Wade* finding that a "right of privacy" it had earlier discovered was "broad enough to encompass" a right to abortion, and adopted a trimester scheme of pregnancy. In the first trimester, a state could not enforce any regulations. In the second trimester, the state could enact some regulation, but only for the purpose of protecting a mother's maternal health. In the third trimester, a state could prescribe an abortion only to preserve the life and health of the woman seeking the abortion.

ROE v. WADE
HISTORY

1959—The American Law Institute (ALI) proposes a model penal code for state abortion laws. The code advocates legalizing abortion for reasons including the mental or physical health of the mother, pregnancy due to rape and incest, and fetal deformity.

1967—April 25: Colorado Governor John A. Love signs the first "liberalized" ALI-model abortion law in the United States, allowing abortion in cases of permanent mental or physical disability of either the child or mother or in the cases of rape or incest. Similar laws are passed in California, Oregon, and North Carolina.

1970—April 11: New York allows abortion on demand up to the twenty-fourth week of pregnancy, as Governor Nelson A. Rockefeller signs a bill repealing the state's 1830 law that banned abortion after quickening except to save a woman's life. Similar laws are passed in Alaska, Hawaii, and Washington State.

1971—April 21: The U.S. Supreme Court rules on its first case involving abortion in *United States v. Vuitch,* upholding a District of Columbia law permitting abortion only to preserve a woman's life or "health." However, the Court makes it clear that by "health" it means "psychological and physical well-being," effectively allowing abortion for any reason.

1972: By year's end a total of thirteen states have an ALI-type law. Four states allow abortion on demand. Mississippi allows abortion for rape and incest (1966) while Alabama allows abortion for the mother's physical health (1954). However, thirty-one states allow abortion only to save the mother's life. New York repeals its 1970 abortion law but Governor Rockefeller vetoes the repeal.

1973—January 22: The U.S. Supreme Court rules in *Roe v. Wade* that a "right of privacy" it had earlier discovered was "broad enough to encompass" a right to an abortion and adopts a trimester scheme of pregnancy. In the first trimester, a state could enact virtually no regulation. In the second trimester, the state could enact some regulation, but only for the purpose of protecting maternal "health." In the third trimester, after viability, a state could ostensibly "proscribe" abortion, provided it made exceptions to preserve the life and "health" of the woman seeking abortion.

Doe v. Bolton—Issued by the U.S. Supreme Court on the same day as *Roe v. Wade, Doe v. Bolton* defines "health" to mean "all factors" that affect the woman, including "physical, emotional, psychological, familial, and the woman's age."

Source: National Right to Life Committee

Doe v. Bolton—which defined "health" to mean "all factors" that affect a woman's "physical, emotional, psychological, familial, and the woman's age"—is where many scholars draw the line. The definition of "health" became too large in scope, because a woman could then give any explanation such as a headache for aborting a fetus. Fast-forward almost three decades, and the position taken by many women is that the decision to have an abortion is solely her right to choose.

A WOMAN'S RIGHT TO CHOOSE?

In all fairness to the pro-choice view, many women do not necessarily support having an abortion, but want to maintain choice over their own bodies to do as they please. On the surface, it sounds a lot like the argument made in support of assisted suicide. While pro-choice may sound reasonable, the woman is not the only actor here. If we grant all abortion rights to the mother, what happens to the rights of the father, grandparents, siblings, and of course, the rights of the unborn? Since it takes two to procreate, shouldn't a father be given as much deference as a mother in the decision-making regarding their unborn child? Just because the unborn is innocent and incapable of communicating does not mean that we have the right to disregard his or her being.

Feminist Marilyn French wrote, "Without the right to abortion, women do not possess the right to physical integrity." Excuse me? What about the physical integrity of a being struggling to come to life? I thought the cornerstone of women's liberation is that oppression of anyone is fundamentally wrong and should be condemned—whether against women, men, children, or the unborn. "When we consider that women are treated as property, it is degrading to women that we should treat our children as property to be disposed of as we see fit," said Elizabeth Cady Stanton. Was it not the early feminists who were so engaged in the abolitionist movement who believed in equality and justice for all?

Some pro-choice advocates fight the fight from a position of selfish posturing and backlash against a common liberal women's perception that we live in a patriarchal society. Other pro-choice advocates state that abortion liberates them. This is an illogical argument, because abortion liberates men, not women. Men are the ones who just get to walk away from bearing the responsibility of raising a child even though they were obviously engaged in conceiving that child. Men are the ones who can force a woman into an abortion through aggression or coercion.

Activists at the Feminists for Life of America believe that there should be respect for all human life, including the life of the unborn. These pro-life women want real choice for women as there are real choices to make in employing effective birth control, and real choices to make whether to have a career or to recognize the value of making a choice to stay home and raise a family. These activists also believe that men, too, should be able to hold a strong voice for the life of a child. Finally, pro-life feminists reject abortion. For aborting a child is the devaluing of human life—period.

HEALTH RISKS OF ABORTION

Most people haven't read the body of literature about the health risks of abortions, but there is strong evidence supporting the physical dangers. According to medical ethicist and author David Reardon, nine of the most common major complications include: infection, excessive bleeding, embolism, ripping or perforation of the uterus, anesthesia complications, convulsions, hemorrhage, cervical injury, and endotoxic shock. There is also strong epidermiological evidence linking abortions to breast cancer where thirteen of fifteen U.S. studies show increased risk. In fact, 10 percent of women who undergo abortions suffer from immediate complications, of which 2 percent are considered serious. Over one hundred other complications have been associated with induced abortions, including: minor infections, bleeding, fevers, chronic abdominal pain, gastrointestinal disturbances, vomiting, and Rh sensitization. Abortions can even cause irreparable harm leading to death.

According to the *Miami Herald,* Carolina Guiterrez bought into the myth that abortion was safe. She was twenty-one years old, married, and the mother of two small children. In December of 1995, Carolina underwent an abortion at a women's clinic in Miami's Little Havana, and was sent home despite insurmountable pain in her abdomen. She made several calls to the clinic, and was first hung up on by clinic staff and later left several messages on the clinic answering machine. No one from the clinic ever got back to Carolina. Two days later, Carolina could barely breathe, so she phoned 911 and was rushed to the hospital where she was diagnosed with a blood infection so severe that it sent her body into septic shock. Her uterus had been perforated in two places from the abortion. Gangrene forced the doctors to amputate her feet and some of her fingers, but nothing seemed to help. Less than six weeks later, Carolina Guiterrez was dead.

For other women who are fortunate enough not to experience serious repercussions, there is the emotional aftermath of guilt. While the immediate reaction of a woman may be relief that the procedure is over, these temporary feelings are followed by what psychiatrists describe as emotional "paralysis," or post-abortion "numbness." It is a similar mind-set to what soldiers feel after experiencing the killing of another human being in battle. According to David Reardon, within eight weeks after their abortions, 55 percent expressed guilt, 44 percent complained of nervous disorders, 36 percent had experienced sleep disturbances, 31 percent had regrets about their decision, and 11 percent had been prescribed psychotropic medicine by their family doctor. The health risks are rarely discussed in pro-choice circles, because the political battle for victory has outweighed the need to inform people of the physical dangers associated with induced abortions.

A REPUBLICAN STAND

The Republican Party tolerates both the pro-life and pro-choice view. Antiabortionists have dominated the past 1996 and 2000 Republican Convention platforms and included it as a priority, but earlier Republican convention platforms have been subjugated by pro-choice views. And, there is flexed muscle among pro-choice Republicans in the party. Some of the outspoken advocates of pro-choice views are EPA Administrator and former New Jersey governor Christine Todd Whitman, Homeland Security chief and former Pennsylvania governor Tom Ridge, and former member of Congress Susan Molinari. Even President George Bush—despite his allegiance to the religious right—affirmed he would do very little to overturn *Roe v. Wade* since roughly two-thirds of Americans think abortion should stay legal even if in a limited capacity.

For me personally, I take a position more consistent with the majority of my party. In my own view, abortion is the exercise of the strong over the powerless. I find it morally reprehensible that we are accepting of scraping off or sucking out something that clearly is the origins of human life, and walk away as if we haven't committed an act of murder. Abortion can only be described as "cruel and unusual punishment." I believe in the rights of the mother and father, grandparents, siblings, and the unborn child, and don't support federal funding of abortions, not even for Medicaid recipients. I don't think our government should be in the business of killing babies.

All aside, we should really just ask ourselves whether we have grown into a culture that has devalued life. That's what happened in Boston when a man shot his pregnant wife (and staged an elaborate scheme to frame an innocent man) because it interfered with his ambitions as a restauranteur. Have we grown into a society that says, "I'm too busy or it's not convenient to have a baby now, so, I'll just abort it and go on with my life"? That's what lawyer Heather King said after having three abortions—which she now vehemently regrets—because it would have interfered with her legal career.

On the other hand, there are conditions when a woman may have to abort a child, such as in the case of rape or incest. In life, unfortunate things happen like in the case of Barbara Hernandez, who is Catholic and supports an antiabortion view. One night Barbara was raped by her brother-in-law, Joe, and faced the difficult decision of going against everything she believed in or to be continuously reminded of the horrors of one tragic evening. Barbara wrote about her encounter in the book *Abortion: My Choice, God's Grace: Christian Women Tell Their Stories.*

Irrespective of Barbara's tragedy and the tens of thousands of other cases of rape and incest, we are at a point in the debate where we need to reevaluate why we entered the fight in the first place. We need to take a step backward, depoliticize the issue, and seek viable alternatives to abortion such as adoption. There are nearly three thousand Crisis Pregnancy Centers to help women facing unexpected pregnancies. In addition to providing pregnancy tests and counseling, the centers assist women with obtaining housing, maternity and baby clothes, baby furniture, pre- and postnatal counseling and care, legal and financial assistance, and even offer advice on how a woman in school can continue her education.

As the battle continues over abortion politics, perhaps there is a place where like-minded soldiers on opposite sides of an issue can jettison their weaponry and seek middle ground to a debate that has consumed American politics. Anything is possible. President George Bush very handedly found a mainstream approach to the stem cell research debate. While he certainly did not please all of his constituencies, he, with great diplomacy, found a place where the waters in the stem cell research debate are relatively calm.

Norma McCorvey, the "Jane Roe" of *Roe v. Wade*, knows the rough waters of abortion. In 1998, Norma testified before a Senate panel and talked about the millions of "children who will never know the warmth of a father's embrace, or the strength of a mother's love. We need to recapture an American culture where life is cherished, motherhood is honored, and children are valued."

RESOURCES FOR THE RIGHT

NATIONAL RIGHT TO LIFE COMMITTEE
This organization dedicates itself entirely to protecting all human life.
419 seventh Street

NW Suite 500
Washington, DC 20004
202-626-8800
www.nrlc.org

CONCERNED WOMEN FOR AMERICA

This organization is for women and like-minded men, from all walks of life, and dedicates its mission to restoring the family to its traditional purpose.
1015 Fifteenth Street, NW
Washington, DC 20005
202-488-7000
www.cwfa.org

FAMILY RESEARCH COUNCIL

This organization "champions marriage and family as the foundation of civilization, the seedbed of virtue, and the wellspring of society."
801 G Street, NW
Washington, DC 20001
202-393-2100
www.frc.org

COMMON GROUND

- While we disagree about abortion, we do believe the issue has been overly **politicized.** Particularly in the political process, we would like to see abortion less of a political lightning rod as in other countries.

- We both believe that **no woman chooses abortion as an option easily,** as there are many circumstances why a woman would have to do so, such as when a pregnancy jeopardizes the mother's health. Deborah would add that the woman is not the only actor to determine the outcome of the fetus. Julianne feels that with more reproductive health education and reproductive health options, fewer women will choose abortion.

• Young men and women should learn **abstinence,** because until a young person is ready to take responsibility for the birth of a child, he or she should abstain from sexual intercourse.

9

FOREIGN POLICY AND GLOBALIZATION

DEBORAH PERRY

When they killed my father, who was a beautiful man . . . I couldn't comprehend what happened. I was seventeen years old . . . and I refused to go back to the barracks because I didn't care for life . . . Thirty yards away or so were the gas chambers . . . I remember that many times in Auschwitz-Birkenau I wished for an air-raid by the Americans or Russians or British, not just for the destruction of Auschwitz-Birkenau but also for my own destruction . . .

ARNOST LUSTIG
AN EXCERPT FROM *VOICES FROM THE HOLOCAUST*
BY HARRY JAMES CARGAS

"Never again!" roar the cries of Jewish people worldwide in the aftermath of the Holocaust during World War II, when the innocent slaughter of six million European Jews occurred solely because Nazis loathed their successes and their religion. Still up for debate (on the numbers) but not forgotten, over twenty million Russians perished in Joseph Stalin's gulags for not supporting "Big Brother's" totalitarian dictatorship in a land where the property of the state was deemed larger than the life of an individual. In South Africa, an entire population of blacks and "non-whites" lived in apartheid and inhumane conditions under an authoritarian regime clinging to its colonial privileges. Massive genocide in Rwanda slaughtered hundreds of thousands of lives during the bloodbath in its civil war. And in Bosnia . . . a modern Holocaust occurred that took away mothers and daughters, and brothers and fathers, and burn in the souls of those who survived.

Where was United States leadership during these historic tragedies? Americans roughly went on about their business, largely ignoring the cries of men, women, and children's torture, in part because too many Americans hold a mentality of "it's just a small group of individuals whom I have no relation to, so it doesn't affect me." And, why should it? The United States is separated by two vast oceans, and safely insulated from the rest of the world. We tend to get involved in the affairs of the world when it serves our interest, or at the demand of the United Nations, and seldom for human rights' abuses.

September 11, 2001, stood as America's last day of vacation from ignoring the atrocities throughout the rest of the world. When President Bush stood before firemen and relief workers at the base at ground zero of the World Trade Center wreckage and said, "I can hear you . . . and the rest of the rest of the world will hear you, too," his words marked a turning point for Americans. While we should have been mindful before and worked to save the lives of millions of innocent people, now we have a personal reason to open our eyes and engage in the world around us. The time has come to balance out the realpolitik and humanitarian interests.

WOMEN AROUND THE WORLD

Mavis Leno, the wife of NBC's *Tonight Show* host Jay Leno, brought to the forefront the plight of oppressed women in Afghanistan long before September 11. Like Afghanistan, there are too many countries that spend energy thwarting half their population from education and work opportunities. And because of this they will never prosper. Author Ralph Peters writes in *Fighting for the Future: Will America Triumph?*, "From Greece to the Ganges, half the world is afraid of girls and gratified by their subjugation. It is a prescription for cultural mediocrity, economic failure, and inexpressible boredom." Restrictive activity on women in these countries is all about male insecurity that women will thrive, create economic independence, and create social change in societies that relish in the oppression of women.

I encourage any woman to read the State Department's annual report on human rights around the world, where you will always find deplorable realities on the status of women and children. Women and children make up 80 percent of all refugees and displaced persons globally, two out of three of the world's 1.3 billion poor are women, and today 6,000 girls were genitally mutilated. Women should care about foreign policy and globalization, because we don't want anyone to live in poverty and shame without the basic human rights that we enjoy in the United States. Some of the most rampant issues affecting women and children: slavery and prostitution, female genital mutilation, enforced child labor, and infanticide of baby girls. Not pleasant topics to delineate, but necessary if we want to end the subjugation of women all over the world.

SLAVERY AND PROSTITUTION

Every year, thousands of women in eastern Europe and Asia are promised viable employment abroad. These occurrences tend to be more prevalent among women in countries where economic conditions have forced them into a life chasing desperation. Due to economic hopelessness, these women leave their families for an unspecified period of time in hopes of being able to provide a better life for their children. Unfortunately, what they learn when they arrive in a foreign country is that they were tricked and coerced into a slavelike prostitution arena and forced to live in brothels where they are often locked up and beaten. Reports of involvement in international trafficking by state officials and police are routinely reported to the trafficking office at the U.S. Department of State, and can now employ economic sanctions against a country if it does not crack down on trafficking.

In India and other places throughout Asia and Africa, forced prostitution takes on a slightly different variation. Many cities, such as Bombay, have become major hubs for the international buying and selling of young girls and women. Traffickers scour train stations, streets, and villages for females and families in need of housing, money, television sets, or anything else which is worth the trade of one's young daughter. Some traffickers even hold beauty pageants in villages to lure parents to bring their daughters out. It is hard to fathom that some girls are as young as nine and ten years old, and are forced to have sex ten to twenty times a day. In lower-rent brothels, four out of five girls contract the AIDS virus. In more upscale brothels where condoms are required, the deadly virus infects one out of five girls. The worst part is that even if a girl escapes or is sent back to her village, she is usually ridiculed and shamed out of her community and is often unaccepted back into her own family. Rarely are the traffickers prosecuted; rather it is usually the girls who get in trouble for illegal prostitution.

FEMALE GENITAL MUTILATION

For many people not familiar with the practice of female genital mutilation (FGM), it is often compared to a male circumcision during infancy; only it is done to girls and women in a harmful, sometimes deadly manner. Genital mutilation is the process of removing the clitoris and often the remaining outer genitalia as a means of maintaining cultural or religious practices and to ensure a female's cleanliness and fidelity as well as to increase male sexual pleasure. A "traditional" practitioner usually performs the mutilation with crude instruments and without anesthesia. Hence the term "mutilation." This epidemic has reached staggering numbers as it is estimated that more than 130 million girls and women worldwide have been victims of this heinous practice.

According to the World Health Organization, immediate health consequences of this procedure include severe pain, shock, hemorrhage, urine retention, ulceration of the genital region, and injury to adjacent tissue. It is the repercussions of hemorrhage and infection that lead to death. Long-term consequences include cysts and abscesses, keloid scar formation, damage to the urethra resulting in urinary incontinence, painful sexual intercourse, and difficulties with childbirth. Then there are the psychological effects: Mutilation leaves a lasting mark on the life and mind of the females who have undergone it. These women suffer feelings of incompleteness, anxiety, and depression. Although most common in African and Muslim cultures, the practice does occur in the United States, Europe, Australia, and Canada, primarily among immigrants from African and Muslim countries.

FORCED CHILD LABOR

I've personally witnessed child labor in Third World countries. According to the International Labor Organization (ILO), between 100 and 200 million children are forced to work endless hours such as sixteen-hour days and are deprived of education and a childhood, at times to support their own family, and at other times for the profit of others. I saw it in Egypt at a carpet store where five- and six-year-old girls were needed for their tiny hands to weave the miles of carpet in the showroom. U.S. Representative Christopher Smith, a Republican from New Jersey, was horrified to observe a three-year-old girl who was forced to stitch soccer balls for hours on end; children walking barefoot amidst piles of used syringes, removing hypodermic needles in preparation for recycling; or other boys and girls who were removed from their homes by abusive masters as collateral for loans. A ghastly cornerstone of many Third World countries, pressure needs to be placed on *tolerating* governments to do a better job to take care of their future generations.

INFANTICIDE OF BABY GIRLS

In many Third World countries, it's no secret that a higher value is placed on the life of a baby boy. In China, prenatal sex selection results in disproportionate abortions of girls in comparison to the discarding of boy fetuses. This practice is commonly dubbed the "Holocaust of Little Girls." After 1949, the Communist Party worked to eradicate the practice of female infanticide, and imposed strict penalties on those caught. But, in 1979, this same Communist Party dictated strict family planning and adopted a one-child policy in an attempt to control China's massive population. And since the 1980s, an estimated 15 million baby girls have turned up drowned, suffocated, or have overpopulated Chinese orphanages.

Here is the story of one little girl who died from neglect in a Chinese orphanage as reported in a controversial article from the June 25, 1995, *South China Morning Post* entitled "Waiting to Die":

> Mei Ming has lain this way for ten days now: tied up in urine-soaked blankets, scabs of dried mucus growing across her eyes, her face shrinking to a skull, malnutrition slowly shriveling her two-year-old body.
>
> Each morning a fellow inmate at her Guangdong orphanage goes into the dark fetid room where she lies alone to see if she is dead. The orphanage staff, paid to look after her, do not visit. They call her room the "dying room" and they have abandoned her there for the same reason her parents abandoned her shortly after she was born. Her problem is simple and tragic: She has a condition which in modern China makes her next to useless, a burden on the state with an almost zero chance of adoption. She is a girl.

When she dies four days later it will not be of some termi-
nal, incurable illness, it will be of sheer neglect. Afterwards the
orphanage will dispose of her desiccated corpse and deny she
ever existed. She will just be another victim of the collision between China's one-child policy and its traditional preference for
male heirs. The name the orphanage gave her articulates precisely the futility of struggle to survive in a society that holds no
value for her. In Putonghua, Mei-ming means "no name."

According to Gendercide Watch, an organization dedicated to raising awareness of infanticide around the world, no one is aware of the overall statistics
on the numbers of baby girls who die annually from infanticide. However,
a minimum estimate would place the casualties in the hundreds of
thousands, and sex-selective abortions likely account for an even greater
number of deaths to little girls. The only good news out of the above story
is that it forced many people to pay attention, and fortuitously, there is a
growing trend around the world for families and individuals to adopt these
little girls.

GLOBALIZATION

The plight of women and children around the world can only change
through democratic development, improved human rights and education,
and through globalization: free trade, microenterprise lending, private property rights, telecommunications, and technology. First, global free trade fosters economic development and better working opportunities for women.
The more exposed less developed labor entities are to the economically
progressive world, the more their labor resources and practices will change
for the better.

Second, microenterprise lending has had an enormous impact on some
of the world's poorest people and is designed to provide minimum amounts
of credit to build a small business. Many times with the help of just $100

in countries like Tanzania or Honduras, a small craftswoman is enabled to expand her business beyond her immediate market. For example, according to Accion International, BancoSol, a microlending bank, is dedicated to the financial needs of Bolivia's microentrepreneurs. In 2000, 74 percent of BancoSol clientele were women who make their living as market vendors, seamstresses, bakers, candy makers, and others. With first loans as low as fifty dollars, BancoSol has lifted up Bolivia's poorest population at a portfolio risk rate of less than 10 percent. Because of its success, BancoSol introduced a new line of housing credit, for the purchase or reconstruction of homes, and began issuing credit cards and debit cards.

Third, private property rights and the recognition of that property is also a contributor to the advancing of economic progress. According to the Heritage Foundation, unfortunately, about 70 percent of poor people's property in the developing world is not recognized by the national government. It is something we tend to take for granted in this country, but without secure private property rights, most of the world's less fortunate cannot use collateral to obtain a loan. The Institute for Liberty and Democracy, a Peruvian think tank, found that where poor people's property in Peru was registered, new businesses were created, production increased, asset values rose by 200 percent, and credit became available.

Finally, the phenomenal advancements in telecommunications and the Internet makes the world an even smaller place and forges stronger links between countries and people. Not since the development of the industrial revolution have we had such great opportunities for great social change.

Whether it is the slaughter of innocent baby girls, the enforcement of child labor, female genital mutilation, or slavery and prostitution, we can make a difference for the women and children of the world. There are fundamental rights in a society such as a rule of law, education and literacy, and a social safety net and subsistence that can provide women a lift up. Globalization does enhance economic and social progress and fundamental human rights. But it is not just up to government, multinational corporations, or even nongovernmental organizations to do the work for us. We all have to do our part.

September 11, 2001, is a day we, as a nation, will be mourning for the rest of human existence. But out of this tragedy comes the opportunity to learn about the people who do not believe in egalitarian societies, to take a proactive approach in getting involved, and to say "Never Again!" just as the Jews did after the Holocaust. Write to your member of Congress and offer language to legislation (see chapter twelve, "Seven Ways to Lift Your Voice") in support of a woman's or child's cause in the world. Get involved with an organization (such as the ones below) or even galvanize a group of women with like-minded interests to start your own organization and advocate. It's that simple.

As American women, we have the power to restore hope in humanity and foster self-respect for so many women and children around the world. We are one of the few countries that can provide the light of democracy against the darkness of evil. We are living in a time where it has never been easier to make a healthier difference for the common good. We have a golden opportunity to send a powerful message around the world . . . people can progress. All we need to do is open our mouths, end the silence, and let our voices be heard.

RESOURCES FOR THE RIGHT

WOMEN FOR WOMEN INTERNATIONAL

This organization provides women with tools and resources to move out of crises and poverty and into stability and self-sufficiency one woman at a time.
733 Fifteenth Street, NW
Suite 340
Washington, DC 20005
202-737-7705
www.womenforwomen.org

FORWARD USA, INC.

This organization has a two-fold mission: "Eliminate Female Genital Mutilation (FGM) wherever it exists on the planet; and provide support services to those young girls and women who are victims of FGM."
89 Wabash Avenue
Suite 1
San Jose, CA 95128
408-298-1653
www.forwardusa.org

FREE THE CHILDREN USA

This organization has two main purposes: "To free children from poverty, exploitation, and abuse, and to give children a voice, leadership training, and opportunities to take action on issues which affect them from a local to an international level."
P.O. Box 32099
Hartford, CT 06150-2099
800-203-9091; Fax: 905-760-9157
www.freethechildren.org

GENDERCIDE WATCH

This organization is working to "raise awareness, conduct research, and produce educational resources on gendercide" and female infanticide.
10011 116th Street
Suite 501
Edmonton, Alberta
Canada T5K 1V4
www.gendercide.org

JULIANNE MALVEAUX

At the dawn of the new millennium, the United States is enjoying a preeminence unrivaled by even the greatest empires of the past. From weaponry to entrepreneurship, from science to technology, from higher education to popular culture, America exercises an unparalleled ascendance around the globe.
HENRY KISSINGER, *DOES AMERICA NEED A FOREIGN POLICY?*

A decade ago, as the cold war ended, it was unclear whether the United States would maintain its position of world superpower. We were unsure what our policies should be in the wake of the cold war against the former Soviet Union and the "evil forces" of communism. Our foreign policy, if we had one, had evolved into an episodic intervention into global conflicts, coupled with the granting of foreign aid, partly to help allies or to shore up our interests in developing countries, and partly out of habit. Even as we were the biggest and the baddest player on the world stage, we weren't always a cooperative one. We'd developed a defensive posture with the United Nations, amassing back dues of more than $800 million. Further, we'd said we would not support the U.N. to the extent that it was "anti-American." We seemed not to understand that some criticisms of the United States were criticisms of the status quo, of our hegemony over smaller countries, with an economic inequality that chafed the rest of the world, especially the developing world.

As the United States moved into the twenty-first century, though, we moved in a position of strength and superiority. Much of our strength has had to do with the globalization of the economy, and the fact that we are among the countries best able to benefit from globalization. Just as our size engenders resentment, so does globalization—though it is inevitable—because in some cases it exacerbates already existing inequalities, maximizing the influence of the large and strong, and marginalizing the influence of the smaller and weaker countries. Our nation's policy toward Africa is an example of the marginalization. The Bush administration has repeatedly said that involvement in Africa is not in our country's "strategic interest." The administration snubbed the world Conference Against Racism, and pledged a piffling sum to the U.N. effort to fight AIDS in Africa, despite the fact that 80 percent of all children suffering from AIDS are located there. Until the tragic events of September 11, 2001, the administration's foreign policy position might well have been described as "constructive disengagement."

The terrorist attacks on the United States that resulted in the loss of nearly three thousand lives and the destruction of billions of dollars of property may have changed the lens through which the United States sees the world. Countries that we hardly bothered to speak to on September 10, 2001, were asked to join us in a "war against terrorism." A $582 million installment on long-overdue United Nations dues was paid. President Bush met with more foreign leaders in a month than in the prior nine months of his term in office. In the wake of terrorism, we seemed to learn that while we are still the world's mightiest nation, we are also a nation that cannot survive without the help of our neighbors.

What does this mean to women in the foreign policy context? At home, the events of September 11, and subsequent military actions, will cause a crowding out of domestic programs that help women. For all the talk of "homeland security," many women lack basic economic security, and their insecurity was exacerbated by September 11, when loss of life was compounded by the thousands of workers who lost their jobs. Internationally, the United States has been reminded of the strength in alliances. To the extent that September 11 heightens our international awareness and involvement, some of that awareness must be focused on women. Especially in the developing world, women are the poorest of the poor, the least literate, and yet the nurturers of nations. Constance Berry Newman, assistant administrator of the Bureau for Africa for the U.S. Agency for International Development, says that funds we spend on development must focus to some extent on women.

Women in the United States can play key roles in improving the status of women around the world. We can be active in organizations like MADRE, the international women's human rights organization, and the Women's International League for Peace and Freedom (WILPF). We can support the export efforts of women in developing countries through groups like the Global Exchange Network. And, we can become involved in the foreign policy debate, placing a special focus on women and women's issues.

From a foreign policy perspective, are we to be all things to all nations? Are we also a nation to be held responsible for the flaws and excesses of the international agencies in which we play a role, such as the World Bank and the International Monetary Fund? In many arenas we have not so much absolute authority but mere influence. We can play a role in stabilizing the world economy, but have only a limited ability to maintain economic stability in any given country.

From a human rights perspective, we must be cognizant of then–First Lady Hillary Clinton's assertion that "women's rights are human rights." We can take a position on the education of girls or the abhorrence Americans feel toward policies like female genital mutilation. But unless our statements are accompanied by sanctions, we cannot force countries to our way of thinking. Indeed, we have frequently allowed our economic concerns to overshadow our beliefs as our continuing trade with China illustrates. China is the world's fourth largest economy, some say too large to antagonize because of our human rights concerns. But when we preach human rights to some countries, while ignoring violations in others, accusations of double standards can be easily raised.

We do not have the resources to be all things to all nations, and we may have fewer resources in the wake of September 11. Indeed, almost anything that one could say about foreign policy has been altered by the attack on the United States. I had written that the "defense" budget should not rise by $33 billion, which President Bush had requested before the attack on the World Trade Center. And I had written that Mr. Bush's plan to build a missile defense system within four years was senseless, and still is, in my opinion.

Now, we are placed in a position of having to defend ourselves. President Bush projects spending $2 trillion more on defense in the next five years. Billions will be spent on military preparedness, on air strikes on Afghanistan and other countries we describe as terrorist. I don't think the countries themselves are terrorists, though irresponsible forces in those countries, such as the Taliban, certainly are. I don't think there is a "left" or "right" position on our response to the attack on us, though I applaud Congresswoman Barbara Lee (D-CA) for her lone vote in opposition to giving Mr. Bush the power to declare war. Lee neither condoned terrorism nor eschewed retaliation, but urged deliberation instead of a rush to war. Indeed, while Barbara Lee declined to define herself as the pacifist many said she was, her statement and her vote came out of the best of the left tradition.

After September 11, there seems to be less tolerance for dissent, especially around foreign policy issues. Yet, if the response to terrorism is to mute free speech or eliminate divergent views, then terrorists have won their war against the United States. The vast majority of Americans said, when polled, they wanted to retaliate against terrorists and supported the air strikes that began on October 7. Still, many feel that nothing is served if we use the tragic events of September 11 as an opportunity simply to pour money into defense-related matters. Just as other federal programs require fiscal prudence, so does the matter of defense. September 11 should not become an opportunity to build up a missile defense that we might not need, and we should be especially aware of ways that defense spending crowds out other spending.

President Bush had described education as his top priority but asked for a budget increase of just $4.5 billion in the educational arena. At the same time, defense was slated to get a $33 billion increase. Meanwhile, spending on "public diplomacy" has declined, with cuts in the Foreign Service, the marginalization of Voice of America in the Middle East, and the elimination of the U.S. Information Agency (USIA). The impulse to spend on weaponry, not the tools of diplomacy, then, existed even before our nation was attacked.

The desire for safety and a strong national defense is nearly universal, but questions must still be raised about some of our foreign policy decisions. From my left perspective I'd like our foreign policy to be fairer, and to promote more economic equality. I'd like us to behave as a good and collaborative world citizen, and to exercise more of our influence in the human rights (and women's rights) arena. And while our strategic interests dictate some of our economic alliances and the grants of foreign aid, I'd like us to be more balanced in the ways that we treat countries throughout the world, especially in the Middle East.

FAIRNESS

How can we justify billions of dollars of foreign aid to one country (case in point, Russia, which siphoned off $1.2 billion of International Monetary Fund aid to a shell corporation in 1996), but only loan guarantees to another (now I'm thinking South Africa and our more limited economic involvement)? Or how can we advocate military intervention in Bosnia but not in Rwanda? The words "strategic interests" are likely to be used in any official explanation, but from where I sit, something other than strategy dictates our involvement. Sometimes, ethnic lobbies determine who gets what and when, and in other cases our own legislative myopia makes us behave as if a Bosnian life is more valuable than a Rwandan life.

These double standards bleed into our immigration policies, where it is easier for people from some countries (again, I'm thinking Russia) to come to the United States than it is for people from neighboring Mexico. From an economic standpoint, it makes sense for us to speak of managing immigration, but it seems hypocritical for us to benefit from globalization on one hand, and try to contain one of the effects of globalization on the other. In other words, globalization works because of the free flow of capital, yet we would restrict the flow of labor.

Of course, I have mixed feelings about labor mobility, especially when, in expanding economies, some people in the United States cannot get jobs or training while corporations are hollering "labor shortage." The H1B programs that facilitated the migration of skilled workers to the United States in the late 1990s provided world opportunities, but there were people in the United States who could also have benefited from those opportunities. The H1B program, also, is skewed toward men since women in the developing world are less likely to have access to technological education. Women are likely to come to this country undocumented and are often exploited as household workers, sweatshop workers, and other marginal workers.

How can we chastise some countries for their political systems, criticizing them for being "nondemocratic" while being silent when others are equally so? In the Africa Growth and Opportunity Act, for example, favorable trading relations are awarded to those countries that, among other things, embrace democratic principles. At the same time we are trading briskly with totalitarian China, imposing no conditions on our trade relationship with them. Of course, a quarter of the world's population lives in China, a major consumer market for our goods. We are in a far better position to scold Africa than we are to scold China. Our standard of democracy, then, is not absolute but driven by a set of market considerations. That may be in our best economic strategic interest, but it certainly is not fair.

PROMOTING ECONOMIC EQUITY

So-called free trade is the engine that has turned both markets and governance global, with the establishment of the World Trade Organization and other global adjudicating bodies. The United States has been a primary beneficiary of this globalization because it has provided us with more markets for distributing our goods and services. While globalization may have boosted the economic well-being of the United States, unrestricted free trade hurts the world's poor, especially poor women. The World Bank says that globalization "reduces poverty because integrated economies tend to grow faster and this growth is usually more widely diffused." Researchers at the Economic Policy Institute have shown that in 2001, after twenty years of global economic deregulation, poverty and inequality are as pervasive as ever. In 1980, median income in the richest 10 percent of countries was seventy-seven times greater than the poorest 10 percent. The gap widened to 122 times by 1999. While poverty rates have fallen in the United States, they have risen in other parts of the world, especially in the world's poorest countries. Much of the world's poverty is concentrated among women and children.

The United States has been one of the advocates for free trade and for the rapid mobility of capital around the world. If capital mobility hurts developing countries, our policies ought to mitigate that hardship with foreign aid, especially in the human development sector of a country's budget. Instead, some developing countries are forced to limit government spending that could reduce poverty because of the conditions of their loans with the International Monetary Fund.

Debt relief is one way the United States could promote economic empowerment and economic equity in developing countries. While we have provided some lip service on the issue, we've not done enough to lower the debt owed by poor countries around the world. When Europe was devastated at the end of World War II, the United States embarked on the Marshall Plan, spending $13.3 billion over three years on developing Europe. We've not managed to join with European allies in doing that in Africa or other parts of the developing world, though a July 2001 meeting of the world's largest economies, the G8 countries, focused on issues of world poverty. Historically, aid and development efforts have been implemented in a patchwork manner that often leave countries worse off than before they got foreign aid. In some West African countries half completed highways careen off to nowhere, serving no one, because of poor planning and heavy-handed international intervention. The money borrowed to build those useless roads still has to be repaid, despite the fact that foreign corporations profited by these unnecessary "development projects" and even though that money might be better used building schools or providing basic health care to sick children. The debt situation is so acute that spirited protests have been organized against the World Trade Organization, the World Bank, and the United States. These protests have successfully raised concerns about the impact that globalization has on poor populations all over the world.

Women have been especially affected by the globalization of manufacturing. Women are more likely to be hired at low wages to work outside the home manufacturing light consumer goods (such as athletic shoes and clothing). Working in conditions that are often harshly exploitative, they are also responsible for the maintenance of their homes and the sustenance of their children. United States corporations have often been the agents of exploitation. But they have argued that the jobs they bring are better than no jobs at all, and governments often go along with them. Our country could provide leadership on issues of economic fairness, but our country has consistently failed to provide real leadership on issues of economics.

World organizations have responded to the needs of women in a number of ways. The World Bank has made some funds available for microenterprise lending programs around the world. These programs provide women with just a few dollars—often under $500—to help start or sustain a business. Though the dollars are few, the amounts are significant enough for women to buy a sewing machine for a clothing shop, a computer for a word-processing business, or a used automobile for a taxi service. Such programs make the difference between poverty and sustenance for some women.

WORLD CITIZENSHIP

In our dealings with the United Nations and other bodies, the United States has operated as a poor world citizen, with a "my way or the highway" attitude that is dictatorial and noncooperative. Our relationship with the United Nations is a good example of the ways that we have failed to cooperate internationally. In the early 1990s, the United States demanded that the United Nations implement management improvements, and withheld its dues—which are set at 25 percent of the U.N.'s operating expenses—until reforms were made. The United States also asked that our dues decrease from 25 percent to 22 percent, but this penny-pinching seems pathetic when it comes from a country that so frequently brags about how large and powerful we are.

In the past decade, the United Nations has responded to calls for reform by creating an inspector-general's office, reducing staff by one thousand people, changing the budgeting process, and operating on a no-growth budget since 1996. While many of these changes were necessary and fiscally prudent, the United States took a heavy-handed approach that alienated our allies. It took terrorism to shake loose the $582 million the United States owed the United Nations largely because political considerations in our country slowed the paying of dues.

Just as we balked on paying United Nations dues, we balk on joining international agreements, and on implementing them. And we've balked on behaving cooperatively with other nations. Yet some world problems require a cooperative approach. For example, the international trafficking in women and children by crime syndicates begs for a regional and world approach, not just a national approach. Suphanvasa Chotikajan of Thailand's ministry of foreign affairs noted that "trafficking rings often try to exploit laws in individual countries and that needs to end. A regional response will make it difficult for the traffickers. Organizations like the United Nations provide countries with the forum to discuss these issues and to develop solutions. It is my hope that the spirit of cooperation and coalition that has come together to fight terrorism will stay together to address other pressing world issues."

Human Rights Activism

The World Conference on Human Rights was held from June 14 to 25, 1993, in Vienna, Austria. The final document from the conference recognized the interdependence between democracy, development, and human rights, and included the right to development as a human right. The conference also took historic steps to promote and protect the rights of women, children, and indigenous people, and called for the creation of a high commissioner of human rights by the United Nations General Assembly. In his final address to the conference Ibrahima Fall, secretary-general of the body, said, "In adopting this declaration, the member states of the United Nations have solemnly pledged to respect human rights and fundamental freedoms and to undertake individually and collectively actions and programs to make the enjoyment of human rights a reality for every human being." These are lofty words, but they are rarely enforced.

In Iran, where the United States has little influence, women who are found guilty of adultery are lashed and then put to death by stoning. Around the world, there is indifference to violence against women. Human Rights Watch reports that 12,000 Russian women die annually as a result of domestic violence. In South Africa there are 49,280 rapes. In the United States, there is a serious problem of sexual abuse of women in state and federal prisons. Human Rights Watch has called on world governments to repeal and revise all laws that discriminate against women and deny them access to justice. The United States could take leadership in this area but, perhaps haunted by our own human rights abuses, we are largely silent.

Assaults on women were used as a weapon of war in every conflict waged in the world in 1999. Human Rights Watch gathered information from Algeria, East Timor, Sierra Leone, and Bosnia and found a disturbingly repetitive pattern of abuse of women. Still, women seeking asylum in the United States and Europe were often denied the opportunity to immigrate, in some cases because their abuse did not take place because of their political opinions or membership in a social group. In these cases, immigration authorities fail to recognize gender as a social group, and fail to recognize the extent to which societal gender bias can cause the persecution of women.

The United States can play a role in improving the status of women around the globe. The International Women's Health Coalition, a New York–based organization that works around the world on women's health and rights, has helped implement efforts in Nigeria that focus on girls' and women's empowerment. The Girls' Power Initiative (GPI), Action Health Incorporated (AHI), and the Adolescent Health Information Project (AHIP) educate girls and boys on reproductive health, women's rights, and issues such as female genital mutilation and HIV/AIDS. None of these projects have government funding in Nigeria, but none of the girls who have participated in GPI have had an unwanted pregnancy since their enrollment. Nongovernmental organizations in the United States can make a difference in the status of women around the world.

We can also improve the status of children, since child labor is an issue both at home and abroad. Child labor is especially an issue in Latin America and Asia, but in war-torn parts of Africa, children are forced into the military before they reach their teens. In China, childbearing policies often force the slaughter of girl children. In Afghanistan, women are forced to wear traditional attire and are publicly beaten if they do not. Since the Taliban came into power, the education of girls has been forbidden and professional women have been forbidden to work. Now, things are changing slowly in Afghanistan and women again have access to education.

In the face of these human rights violations, the United States could play a more significant role in, as Mr. Fall challenged, "undertaking actions and programs to make the enjoyment of human rights a reality for every human being." We could be influential through our advocacy, through legislation, and through asylum policies. All too often, though, indifference, sociopolitical concerns, and economic considerations trump our human rights concerns and a range of issues that especially affect women and children go unaddressed.

RESOURCES FOR THE LEFT

MADRE: AN INTERNATIONAL WOMEN'S HUMAN RIGHTS ORGANIZATION

"Since 1983, MADRE has worked in partnership with community-based women's organizations in conflict areas worldwide to address is-

sues of health, education, economic development, and other human rights."
121 West 27th Street
Room 301
New York, NY 10001
212-627-0444
www.madre.org

AMNESTY INTERNATIONAL

"Amnesty International is a worldwide campaigning movement that works to promote all the human rights enshrined in the Universal Declaration of Human Rights and other international standards."
322 eighth Avenue
New York, NY 10001
212-807-8400
www.amnesty.org; U.S.A chapter: www.aiusa.org

WOMEN'S INTERNATIONAL LEAGUE FOR PEACE AND FREEDOM

"The Women's International League for Peace and Freedom was founded in 1915 during World War I, with Jane Addams as its first president. WILPF works to achieve through peaceful means world disarmament, full rights for women, racial and economic justice, an end to all forms of violence, and to establish those political, social, and psychological conditions which can assure peace, freedom, and justice for all."
1213 Race Street
Philadelphia, PA 19107
215-563-7110
www.wilpf.org.

FACE TO FACE INTERNATIONAL

"Face to Face is an international campaign to give voice to the millions of women denied basic human rights and freedoms. The goal of Face

to Face is to increase global awareness that women's rights are human rights."
www.facecampaign.org/main.html
212-809-6539

AFRICARE

"Africare seeks to improve the quality of life in rural Africa through development of water resources, increased food production, and delivery of health services."
440 R Street, NW
Washington, DC 20001
202-462-3614
www.africare.org

COMMON GROUND

- **September 11, 2001**, changed the United States' engagement in the world.

- As the richest country in the world, the United States shall play a role in **stabilizing the world economy**. While Julianne believes this can be achieved primarily through foreign aid and fairer trade policies, Deborah makes the case for globalization to provide poor people around the world a glance at a better life and a chance for hope.

- **Human rights, the plight of women, and the education of girls worldwide** should be priorities for the United States.

- While **foreign aid** certainly has a role to play in foreign policy, economic development opportunities through **microenterprise lending** can help lift people.

10

THE ENVIRONMENT

JULIANNE MALVEAUX

We can use artificial fertilisers, but only if they improve the soil quality rather than destroying it. All the methods need to pass a test: They shouldn't be allowed to disrupt natural cycles and processes. Bio-farming is no longer a luxury for us. It is our only remaining hope.
DR. TEWOLDE EGZIABHER
INSTITUTE FOR SUSTAINABLE DEVELOPMENT, ETHIOPIA
AN INTERVIEW WITH GREENPEACE, 2001

The polluter establishment wants us to believe that environmentalism is the domain of the elites, that the Great Unwashed majority is much too preoccupied with scraping together a living to spend time worrying about such prissy concerns as factory emissions and oil spills. Just get government the hell out of the way, they say, so developers can build, factories can roar, money can be made, and the marketplace can work its magic in solving both our economic and our environmental problems. The purveyors of this conventional wisdom intentionally overlook the common sense of the ordinary American.

*There is a solid, unshakable, and highly agitated environmental ma-
jority in our country—people who are not interested in some phony
tradeoff between their families' environmental health and their economic health. They want unpolluted water, air, land, and food, period. Such folks are not likely to belong to the Audobon Society, most
would not call themselves "environmentalists," and they probably
know more about the PTA than the EPA—but they damn sure know
pollution when it hits them. These are the "pollutees," and they are
sick of the platitudes and pussyfooting they get from politicians when
it comes to protecting their families.*

JIM HIGHTOWER
*THERE'S NOTHING IN THE MIDDLE OF THE ROAD BUT YELLOW STRIPES
AND DEAD ARMADILLOS*

When I am able to go hiking, inevitably, by the nature of the activity, it is in a beautiful mountain setting, with views for miles, ideally. I enjoy this rare time because remaining cooped up in the geological depression that is Washington, D.C., for too long when it's too hot can wreak havoc on the psyche. Fortunately, hiking is a recreational activity that for years has been nurtured and protected by government agencies, through the Clean Air Act, Endangered Species Act, and related policies. And I, as well as the rest of the world who enjoy Yellowstone National Park in Wyoming, the Black Hills of South Dakota, and Arizona's Grand Canyon, appreciate this. My concern now rests in the enjoyment of not only recreational activities such as hiking, but in the enjoyment of a healthy life for those who are not as fortunate. Millions of people around the world agree: The new environmental war is taking place not so much in national parks and major rivers as it is taking place in backyards and playgrounds— and as women are socially responsible for homes and kids, the task of protecting their children, families, and neighborhoods falls on them.

Environmental Justice Versus Environmental Protection

For the greater part of the last century, environmentalism was seen as a radical movement against corporations and for animals and trees. Students chained themselves to great California redwoods. Greenpeace members sailed the seas protesting major oil companies like Exxon. People for the Ethical Treatment of Animals sprayed wearers of real fur with fake blood. But the new environmentalism is not content with the protection of furry animals and big trees. Organizations like the Environmental Justice Resource Center at Clark Atlanta University have helped to turn environmentalism on its head—and made it that much more difficult to ignore. In the new millennium, environmentalism means protecting the lives and livelihood of human beings as much as the lives of endangered species. The new face of environmentalism—that of environmental justice versus environmental protection of animals and trees—is more readily accepted by mainstream culture, partly because environmental injustice has become more pervasive and visible and partly because it is seen as less radical to protect humans than trees. The blockbuster movie *Erin Brockovich* made environmental justice sexy; the task at hand for contemporary environmentalists is to make environmental justice make sense.

Increasingly, issues of environmental justice center around communities of poverty and color. While Love Canal and Three Mile Island are the environmental horror stories of days gone by, in 2001 Cancer Alley is the nickname for the Louisiana corridor home to some of the United States' most impoverished communities and most polluting industries—and thus the home to environmental injustices of the most grievous order. The Tulane University School of Law Environmental Law Clinic, which represents low-income clients in matters of environmental justice, is one of the toughest opponents to the heavy and toxic industry that threatens the lives of mostly black and Hispanic Louisiana residents. The school, along with local community action agencies in towns like Bogalusa, Oakville, and Perryville, has garnered victories over solid waste facilities and power plants. The school has been so successful in recent years that the Fifth Circuit Court attempted to restrict student practice of law (through university legal clinics) and raise the minimum income that would make low-income clients eligible to receive legal assistance. It should come as no surprise that in Louisiana, where judges are popularly elected, the judiciary would respond to the influence of industry bigwigs. The corruption of American politics has again lent itself to the corruption of our values: It is the corporation that is of paramount importance, not the citizen.

Again, not surprisingly, asthma accounts for 10 million missed school days, millions of emergency room visits, 15 million outpatient visits and hospitalizations, and 18 million days of restricted activity every year—with the majority of these victims being inner city children and adults (whom we know are more likely to be of color), as they have the highest rates for asthma prevalence, hospitalization, and mortality. If that weren't enough, African Americans are three times more likely than whites to die from asthma and asthma complications. For the inner city mothers who work three jobs and must take off of work when their child needs to visit the physician, for the teachers who miss students on a daily basis due to almost entirely preventable ailments, for the employers who lose money every time an employee is out sick, the signs are there: Where we live can impact our productivity and ability now more than ever. We must not forget that the issue of environmental justice is wedded to the idea of sound public health. Just as women who lack the autonomy to control their reproduction, people who lack the security in knowing the air they breathe is clean and the water they drink is safe also lack the ability to participate in our cultural life. Healthy individuals are key to a sound economy and a sound social structure. It boggles my mind to see that our lawmakers fail to see the relationship between healthy citizens and a healthy society.

MONEY, OIL, AND AIR

The fact that environmentalism now takes place in poor communities across the United States and the globe has not gone unnoticed by those who stand to gain from putting the lives of blacks and Hispanics at risk. In 2000, the Center for Energy and Economic Development spent $40,000 vilifying the Kyoto Protocol for the harmful impact it would have on people of color, according to Clark Atlanta University's Environmental Justice Resource Center. The protocol was a result of a conference of 160 nations in 1997 meeting to discuss binding limitations on greenhouse gas emissions for the developed nations, pursuant to the objectives of the Framework Convention on Climate Change held in 1992 where developed nations agreed to reduce greenhouse gas emissions relative to the 1990 levels. The United States agreed in Kyoto to reduce its emissions by 7 percent during the period from 2008 to 2012. At last check, however, the United States will not be keeping its word: President Bush and EPA Administrator Christine Whitman announced in 2001 that the United States has "no interest" in agreeing to the Kyoto Protocol, fearing the detrimental effect it could have on big energy businesses and production.

Organizations like the A. Philip Randolph Institute, the Labor Council for Latin American Advancement, the National Black Chamber of Commerce, the National Institute for Latino Development, and the United States Hispanic Chamber of Commerce strongly supported the Center for Energy and Economic Development report—even though none of them has an environmental justice track record, according to the Environmental Justice Resource Center. Further, every opportunity to improve air quality is trumped by American fuel interests, both internationally and nationally. The Kyoto Protocol? Forget it. More stringent emissions standards for American cars and trucks? Not so long as United States automakers continue to produce and introduce brand-new gas-guzzling sport-utility vehicles. Does anyone else find it eerily ironic that while we claim we can't reduce harmful emissions without reducing profit and productivity, we can still find the energy to create vehicles that get eight miles per gallon on the highway? While Japan has spent the bulk of their research and development capital over the last twenty years on designing and building lighter, more fuel-efficient, and more economical cars, the United States has continued to allow our conventional wisdom that bigger is better to dominate production of our automobiles—even though we have, although only recently, seen a small shift toward research and design of more economical cars.

And who suffers? In the United States it's disproportionately persons of color, although the entire world loses when the globe's biggest fuel consumer and biggest producer of harmful gaseous emissions perpetuates its acid rain on everyone's parade. According to Argonne National Laboratory researchers, 57 percent of whites, 65 percent of African Americans, and 80 percent of Hispanics live in 437 counties with substandard air quality. And in Atlanta, which has had its federal highway funding snatched away on more than one occasion for its failure to improve air quality, ground-level ozone continues to contribute to its smog problem, according to the Environmental Protection Agency. As growing metropolises like Atlanta and Tampa and Charlotte are flooded with new immigrants from our neighbor Mexico, migrants from other parts of the country looking to work in the most bustling region of the United States, and African Americans returning to their roots, and as places like Salt Lake City continue their reproduction boom, roads—especially in the South and the West—will get wider and cars will multiply. This is part of the new urban paradigm. This should also be a weighty concern when one considers that air pollution from vehicle emissions causes significant amounts of illness, hospitalization, and in some cases, premature death. Conservatives will tell you that we can't "prove" that automobile emissions cause illness, hospitalization, and premature death. If we believe that secondhand smoke can kill us, why is it not possible that the exhaust spat out every day by buses, cars, and tractor-trailer trucks can do the same thing? The dollar amount of the damage done by cars and fuel? Estimates run from $10 billion to $200 billion annually. The average Washington, D.C.–area resident spends more than an hour in their car per day commuting. The average Los Angeles–area resident spends more than two hours in their car per day commuting. And the chances that either of these average commuters carpools is as slim as ever.

Women can drive lighter, more fuel efficient minivans and cars instead of SUVs and trucks. We can protest the placement of factories in residential neighborhoods—be the neighborhoods rich or poor, black or white. We can, indeed, carpool. We can ask our representatives in Congress to support global treaties that aim to protect the environment—treaties like the Kyoto Protocol—and we can ask them to oppose drilling in the Arctic National Wildlife Refuge, which, by name, is supposed to be a safe haven for wildlife in the region. It is not clear whether drilling for oil in the Alaskan tundra will wipe out species, but the risk appears to be far greater than any potential benefit as it is also not clear or certain how much oil we can glean from this particular source. And while it is likely that more men than women share the president's belief that we must "lessen our dependence on foreign oil," exactly how much oil from the Arctic National Wildlife Refuge can contribute to that dependency reduction is sketchy at best.

A Cleaner United States

It is important to note that often, as countries become more industrialized, they also become cleaner. Yes, the United States as a whole has become a cleaner nation—with more stringent policies regarding air and water quality—but the effects of the pollution that continues to be produced are concentrated in poorer areas. What persists and what has multiplied—garbage, for example—now invades landfill facilities that I can guarantee you are not located in the affluent areas of Cherry Hill, New Jersey, Farmington Hills, Michigan, or La Jolla, California. Americans who believe they are doing a world of good by recycling may be being duped in the process: Barges of recyclable material routinely sail the seas and end up on Indonesian mountainsides.

Waste

Waste not, want not. Reduce, reuse, recycle. It should come as no surprise that the United States is the most wasteful nation in the world. We are 4 percent of the world's population, but we emit 22 percent of greenhouse gasses and produce 37 percent of its garbage. To be sure, we use so much oil and electricity and produce so much waste because we are the most productive country in the world. High levels of productivity, however, do not give us free reign to pollute and punish the earth for no reason. Take commercial farming for example: When one considers total output from farms, small farms are more efficient—to a degree—and the environmental effects of factory farms could be construed as devastating.

- The U.S livestock industry produces 2.7 million tons of waste each year—which is 130 million times the volume of human waste;

- In 1995, Premium Standard Farms' operation in Missouri generated five times as much sewage as Kansas City;

- Waste leads to permanent soil toxicity, poisoning the land forever.

Further,

- Just four corporations control 58 percent of pork processing in the United States.

- Between 1950 and 1999, the number of U.S. hog farms fell from 2.1 million to just 98,000;

- When factory farms move in, poverty rises, unemployment rises, migration rises, and pollution levels rise—especially in "isolated rural communities" (particularly in North Carolina, Missouri, Iowa, Minnesota, Ohio, and Illinois).

Here we are confronted with the idea that women are expected to protect their children, yet no amount of maternal protection will shield kids from the harm caused by waste and pollution.

FARMING AND AGRICULTURE

Third only to motherhood and prostitution (proof that women are the real workers in every society), farming has been one of the oldest and most stable occupations of all time. We all must eat, after all. With increased population and industrialization came the insufficiency of mere hunting and gathering. Enter small-scale farming. And farming, because it is the only way to feed large amounts of people without consuming the energy of every individual (as does hunting and gathering), has lasted as the world's primary food source and the source of livelihood for millions worldwide. The millions of worldwide farmers who up until the last twenty years have been able to provide for their families by farming are finding that they cannot compete with big business: The number of people for whom farming remains as an adequate source of livelihood is dropping precipitously. American farms are dropping like flies—especially small and minority farms according to Oxfam America and the Federation of Southern Cooperatives, as well as community groups in states like Texas and Nebraska who are also monitoring what William Greider termed "the last farm crisis" in *The Nation*. Globally, fewer and fewer families are able to be self-sufficient with farming as their primary occupation. Marika McCauley, a consultant to Oxfam America's Washington, D.C., office now working in the Mekong delta of Vietnam, finds that "farmers in both the global north and south are facing barriers to survival in an era of large-scale, industrial agriculture. The sustainable small farm models are rapidly being replaced by profit- and production-oriented corporate models." Most sadly, when one considers all of this information, is that this earth is producing more food than ever before, yet family farms are going out of business and the number of hungry children and adults across the globe has increased. There is something wrong with this picture and I can tell you what it is: agribusiness.

Take the agribusiness giant Monsanto, based in St. Louis, Missouri. Now is a good time to mention that a friend of one of the young women in my office grew up blocks away from the huge Monsanto facility in St. Louis. He reports having seen blue snow on their grounds on more than one occasion. This having been said, Monsanto historically has been in-volved in some extremely useful and innovative projects—the same assistant with the friend from St. Louis has a friend whose grandfather was a Mon-santo vice president for a number of years. The flush toilet? We have Mon-santo to thank for that. Unfortunately, they've also been party to a great deal of insecticide and herbicide production, chemicals used to treat crops to prevent destruction from insects and weeds. It's too bad human beings can't be treated with chemicals to prevent destruction from insecticide and herbicide since these same chemicals on which we have depended to pro-tect our food have been endangering our lives: Fifty thousand American women die each year of breast cancer. The most likely culprit is the chem-ical poisoning of the air we breathe, the water we drink, and the foods we eat.

Professional muckraker Jim Hightower reported in 1998 that when a Texas farmer tried to use the food chain to prevent insect destruction—that is, placing bugs that eat plant-eating bugs in the same proximity—the federal government intervened and said no way. The FDA and EPA even-tually backed off, but not after years of arguing over what was safer: a few extra bugs in grain or the effects of permanent toxicity that can result from widespread use of herbicides and pesticides. Monsanto, though, has now decided that the wave of the future is not in chemical herbicides and pes-ticides. Instead, they're all about creating crops. Creating crops? Yes. They're creating the genetically modified organisms (GMOs) that we've all been hearing about for the past ten years. Companies like Monsanto and Archer Daniels Midland ("supermarket to the world") are all in cahoots in this brand-new biotechnology field. We're talking the production—inven-tion, if you will—of crops modified by genes that make them resistant to weeds and bugs. We're talking about soybean crops that can yield ten times more soybean per plant per acre than strains found in nature. ADM and Monsanto would have you believe that the world's hunger problem can be solved by their technology. Unfortunately, the world's hunger problem is not a product of a lack of food. It's the result of, quite possibly, every other factor besides food itself. Civil war, wage gaps, unemployment, unsound infrastructure in developing nations . . . all of these factors confluence to keep hungry children and adults worldwide in starvation. Just as problematic employment prospects for people of color in the United States are less the result of employment problems than they are the result of race problems, the food problem must be solved in every other way besides the production of food.

WHAT YOU CAN DO

Eating certified organic or homegrown foods is one way to ensure the health and safety of your produce, but is, regrettably, a luxury afforded only to those who can pay the higher prices for safer foods. Just as when one thinks of safe cars, one thinks of Volvos and Mercedes Benzes, when one thinks of safer foods, fresh and organic produce purchased at upscale, nationwide chains such as Trader Joe's or Whole Foods Market come to mind. Buying organic is not inexpensive, but for those for whom it is a luxury, growing one's own vegetables is another option. Many cities across the country have urban or community gardens (visit the U.S. Department of Agriculture website www.usda.gov for more information) where neighborhood residents are responsible for the upkeep and maintenance of relatively large plots of land where they can grow their own fruits and vegetables. In some localities, residents pay for nothing; in others, they are expected to cover the cost of seeds.

Genetically modified organisms have not (yet) proven to be harmful to consumers' health, but they have also not proven to be necessarily good for it either. A healthy dose of skepticism, I believe, is in order. Avoiding genetically modified organisms is becoming increasingly difficult, as European countries especially report contamination of non-GMO foods with strains of crops that have been genetically modified. Again, shopping at whole foods stores and organic and farmers' markets, and growing your own produce is a way to avoid the potential repercussions of the unknown.

Being a vegetarian or vegan is another option if one wants to help the planet, though I must admit I'm not there yet, usually passing up red meat in favor of seafood or poultry. Many vegetarians are not vegetarians because their food once "had a face;" some of us are vegetarians for weight-control purposes, but many people who do not eat meat do so out of respect for the environment as a whole. The meat industry uses acres and acres of open space for grazing, billions of gallons of water yearly, and, as stated earlier, produces more waste per capita than human beings.

It's interesting to note that opponents to taking care of the environment think that every doomsday statistic is out to scare you. Is it so hard to believe that pollution causes cancer? Is it so unlikely that billions of pounds of CFCs released into the atmosphere each year could very well cause or contribute to a greenhouse effect? Could it not be possible that giving cows artificial hormones has a negative effect on the humans who eat them? And if it all is possible—even if not proven—wouldn't you like to know and be given the chance to make informed decisions for the health of your children, your family, and the future of the environment?

RESOURCES FOR THE LEFT

GREENPEACE USA
Greenpeace International works to protect the environment on six basic fronts: climate, genetic engineering, forests, toxins, oceans, and nuclear disarmament. They have Greenpeace offices worldwide, including the United States and Canada.
702 H Street, NW
Washington, DC 20001
800-326-0959
www.greenpeaceusa.org

OXFAM AMERICA
Oxfam America, the North American office of the U.K.-based Oxfam, "invests privately raised funds and technical expertise in local organi-

zations around the world that hold promise in their efforts to help poor people move out of poverty. [Further, they] are equally dedicated to educating the public—in all quarters of the world—on the realities of poverty and on the universal obligation we have to establish a future that is equitable, environmentally sustainable, and respectful of the rights of all peoples."

26 West Street
Boston, MA 02111-1206
800-77-OXFAM (800-776-9326); Fax: 617-728-2594
www.oxfamamerica.org

PRIMAL SEEDS
Primal Seeds is "a network to actively engage in protecting biodiversity and creating local food security."
www.primalseeds.org

Deborah Perry

My first night's sleep in the Amazon rain forest was mind-boggling—a story that I have been indulging my friends and family with for years. I was insistent on seeing the Amazon during my three-month travels in Brazil. My friend and traveling companion, Eduardo, was not. There we were walking the boardwalk in Manaus, one of the main ports leading into the Amazon, in search of a true Amazonian Indian who would be willing to take us into the rain forest. As luck would have it, we met a sun-scorched middle-aged Indian who had grown up in a village deep in the jungle. He and his wife moved beyond village life and bought a boat (if you can call it that) to lure humble travelers like myself into the vastness of the jungle. We bought in and traveled for five nights onto two of the thousands of rivers that comprise the Amazon.

Nightfall emerged, and the first thing I noticed was the interminable, beaming sky displaying the brightest stars I have ever seen. As my eyesight leveled off to the river, I saw laser pointer–like red dots everywhere. I asked in broken Portuguese, "What are those?" The response was nothing I wanted to hear. It was the dozens of alligators—surrounding our boat— that come alive after nightfall. "Great!" I thought, as I was about to sleep on a hammock in a flimsy, open boat, barely hovering above the water. Oh, and it is vociferous in the Amazon at night. Everything comes alive at night as many of earth's creatures sleep during the day.

It was late, and we all decided to turn in to our hammocks. Eduardo's was next to mine, and the Indian's and his wife's hammocks were at the stern of the boat. I couldn't sleep because all I could think about was that I was sleeping in the (expletive) Amazon, and I had four more nights to go. At some point in the middle of the night, I finally fell asleep . . . but not for long. I heard a high-pitched noise, getting louder and louder. Boom! Something attacked me. A troop of huge flying cockroaches were all over me (everything is magnified in the Amazon, and these suckers are titanic).

My heart was pounding uncontrollably, and I was trying to be as quiet as I could since everyone else was asleep. I pulled these things out of my hair, enclosed myself in the hammock, and attempted to go back to sleep.

I, once again, fell asleep. I, once again, woke up. This time it was to the sound of salt and pepper shakers flying across the dinner table. I cautiously peered over to my left, and less than two feet away was an anaconda snake (you know . . . the one they made the movie about). But it's okay, because the thing was so big that I didn't see its head or its tail, just the enormity of its body. This time I had an out-of-body experience, jumped from my hammock into Eduardo's without touching the ground. Fortuitously, the Indian also heard the flyings of salt and pepper shakers, rose to investigate, and threw the mammoth thing back into the water. Then we all went back to sleep.

Five days later, as we left the rain forest behind and headed back to Manaus, my friend looked deep into my eyes and with considerable passion said, "You are as free as a bird." Without any explanation, I knew what he meant. You can't help but to take away life lessons from the milieu of the Amazon. While being "free as a bird" may have more to do with my attitude in life today, it has always been the great outdoors that puts me at peace.

Whether we are Amazon travelers or couch potatoes, we hold a contributory relationship with the environment, as generations of populations and a bounty of uncontrollable factors dramatically alter the course of conditions of our planet. We are all reliant on the environment and its resources. It can be as simplistic as the usage of a paper towel made from trees, fuel for our cars, or the correlated relationship between our health and the environment. It is the air we breathe and the water we drink that can dictate the wellness of our health—from conception to death.

The debate today is not whether we want to protect the environment, but how best to protect it. This is easier than it sounds. Over the last thirty years, the United States was tasked with a clear agenda, and tackled the most glaring environmental problems such as clean air and water. Now we are expected to make environmental gains in less obvious, but more contentious issues such as arsenic in drinking water or global warming. While

these and other obscure environmental issues seem straight forward to reduce, we have to weigh practical solutions with associated costs. Consider
the following delineations and costs of reducing arsenic and global warming.

In recent years, there has been much discussion about reducing arsenic
(from fifty to ten parts per billion) in drinking water. Arsenic is a natural
chemical element found in soil, the ocean, lakes and streams, and in plants
and animals. The Food and Drug Administration estimates that the average
adult ingests about fifty-three micrograms of predominately organic arsenic
a day. But the vast number of Americans will never need to think about
arsenic in their water as they receive more arsenic in food. Yet, the annual
estimated price tag for reducing arsenic is $180 million, for saving a max-
imum of eight lives from bladder cancer, and twenty-two lives from lung
cancer. Using these figures, the United States would spend between $6
million and $29 million per life saved.

The Kyoto Protocol, despite the falsified claims put into the public
domain, will not prevent global warming—it instead reduces emissions by
a mere five percent in industrialized nations only, and only saves the world
six years. This may sound like a good thing until you look at the projected
total cost between $5 and $8 trillion (the United States' share is estimated
near $1 trillion). There are more important health-related problems that are
less costly, such as solving the number one health issue around the world:
safe drinking water and sanitation coverage.

While it is noble to want to eradicate every conceivable pollutant off
the face of the earth, it is unrealistic due to exorbitant costs and in some
cases, unsound science. We have to direct our resources in the direction
that strives for the greatest reductions in health risks. All we know, for sure,
is that the current debate over the environment has become mired in caus-
tic rhetoric by environmental extremists. You can dupe people with statistics
any way you want, but doing business this way will not help to formulate
responsible policies that will improve Americans' well-being.

BLUE SMOKE AND MIRRORS

The environmental extremists make shocking claims to get your attention. They want us to run around petrified; for the more terrified we are, the more they attract media attention, which helps their fund-raising apparatus. For example, Harvard biologist George Wald estimated in April 19, 1970, that "civilization will end within fifteen or thirty years unless immediate action is taken against problems facing mankind." Well, we know this didn't happen.

In a December 20, 1997, article in *The Economist* entitled "Plenty of Gloom," the writer states, "You can be in favour of the environment without being a pessimist." There ought to be room in the environmental movement for those who think that technology and economic freedom will make the world cleaner and will also take the pressure off endangered species. But at the moment such optimists are distinctly unwelcome among environmentalists. Environmentalists are quick to accuse their opponents in business of having vested interests. But their own incomes, their advancement, their fame, and their very existence can depend on supporting the most alarming versions of every environmental scare. "The whole aim of practical politics," said H. L. Mencken, "is to keep the populace alarmed—and hence clamorous to be led to safety—by menacing it with an endless series of hobgoblins, all of them imaginary."

These environmental extremist groups receive federal funding and then turn around and advocate against them and/or sue the very federal agencies that provided them funding. According to the Capital Research Center, in the first quarter of 2000, the Natural Resources Defense Council (NRDC) received $378,265 from the Environmental Protection Agency (EPA). On June 29, 2001, the NRDC filed a lawsuit against their benefactors at the EPA, alleging violations of the Safe Drinking Water Act.

Generally, the environmental extremists make most of their money off of four fear factors. They say:

- Air and water pollution are getting much, much worse;

- Population numbers are out of control;

- Biodiversity is suffering; and

- "Greenhouse" emissions are raising world temperatures.

SETTING THE RECORD STRAIGHT

Air Quality Is Good and Getting Better

Has air quality gotten as unhealthy as they say? Quite the contrary. According to the U.S. Environmental Protection Agency (EPA), between 1990 and 1997, emissions of every major pollutant affecting air quality decreased except for emissions of nitrogen dioxide, which increased by 11 percent (by the way, air quality is defined as a measure of six primary pollutants: particulate matter, ozone, lead, carbon monoxide, nitrogen dioxide, and sulfur dioxide). Here's an interesting point. Since the first Earth Day in 1970, the EPA has been monitoring contributing elements of the environment and weighing it against U.S. growth. While sulfur dioxide and carbon monoxide emissions fell by 75 percent since 1970, the EPA snapshot of U.S. people growth looks like this: population increased 29 percent, vehicle miles traveled increased 121 percent, and the gross domestic product (GDP) increased 104 percent.

It is accurate that economic prosperity made its mark in the improving of the environment. United States' wealth fostered cleaner air and water quality, even before the first passage of the Clean Air Act in 1970. As we became richer, our air became cleaner, and the same goes for any other country. The more we help other countries develop economically, the more overall air quality will advance.

Water Quality Continues to Improve

Similar clean trends in air can be found in water. The EPA, in 1992, reported that wastewater treatment had reduced the release of toxic organic waste by 99 percent, and of toxic metals by 98 percent. And a July 1997 report in a United States Department of Agriculture handbook stated that 86 percent of America's rivers, 91 percent of its lakes, and 90 percent of its estuaries are functional for safe use. Since the early '70s, the United States has invested more than $540 billion in water pollution reduction efforts, according to the Pacific Research Center. Even wetlands losses have been slowing since the mid-1950s, and the United States is within 47,000 acres of achieving "no net loss" of wetlands acreage.

Biodiversity Is Alive and Well

While we certainly should monitor the well-being of species and the environments in which they live, we have to be honest with the facts. According to practical environmental leader and statistician Bjorn Lomborg, "Tropical forests are not lost at annual rates of 2-4 percent, as many environmentalists have claimed: The latest U.N. (United Nations) figures indicate a loss of less than 0.5 percent." Any deforestation around the world is due to poor families who are trying to survive by burning patches of the jungle to grow food. So, if we want this practice to stop we need to further come up with creative ways, such as the activities employed by the Nature Conservancy, to help individuals become wealthier.

America's resources are not being lost to suburban "sprawl" either. According to Dr. Sam Staley, director of the Urban Futures Program at the Reason Public Policy Institute, less than 5 percent of the nation's land is developed, and three-quarters of the nations' population lives on 3.5 percent of its land area. Over three-quarters of the states have more than 90 percent of their land in rural use, including forests, cropland, pasture, wildlife reserves, and parks. According to the U.S. Geological Survey, it is estimated that about 0.07 percent of land is being developed. In fact, the "sprawl index," a simple comparison of population growth and rate of urbanization, has actually declined since 1980.

Population Exploding, Resources Imploding

Stanford University biologist Dr. Paul Ehrlich told *Mademoiselle* in April of 1970 that "the death rate will increase [and] at least 100-200 million people per year will be starving to death during the next ten years." While it is an abysmal reality that far too many people remain poor and hungry in the world, food production today, according to Lomborg, has increased to 52 percent per person since 1961. Poorer people are receiving 2,650 calories in their daily diets as compared to 1,932 calories in 1961. According to Lomborg, this caloric intake is expected to rise to 3,020 calories in the year 2030. Along with that, the World Bank claims that food production is also at its cheapest—by more than 90 percent since 1800—and has constructively outpaced population growth. Where we have witnessed famine such as in Ethiopia or Somalia in recent times, it is the outcome of political instability and civil war.

Resources such as wheat, oil, gold, you name it, are everywhere and cheap, and environmentalists are burying their faces over the fact that many claimed the planet's resources are so limited that they place rigid limits on human numbers and human prosperity. Dr. Ehrlich was so confident that this was going to be the case, he bet environmental leader Julian Simon $1,000 any resource would not be cheaper at any future date. Just the opposite happen, population exploded and resources imploded. Ehrlich paid up.

World Temperatures Are Decreasing

Global warming . . . global warming . . . global warming. The world is not coming off its hinges, and temperatures have shown marginal change in natural cycles. According to Thomas Gale Moore in his book, *Climate of Fear: Why We Shouldn't Worry about Global Warming*, temperatures over the past hundred years have risen one degree Fahrenheit or less. This is inconsequential to the human race. Much of this temperature rising took place between the 1920s and 1940s during the industrial revolution. According to atmospheric physicist S. Fred Singer, "The climate warms and cools naturally all the time. It changes from day to day, month to month, season to season, year to year, and so on. At times, there is global warming; at other times there is global cooling. Some climate changes are predictable and some are not . . ." While variations in temperature are real, President Bush has committed the United States to do research in both the science and the means of mitigating its effects through the president's Climate Change Research Initiative and his National Climate Change Technology Initiatives, which will add to the more than $18 billion spent on climate research since 1990.

The Bridge Between Public and Private Conservation

Republican President Theodore Roosevelt was a crafter of conservationism, and it grew into the political heritage of the conservative movement. To truly protect the planet for future generations, we need to employ evidence before action and a belief in the power of conservationism and private property rights. The conservationist manifesto is "Wise use of resources and a respect for nature's wonders that is balanced by an understanding of the importance of free-market incentives and property rights in solving environmental problems." Flexibility is needed so that the federal government can concentrate on the big picture such as an energy policy, and state and local governments, businesses, and individuals can decide on the best environmental solutions for their own individualized needs.

We Need to Be Less Dependent on Foreign Oil

For far too long, the United States has been reliant on foreign energy supply, as we import nearly 60 percent of our crude oil, an all-time high in history. This reliance on oil imports gives foreign governments the ability to have undue influence in America's economy.

President Bush—the most responsible energy president of our time—realizes that until we discover efficient, alternative energy sources, natural resources have to be located somewhere on or around the continental United States in order to avoid an energy crisis. So called "environmentally friendly" politicians protest oil drilling in the Arctic National Wildlife Refuge (ANWR), but offer no alternatives while being chauffeured around in their gas-guzzling limousines. We can't have another California energy crisis on our hands, as it had a death-defying effect on the state's economy.

I have not been to ANWR, but *National Review*'s Jonah Goldberg has and says that it is a snippet of land on the northern coast that is devoid of beauty, and is not the breathtaking landscape we all saw on the evening news. According to Goldberg, the caribou would not be stupid enough to venture into it because of its swampy tracks and the zillions of mosquitoes that inhabit the area. The oil industry has come a long way in its efficiency in drilling, which could be done in the dead of winter, as no human nor animal will make its way into the area when below freezing temperatures last for a straight fifty-eight days. Even the Inupiat Eskimos support drilling in their homeland. The bottom line is Americans cannot continue to air-condition their homes and offices at a cool seventy-two degrees and snub our responsibility in search of alternative fueling resources.

We Can Protect Endangered Species Through Private Landowners

The federal government has done little to truly protect endangered species. The National Wilderness Institute (NWI) reported in 1997 that of the twenty-seven endangered or threatened species that had been removed from the list since passage of the Endangered Species Act (ESA), not one had been removed because of improved numbers. Rather, seven of the twenty-seven species had been removed from the list because they were extinct, and nine had been removed because erroneous data had been used to justify their original listing.

Congress has the opportunity to seek reforms that would make the ESA less stringent in terms of landowners being forced to chase off endangered species for fear of government regulation. According to Angela Antonelli of the Heritage Foundation, until Congress weighs in "on the constitutional first principles of property rights and just compensation, both endangered species and landowners will continue to suffer."

As we continue to seek solutions to more elusive problems, more scientific research and development of technologies must be done to learn more about the risks and the effective response to the many uncertainties. Again in the case of global warming, there are endless unanswered questions. We don't know how much or if the climate will change in the future. If global temperature increases or decreases, how much is related to natural fluctuations? If we take action, we don't know the consequences our actions may have. We do not even know with any certainty what constitutes a dangerous level of global warming that must be avoided.

President Roosevelt loved the outdoors so much that he became our first president who truly dedicated his presidency to conserving America's natural beauty. We work so hard in conserving our historical documents, paintings, and buildings so that future generations can learn about America's inception in a practical, hands-on setting. Why not commit to protect the environment that has been here for thousands of years before in a sensible manner based on evidence, and not on senseless actions invoked by fear? Conservationism works to preserve the great outdoors and wildlife, and natural heritages, which occupy it by affirming it, not abandoning it.

Resources for the Right

The Cooler Heads Coalition
A subgroup of the National Consumer Coalition, founded by Consumer Alert, focused on the issue of global warming.
Cooler Heads Coalition
Competitive Enterprise Institute

1001 Connecticut Avenue, NW
Suite 1250
Washington, DC 20036
202-331-1010
www.cei.org

COALITION FOR REPUBLICAN ENVIRONMENTAL POLICY

This organization wants to restore natural conservation and sound environmental protection as fundamental elements of the Republican Party's vision for America.
P.O. Box 7073
Deerfield, IL 60015
847-940-0320
www.repamerica.org

COMMON GROUND

- We agree that the environment, like reproductive rights and abortion, is another issue that has been highly **politicized**.

- We both believe that **we need to care for the environment,** although we would disagree on the methods employed to do so. Our clean environment is something in the United States we take for granted and we forget that it is not an unlimited resource. Julianne believes that treaties such as the Kyoto Protocol, regulations, and government intervention will help solve the world's environmental problems. Deborah thinks policymakers and the public should possess accurate information and research before employing costly strategies.

- We also agree that **purchasing organic foods or growing one's own,** either through home gardens or community gardens, is a way to ensure the quality and safety of one's food.

11

Where Do Women Go From Here?

JULIANNE MALVEAUX AND DEBORAH PERRY

We came to this project with divergent voices, and our voices remain sharply divergent. As we wrote the sections in this book, exploring issues important to women, we found a few areas of common ground, but the most important thing we agree upon is the overarching sense that women's voices are not sufficiently heard, that women need to be more active participants in the political process, and that women can shape the quality of their lives and those of their families and communities through their involvement. Such was our disagreement about issues that we decided to take a unique approach to this closing chapter. We wanted to write in one voice, to the extent that we could, to attempt to explore some of our differences instead of just confronting them. Thus, we taped a conversation we had toward the end of our process about the issues we continued to focus on with an eye toward the future. And we edited that conversation, speaking in one voice whenever we could, and highlighting our differences when it made sense to do so.

Historical factors often prevent women from being involved. Julianne likes to say that if black folks went along to get along they'd still be picking cotton. What that means is that people do what they are accustomed to doing, without being aware that their actions are often shaped both by history and custom. Women often don't get involved because they haven't been involved. But that's changing and we see more and more women embracing the political process. Deborah likes to acknowledge that women have made great advancements in politics and the workforce, and that we have to appreciate how far we've come in a relatively short time.

There are biases that discourage women's involvement, though. Politics is an "old boy" network and no one is planning a welcoming reception for women. In the 1970s and 1980s, activist women's organizations held political trainings especially for women, and groups like EMILY's List (pro-choice Democrats) and the WISH List (pro-choice Republicans) were developed to funnel money to women candidates who often have a harder time raising money than male candidates do.

Mentioning EMILY's List and the WISH List, though, raised questions about women's differences, and these were differences that we were constantly confronted with as we worked together. What if women's voices *were* more involved in the political process? Would the outcomes be necessarily different? Which women are we talking about? Pro-choice feminists? Republican traditionalists? We are evidence that gender does not determine ideology. Still, we think that many women, regardless of ideology, bring a different energy and awareness to the political process. And we both think that because we have experienced the marginalization that comes with being female in the political process, many women are sensitive to issues of inclusion because of their own exclusion.

Julianne is especially concerned with women she describes as "the invisible workers." These are the women (and some men) who take care of our children and our elders, who make up the beds in hotel rooms and pour coffee at the local delicatessen. Too often the concerns of these women are swallowed by the enormous class biases that exist in the policy world, where professional workers make policy decisions based on the reality of their own lives. For example, some would like to finance Social Security by raising the retirement age, but there is a real difference between raising the retirement age for a pencil pushing bureaucrat and raising the retirement age for a waitress who is on her feet all day (or, as Julianne's colleague Richard Trumka of the AFL-CIO reminds her, for a mine worker who is doing physical work).

Deborah is concerned that women who support a traditional way of life have their voices drowned out by those of more vocal feminists. Julianne thinks that the feminist movement came about because the traditional way of life was virtually the only way of life available to women. As lifestyles have gradually changed, with the median age for first marriages rising, many women feel they do have other options than the traditional way of life. Julianne thinks that there is a strong conservative women's lobby, and that inside the Washington, D.C., beltway, there are women on the right that have as much, if not more, visibility as women on the left. Because of women's differences, though, we both agree that women are not likely to become a unified lobbying voice.

Deborah would like to see a woman as president, if she is the best person for the job. But she says many women choose to have a traditional family or work that is compatible with family life, and that makes it difficult for women to enter politics. Julianne points to the career of Harriett Woods, former president of the National Women's Political Caucus, former lieutenant governor of Missouri, and a candidate for governor who got involved in politics from the school board. Julianne feels that women like Harriett get involved in politics because they care about people and issues that affect them, not because they care about power.

Deborah feels that the way that women are raised shapes their likelihood for civic participation. The role that family background plays has been a theme between the two of us for as long as we have worked together. Julianne's first political act was pulling the lever in the voting booth when her mother, Proteone Marie, voted for John F. Kennedy in 1960. At eight, she passed out flyers for her mom's friend, David Johnson, who ran for sheriff in San Francisco, and she still remembers Mr. Johnson's campaign literature (he distributed blank notebooks with the heading "My Opponent's List of Achievements"). Julianne can't image *not* being politically involved,

motivated by the Negro National Anthem, "Lift Every Voice and Sing"—
she believes that women should "Lift Every Voice and Vote and Participate."
From the perspective of her travels on the 2000 campaign trail, following
George W. Bush in New Hampshire and South Carolina, Deborah reminds
Julianne of the women she met who still deferred to their husbands for
their political views, and wonders if Julianne's experiences are unique to
her activist background.

Julianne is concerned that high schools don't teach civics as much as
they used to, and that our entire society is becoming more apathetic and
indifferent to politics and political involvement. More and more people
seem to retreat to their homes, or to their worlds, leaving political decisions
to politicians who they are all too eager to criticize when they don't get the
results they want. She lifts up Joe Lieberman's *In Praise of Public Life* as a
book that talks about the many rewards of political involvement and wishes
a woman would write a book like that.

Julianne also thinks of particular women who have shaped the policy
arena and lifts them up as inspirations to other women. Her sorority sister,
Rae Lewis Thornton, was diagnosed with AIDS in her twenties and became
an AIDS activist as a result. Rae was politicized by having AIDS and used
the political process to turn her pain into power and information for other
people. Deborah points out that Republican Mary Fisher played a similar
role, sharing her AIDS status with the nation and galvanizing unlikely support for federal funding of AIDS prevention efforts.

Julianne feels that there is something horribly cynical about the way
Republicans have attacked government and its size, and that this had led
to some of the political cynicism that so many people feel. Deborah feels
that Republicans have more faith in the individual than Democrats do, but
that Democrats have made promises on behalf of government that they
can't keep, such as the promise to take care of retirement through Social
Security. Julianne disagrees, feeling that the so-called Social Security crisis
is a hoax that is perpetuated by folks who want privatization so they can
reduce the size of government.

Julianne says there are some things that government does better than individuals and that some goods are better provided as public goods. She spoke of environmental standards, protective services, and defense issues in particular, and feels that it shows no lack of faith in the individual for government to serve an umbrella function in these cases. Both of us agree that the bureaucracy that comes from "big government" creates inefficiencies, but we disagreed about the magnitude of the inefficiencies. The debate on government is one that we could continue indefinitely. And we almost did!

As sharply as we disagreed about the role of government, we concurred about the matter of women's engagement. Deborah lifted up England's Queen Elizabeth and said that women have always taken leadership roles in our society, citing early feminists, but that somewhere along the way women have just disengaged or turned off from the political process. Julianne laughed out loud at Deborah's view of history, noting that the law prevented women from voting until 1920, and that there have been clear institutional barriers to women's full political involvement. Julianne acknowledged women's indirect role, such as Abigail Adams' influence on her husband, President John Adams. She also is proud of the role African-American women have had in shaping public policy, and thinks of the antilynching campaign of Ida B. Wells-Barnett, or the work of the colored women's club movement of the early twentieth century. Julianne concurs with Deborah that women have always been involved at some level, but notes that institutional sexism has often kept women from being as involved as they might be.

Women need to be more involved though. No matter where we are on the political spectrum, we need to work to make sure that women are involved, that their voices are heard, that support mechanisms for women to get involved in politics should be developed, and that political education is important. We started writing this book because we encountered so many women who wanted to know what to do and how to get involved at the local, state, or federal level.

If Deborah sees the glass as half full, Julianne sees it as half empty. While acknowledging progress, she points to the paucity of women in Congress, as Fortune 500 leaders, and in other positions of influence. She says that it is easy to say women should run for office or get involved, but she points to state party structures and the ways that women may or may not get encouragement. And she feels there is pressure on women to deny the existence of sexism, even though it is alive and well in politics and the corporation. Deborah, on the other hand, feels that there has been little discrimination, and that being a woman has worked to her advantage. She acknowledges that her attitude may be generational.

Deborah believes that we need to mentor more young women to get involved in the political process. The mentorship issue has been a significant one for Deborah, who thinks that "older" women haven't done enough mentoring of younger women and noting that women often work against each other. Julianne has been mentored by, and had access to, many powerful and important African-American women, especially Dr. Phyllis Ann Wallace, the first African-American woman to get a Ph.D. in economics from Yale. She feels less strongly about the mentorship issue than Deborah does and feels that African-American women have created powerful, helping networks. Remembering our 2000 experience with *A Room Full of Women*™, our television pilot, Deborah agrees that she was moved and impressed by the degree of support Julianne was able to get from her African-American sister-friends and colleagues.

Julianne has done diversity training in several corporate and nonprofit settings and challenges Deborah's notion that there is no sexism. She cited women's unequal visibility as pundits and as participants in policy debates, and even in the corporate arena. She notes that some women prefer not to confront discrimination, choosing instead to conform to a male model of engagement and involvement. So, they are silent when they see six men and no women on a panel.

Deborah said that when you see six men on a panel, you may need experts in certain areas, and it just so happens that there are only men. This was another area of sharp disagreement between us. Julianne feels that anytime a panel is all male, or all white male, there is something discriminatory working whether it is overt or covert. Deborah feels that men have been in the workforce longer, contributing more consistently. And she feels that the "old boy" network protects men. Says Julianne, "What is that *but* discrimination?" She thinks the "old boy" network exists because men want to exclude women, not because a group of collegial men are just unwittingly helping each other out.

Deborah says that the existence of the old boys' club should motivate women to form an old girls' club, since women seem less likely to work together than men. Julianne isn't sure that women are consistently working against each other, but considers institutionalized sexism one of the reasons women are excluded.

Deborah says that everyone experiences discrimination, citing people with an accent or white men who are six feet tall. Julianne had no patience with this argument, hissing "oh, please" as Deborah made her point. Julianne noted that there is "personal" discrimination that takes place when you wear a blue blazer, not a white one, and institutional discrimination that takes place when you are excluded because you are a person of color or female.

Deborah doesn't think people exclude so aggressively anymore, citing the Bush administration and the number of women in top positions in that administration. Julianne notes that women are not half of the cabinet members or senior policymakers and that equality means half. She also notes that the Clinton administration was no slouch in appointing women. We agreed that neither party does all it can to include women, nor has any leader made it to that critical mark in appointing women to half of the senior positions in an administration.

What can women do about our exclusion? We'll repeat ourselves by saying that women need to get more active, more involved. We agree that our democracy is an important one, and that we all have a responsibility to get involved civilly and to work to make the world a better place. Julianne feels that even the act of passing around petitions is an empowering act since people need to see other people engaged and involved in issues. She paraphrased Gloria Steinem's comment that when you hear people reflecting the same reality through the stories they tell about their lives, they are talking about something that is political, not personal. Women are time crunched, but in some ways that may be as much a political condition as a personal one. How can we use public policy and public institutions to deal with women's time issues?

Deborah said that women who read traditional women's magazines may be less inclined to get involved since these magazines tend to focus on appearance and relationships, not issues. She said that one of the challenges is to get information out to women, especially information about the conditions of women around the world.

We both agreed that women must vote, be involved in the policy debate in ways ranging from letter writing to offering testimony to policymaking bodies, from joining organizations to starting them. We both like the League of Women Voters as a nonpartisan organization that increases awareness and makes it easier for women to be informed about politics and policy.

At the end of our conversation, we'd answered the question we started with. Where do women go from here? To the polls. We go with our diverse and strong opinions, with our divergent voices, with the cares, concerns, and backgrounds that have shaped our interests in public policy. And the two of us, Deborah and Julianne, go forward as committed to our points of view as ever, but enriched by the opportunity to spend time learning and thinking about another perspective.

Seven Ways to Lift Your Voice

1. Vote!

Voting is the most simple, direct, and powerful way women can affect government. If you think that women's votes "don't really count" you'll be surprised to know that politicians are now well aware of the power of women voters. The issue in recent history has been described as the power of "soccer moms" but it's no laughing matter. In the most famous example of the power of women voters, President Clinton would not have won in 1996 without the votes of women. If only men had voted, Dole would have won.

Women outnumber men in the adult population, and ever since the 1980s women have registered and voted at consistently higher rates than men. These two factors add up to approximately 8 million more registered women voters than men. Politicians have come to recognize that women are a powerful force for change. However, change can only be effected if women continue to participate in voting. Voter turnout in general remains low. In the 1996 election, only 55.5 percent of eligible women voted. In the 20 years prior to the 1996 elections women's turnout did not once exceed 63 percent.

Women only attained the right to vote in the last eighty years. Don't let all the hard work of previous feminists go to waste! Register to vote and mark election days on your calendar. Politicians will listen if you make them. Grab their attention by making your vote count!

2. WRITE A LETTER

Whether it is to the editor, state legislature, or member of Congress, writing a letter is a powerful tool for getting women's voices into public discourse. All too often, however, women do not write, and men's opinions dominate the media.

You may think letters do not make a difference, but the fact is that newspapers use letters to guide their coverage of issues and legislators read letters to make sure they work in concert with their constituents.

3. ATTEND A CITY COUNCIL OR LEGISLATIVE MEETING

Staying informed about issues in your community and state can be a powerful way to make sure your voice is heard. Most city councils offer opportunities for direct citizen government interaction in the legislative process. Attending meetings not only shows legislators that their constituency is paying attention but also allows you to talk directly to the people making laws. Further, it is usually fairly easy to obtain a face-to-face meeting with your city councilperson or state legislator.

4. JOIN OR START AN ADVOCACY GROUP

At the end of every chapter we have listed organizations that might be of interest to the reader. These organizations need members to spread the message, organize meetings, instigate petitions, write letters, and volunteer time. Many organizations such as ACORN or the Public Education Network provide information about how to start chapters in your area and work with larger organizations.

If you have an issue or position that you feel is not fully represented by existing organizations, start your own advocacy group. It can be as small as organizing your neighborhood to improve the community, or as large as a website geared toward women across the nation with your particular issue in mind.

So many organizations started with just a few like-minded individuals joining together to fight for a common cause.

5. HOLD A NEIGHBORHOOD OR TOWN HALL MEETING

What better way to increase activism in your neighborhood than organizing a meeting? All too often residents in the same community have concerns that go unexpressed. Town Hall meetings are becoming increasingly important—just look at the number of times presidential candidates have met in a Town Hall forum. Depending on the size of your town or neighborhood there are often plenty of volunteer opportunities.

6. ORGANIZE A CAPITOL HILL DAY

Many groups organize Capitol Hill Days in order to bring attention to their cause on a national level. Work with your organization of choice to hold an event in Washington, D.C. Often organizations set up workshops to prepare activists to meet with their legislators. Further, Capitol Hill Days can provide a forum for activists across the nation to exchange ideas, heighten awareness, and strengthen ties.

7. RUN FOR PUBLIC OFFICE

Even though women make up the majority of the electorate, too few women run for public office. According to the Center for Voting and Democracy:

> Women have made up an extremely low percentage of general election candidates, particularly for higher office. Since 1972, only 7% of candidates for the U.S. House and U.S. Senate and only 6% of gubernatorial candidates have been women. Just 20% of state legislative candidates were women during the last four election cycles.

Clearly, this level of participation is not enough. Women need to run for office more and force the American public to become accustomed to seeing competent women in positions of power.

Political Glossary

Beauty contest: A preliminary vote usually taken early in the electoral process within a party; it expresses a non-binding preference for one or another of the party's candidates. This preference is not linked to the selection of convention delegates.

Caucus: Literally, it means "a meeting," and it is one of the main mechanisms used by modern American political parties to nominate their candidate for president. In the presidential nomination process, it now denotes a meeting of local party activists at the precinct level who select, in an open forum, delegates to county meetings. These delegates in turn select delegates to state meetings; and these state-level conventions select delegates to the party's national convention. The purpose of this layered caucus system is to open political participation to as many people as possible, and to provide greater incentives to recruitment of fresh talent into party politics than merely voting in a primary election. From February to June of a presidential election year, the major political parties of every state conduct either caucuses or primary elections (primaries). By tradition, the rural, midwestern state of Iowa has the first set of caucuses in the nation (even before the first primary in New Hampshire), and so it has a big impact on the race, even though it is a small state with so few delegates.

Conservative: In American politics, someone who is right-of-center politically. Of the two major parties, the Republicans are generally considered more conservative. In the United States, conservatives usually emphasize free-market economic principles and often prefer state and local governmental power to federal power. Traditionally, conservative support has come from business leaders. Candidates and voters commonly refer to themselves and others as conservative, moderate (or centrist), or liberal.

Convention: A meeting, at state or national level, of delegates from a political party. These delegates vote for the person they want their party to nominate for political office. The nominated candidate will then compete in the general election with the candidates of other parties, and against any independent candidates not endorsed by a political party. In modern U.S. presidential politics, *convention* usually refers to the national conventions of the Democratic and Republican parties, held every four years, during the summer before the general election (which is held in November). These conventions, which include delegates from all states of the Union, the District of Columbia, and U.S. territories, formally nominate the presidential candidate.

Delegate: An official representative selected by members of his or her party to a national or state political convention.

Democratic Party: One of the two current major political parties. Traditionally, the Democrats support an activist role for the federal government in the economic and social sectors. The first Democratic president, Andrew Jackson, was elected in 1828, as the seventh U.S. president. The Democratic party is generally considered to be more liberal or less conservative than the other current major party: the Republican Party.

Electoral base: A politician's "electoral base" is considered to be the heart of his or her constituency, i.e., the groups of people who will usually vote for him or her whatever the prevailing political conditions at any given time, often out of party loyalty (contrast with swing voters) or some other combination of variables such as ethnicity, gender, religion, ideology, military service, geography, or positions on issues. In other countries, "electoral base" is often called the "vote bank."

Electoral College: The electoral college is the group of electors, chosen by voters throughout the U.S. on a state basis on election day, who then meet and formally select the next president of the United States. The selection is by a majority of 270 votes out of the 538 electors. The electoral college system is mandated by the U.S. Constitution.

Get-Out-the-Vote (GOTV) Operations: In the last few days of a campaign, particularly on election day, campaigns usually focus most of their resources on getting their electoral base (see above) out to the polls to vote. Such operations (abbreviated as GOTV by campaign managers) include television and radio broadcasted appeals, telephone banks of volunteers and campaign workers who call voters' homes reminding them to vote, "soundtrucks" with amplified speakers that drive through neighborhoods of likely supporters, volunteer drivers who drive likely supporters (particularly the elderly or disabled) to the polls, "pollwatchers" who ensure the integrity of polling operations, and dissemination of campaign paraphernalia (such as buttons, balloons, brochures, flyers, banners, lawn signs, and posters).

GOP: Stands for Grand Old Party, which is an abbreviated nickname for the Republican Party.

Independent: In U.S. politics, this term denotes a voter, who, when registering to vote, does not declare affiliation with the Republicans, Democrats, or other political parties or does not consider himself or herself to be a member of a political party. Likewise, the term can also refer to a candidate for office who is running on the basis of personal identity rather than party affiliation.

Liberal: In American politics, "liberals" tend to be people who are somewhat ideologically left-of-center. They tend to favor more power at the federal level and federal intervention to regulate economic issues and certain social issues, particularly social issues involving civil liberties, and the rights of minority groups. Of the two major parties, the Democrats are generally considered more liberal. Traditionally, the bases of liberal support have been among minorities, urban voters, labor unions, and academics, though that is evolving as U.S. politics change. Candidates and voters commonly refer to themselves and others as conservative, moderate (or centrist), or liberal.

Midterm elections: This term refers to elections held in-between presidential elections—that is, two years after the previous, and two years before the next, presidential elections. Each midterm election selects one-third of the 100 members of the U.S. Senate and all 435 members of the House of Representatives, as well as many state and local officials.

Persuasion activities: Campaigns frame or define a message that will appeal to the undecided voters, and convey that message through advertising (television, radio, and print); direct-mail to the voters' homes; door-to-door and street-corner campaigning by volunteers or campaign workers; personal appearances and speeches by the candidate; candidate appearances at debates; endorsements and testimonials; and favorable coverage in the news (referred to as "free media" because candidates did not have to buy advertising space or time). Campaigns generally do not waste resources attempting to persuade voters that comprise the opposition's electoral base. As for their own electoral base, campaigns generally target get-out-the-vote resources.

Platform: A formal statement of position on major political issues drafted by a candidate or a political party. In other countries, the "platform" may be called the party "manifesto." The major parties ratify their platforms at their national conventions.

Plurality: A plurality of votes is a total vote received by a candidate greater than that received by any opponent but less than a 50 percent majority of the vote. In other words, if one candidate receives 30 percent of the vote, another candidate receives 30 percent of the vote, and a third candidate receives 40 percent, that third candidate has a plurality of the votes, and wins the election. Abraham Lincoln and Bill Clinton are examples of presidents who received a majority of the electoral vote, but only a plurality of the popular vote in a competitive three-way election contest.

Primary: A "closed" primary is a system of selecting a party's candidate for office in an intraparty election in which *only registered members of that party may vote*. Most state primaries are closed. An "open" primary is a system of selecting a party's candidate for office in which voters registered with *other parties* and *"independent" voters* (i.e., unaffiliated with any party) *may also vote*. This kind of primary is also known as a "cross-over" primary. The major political parties in every state choose delegates for their party's national nominating conventions, by means of either a primary or a caucus. By tradition, the state of New Hampshire has the first primary (soon after the Iowa caucuses), and so it has big impact on setting the stage for the rest of the race, even though it is a small state with so few delegates.

"Reagan Democrats": Democrats who voted for Ronald Reagan for president during the 1980s. It has become a generic term for swing voters in the Democratic party.

Realignment: In U.S. politics, this term refers to occasional historic shifts of public opinion and voter concerns that either undermine or enhance one or another party's traditional base of support. The term is generally applied to national elections which clearly shift the majority and minority status of the two U.S. major political parties, or which replace one of the two major political parties with one that previously had been a "third party." Realignment may be based on many factors, such as the reaction to party positions on a critical issue of national concern (as was the case with the slavery issue in the 1860s), credit or blame for handling a national crisis (such as the Great Depression of 1929), or substantial changes in the demographic make-up of the voting populace.

Republican Party (GOP): One of the two major U.S. political parties. Traditionally, Republican party has favored economic and social policies that are somewhat less re-distributive than Democratic party policies. The first Republican president was Abraham Lincoln, the sixteenth U.S. president, elected in

1860. The Republicans emerged in a major party realignment (see term immediately above), replacing the now defunct Whig Party as a major U.S. party.

Straw poll: In modern presidential politics, a *non-binding* vote, often taken among party activists and usually at a very early stage in a candidate-selection process, to indicate which candidate or candidates are preferred by a local group.

Stump speech: The "standard" speech of a candidate for office—the one he or she is most likely to use, perhaps with slight variations, on normal occasions.

Super Tuesday: Primary elections are often held on Tuesdays, and Super Tuesdays are when primaries and caucuses are held in several states on the same day, with many delegates "up for grabs." If a candidate does particularly well on Super Tuesday, he or she will not only gain many delegates, but also press coverage and momentum. Since Super Tuesdays are seen as big events on the election calendar, they often have a large impact on the perception of where candidates stand in the race, causing front runners to solidify the perception of their invincibility, or lose ground to other candidates that do better than expected. Often, candidates that were lagging in the opinion polls, and that failed to do well in the earlier primaries and caucuses, drop out of the race if they fail to do well on Super Tuesday (they also may find it difficult to raise additional campaign funds, because they are portrayed as not having a chance to win the nomination). Therefore, Super Tuesday may serve as the coup de grace on candidates' campaigns that were already in trouble after disappointing showings in the earlier caucuses and primaries, such as Iowa and New Hampshire.

Swing Voters, Ticket Splitters, and Persuadables: "Swing voters" are those that are not always loyal to a particular political party, and therefore are not part of any party's electoral base. They get their name because they might "swing" from one party to the other in different elections. "Ticket Splitters" is another name for swing voters, because many of them will vote for candidates from opposing parties for different offices on the same ballot (e.g., might vote Democratic for president and Republican for senator, or vice versa). They get their name because they do not necessarily vote for all candidates on the same "ticket" or slate, thus these voters "split" their votes. When swing voters are undecided as to which candidate they will support, they are called "undecideds." Political campaign managers also refer to undecideds as "persuadables," because campaigns concentrate on persuading them, through various persuasion activities, to vote for their candidate. Campaigns generally consider the opposition's "natural" electoral base as unpersuadable, and consider their own "natural" electoral base as already likely to favor their own candidate. Thus, they do not waste resources on the former, and only "target" the latter for motivation or assistance to vote (called get-out-the-vote operations) on election day. Although swing voters are sometimes referred to as independents, they may be registered members of any political party. For example, *Reagan Democrats* is the term used for those Democratic voters who voted for Republican president Ronald Reagan in the 1980s. *Reagan Democrats* is often used today as a generic term for swing voters in the Democratic party.

Third party: In the parlance of American politics, *third party* refers to political parties outside the two-party system which are perceived to have a significant base of support. In the twentieth century, that has come to mean a party that is not the Republican Party or the Democratic Party and can play some role in influencing the outcome of an election.

Source: U.S. Department of State

NOTES

Julianne Malveaux

Introduction

1. Page 1. "More women than men now earn associate's, bachelor's and master's degrees." *Digest of Education Statistics*. National Center for Education Statistics, U.S. Department of Education. 2000.
2. Page 1. "Women now earn 42 percent of the Ph.D. degrees granted in the United States but we are still concentrated in education and the humanities." Townsend, Robert. "More than 1,000 New History Ph.D.s in 1999." *Perspectives Online: The Journal of the American Historical Association*, April 2001.
3. Page 2. "Women make up more than half of the voters but less than 15 percent of elected officials at the federal level." www.gendergap.com/governme.htm
4. Page 4. "Women-owned businesses, to cite a popular statistic, employ more people than Fortune 500 companies." Minority and Women Business Enterprise Program, City of Greensboro, North Carolina. http://www.ci.greensboro.nc.us/mwbe/facts.htm
5. Page 5. "Women are more likely to hold the clerical job than any other." U.S. Bureau of the Census. Current Population Survey, March 2000.

Chapter 1

1. Page 27–28. "Using the most recent data from the Bureau of Labor Statistics, men who work full-time, full-year earn $646 per week, while women with the same work schedule earn $491 per week, or 76 percent of what men earn." *Highlights of Women's Earnings in 2000*. Bureau of Labor Statistics, U.S. Department of Labor. August 2001.
2. Page 28. "According to the Institute for Women's Policy Research, these numbers vary by state with women from Washington, D.C. earning a high 87.5 percent of what men earn while women in Louisiana earn a paltry 64.8 percent of what men earn." State of Women in the States: Institute for Women's Policy Research, 2000.
3. Page 28. "When women are part of collective bargaining organizations, their pay level jumps by 30 percent." *Equal Pay for Working Families: National and State Data on the Pay Gap and Its Costs*. Hartmann, Heidi, Katherine Allen and Christine Owens. Institute for Women's Policy Research and AFL-CIO, 1999.

4. Page 30. "Home health aids earn an average of $8.71 an hour." *2000 National Occupational Wage and Employment Estimates.* Bureau of Labor Statistics, U.S. Department of Labor.

5. Page 30. "A living wage is defined as a wage that yields an above-poverty line wage for a full-time worker; it varies from city to city but is usually between $6.50 and $8.50 an hour." Association of Community Organizations for Reform Now Living Wage Resource Center, www.livingwagecampaign.org.

6. Page 30. "Chauna Brocht noted that there were more than 162,000 federal contract workers who earned less than a living wage." *The Forgotten Worker: More Than One in Ten Federal Contract Workers Earn Less Than the Minimum Wage*: Economic Policy Institute, November 2000.

7. Page 31. "Nearly ten million people earn the minimum wage. More than 70 percent of them are adults, contrary to the myth that most minimum wage workers are teens. Nearly 60 percent of them are women, and these women are disproportionately black and brown. A full-time, full-year minimum wage worker earns $10,700." Annual Averages from the 2001 Current Population Survey. Bureau of Labor Statistics, 2002.

8. Page 32. "Labor shortages push up wages, but while demand for home health aides far exceeds supply, 500,000 more people are needed in that occupation in the next decade, wages have not risen to accommodate increased demand." *Monthly Labor Review,* November 2001. Bureau of Labor Statistics.

9. Page 32. "EEOC received 1,270 equal pay claims in 2000." Equal Employment Opportunity Commission 2000 Enforcement Data.

10. Page 33. "In Lynn, Massachusetts, for example, women custodians at the public schools were called "house workers," and their jobs were to clean the schools, wash lunch tables, mop floors and scrub toilets. Their male coworkers, called junior custodians, were paid $1.50 more per hour for the same duties." Driscoll, Anne. "Equal Pay Victory Is Sweet, At Last, for Charwomen." Sept. 9, 2001, www.womensenews.com.

11. Page 34. "According to writer Anne Driscoll, the Equal Pay Act is 'little-known and underutilized.'" Ibid.

12. Page 34. "Their data show that if single mothers were paid the same as men for work of comparable worth, they'd see a pay adjustment of $4,459, and their poverty rates would drop from 5.3 percent to 12.6 percent." *Equal Pay for Working Families: National and State Data on the Pay Gap and Its Costs.* Hartmann, Heidi, Katherine Allen and Christine Owens. Institute for Women's Policy Research and AFL-CIO, 1999.

13. Page 35. "The EEOC litigates less than 4 percent of the complaints that are filed with it." "Court Recognizes an Exception to Arbitration Agreements." CCH Corporation, January 17, 2002, www.cch.com/press/news/2002/arbitration.htm.

14. Page 35. "In 2002, thirty-two bills in sixteen states have been introduced to prohibit wage discrimination on the basis of sex, race or national origin." *Center for Policy Alternatives News*, February 25, 2002.

CHAPTER 2

1. Page 42. "In the 1950s, nearly 70 percent of African American women were maids." Malveaux, Julianne M. *Low Wage Descriptions: Opportunities and Strategies for Wage Change*. Unpublished paper. National Association for the Advancement of Colored People Legal Defense and Education Fund, 1984a.
2. Page 43. "Marshall Miller, cofounder of the Alternatives to Marriage Project (ATMP) says 'Diverse families, including stepfamilies; single-parent families; gay, lesbian, bisexual and transgender families; and unmarried cohabitors are here to stay. Our challenge as a society is to end prejudice and discrimination so these relationships and families can continue to be healthy and strong.'" Alternatives to Marriage Project website, www.unmarried.org
3. Page 44. "With the unemployment rate rising in February 2002, the Bush administration has proposed to spend $300 million of public assistance dollars to promote marriage to welfare recipients." 2003 Budget of the Bush Administration.
4. Page 45. "According to the Bureau of Labor Statistics, 64 percent of women with children under age three are in the labor force, as are 60 percent with children under age six." *Statistical Abstract of the United States*. U.S. Bureau of the Census, 2000.
5. Page 46. "Single moms who are the sole source of support for their children head approximately 20 percent of white families and more than 40 percent of black ones." America's Families and Living Arrangements. Current Population Reports, U.S. Bureau of the Census. June 2001.
6. Page 46. "One study said that children in daycare are more likely to be aggressive than those who are not, and another study said that low pay contributes to high turnover and staffing problems at child care centers." National Institute of Child Health and Human Development sponsored study on the long-term effects of day care. University of California at Berkeley and the Center for the Child Care Workforce study on turnover rates in child care facilities.
7. Page 48. "As many as forty million Americans do not qualify for family and medical leave." Bargaining Fact Sheet: Family Leave and Expanind the Family and Medical Leave Act. AFL-CIO Working Women's Department and the Labor Project for Working Families. www.aflcio.org/women/family.pdf.
8. Page 49. "The average worker in the U.S. gets sixteen vacation days per year, which is less than the law requires in any of the western European countries on which

the OECD reported in 1998." Working Families in the Global Economy, www. bernie.house.gov.

9. Page 50. "Women represent nearly 70 percent of part-time employees." Bureau of Labor Statistics, 2000 Current Population Survey.

CHAPTER 3

1. Page 77. "Indeed, across class lines, about 95 percent of African American children and 90 percent of white kids go to public schools." *Digest of Education Statistics.* National Center for Education Statistics, U.S. Department of Education, 2000.

2. Page 79. "More than 60 percent of the public schools in every state need some repairs." In D.C. and 25 states, schools needs major repairs or total replacement. Eleven million students, one of every four who attends a public school, goes to a school that is in less than adequate condition, while 3.5 million attend schools that could be described as in "poor" condition." *Condition of Public School Facilities.* National Center for Education Statistics, 2001.

3. Page 79. "In 2000, 60 percent of the classrooms in schools where at least 75 percent of students were eligible for free or reduced price lunch were wired for internet connection, compared to a connection rate of 82 percent for schools with lower concentrations of poverty." *Internet Access in U.S. Public Schools and Classrooms: 1994–2000.* National Center for Education Statistics, 2001.

4. Page 80. "In 2008, it is projected that more than 48 million youngsters will attend public schools. The Department of Education estimates that 6,000 new schools will need to be built to handle new enrollment." The Condition of Education. National Center for Education Statistics, 2000.

CHAPTER 4

1. Page 93–94. "Our gross domestic product, or the value of goods and services that are sold in our economy, was more than $9.3 trillion in the second quarter of 2001. Two-thirds of this money was money that people earned and spent." *Bureau of Economic Analysis News Release.* U.S. Department of Commerce Bureau of Economic Analysis, April 26, 2002.

2. Page 96. "About 35 percent of federal dollars is spent on Social Security and Medicare programs." Public Agenda Online, www.publicagenda.org.

3. Page 97. "The top 5 percent of the population has 20.3 percent of our nation's income, up from 17.9 percent a decade ago." *Current Population Survey,* U.S. Department of Labor Bureau of Labor Statistics, March 2000.

4. Page 97. "When we realize that more than ten million people (mostly women) earn the minimum wage, we are alarmed." Annual Averages from the 2001 Current Population Survey. Bureau of Labor Statistics, 2002.

5. Page 98. "They turned a blind eye to the conflict of interest between Arthur Andersen's consulting and accounting role for Enron, and as a result 21,000 people have lost their pensions." "Ruling Unravels Deal on Enron Pensions," Crenshaw, Albert. *Washington Post*, April 4, 2002.

CHAPTER 5

1. Page 128. "That's a silly notion because the U.S. will spend at least $330 billion on defense this year, far more than we will on social spending—and I would say having a strong defense is a benefit for all citizens, just as is social spending." Budget of the United States. Office of Management and Budget, 2002.

2. Page 128. (including $1.4 billion in "aid" for IBM). *House GOP Stimulus Bill Offers 16 Low-Tax, Large Corporations $7.4 Billion in Instant Tax Rebates.* Citizens for Tax Justice, http://www.ctj.org/html/amtdozen.htm.

3. Page 135. "California's food stamp application can take "hours and hours" to complete and is twenty-one-pages long." *The Red Tape Divide; State by State Review of Food Stamp Applications.* America's Second Harvest, 2001.

4. Page 136. "This being said, how can anyone honestly believe that our current safety net is adequate while anywhere between 700,000 and 2 million people go inadequately housed each year, nearly 11 percent of households go inadequately fed and unreal numbers of people are in the position of having to make $33.60 per hour to afford a two-bedroom apartment in metropolitan areas like San Francisco and San Diego?" *Out of Reach: America's Growing Wage-Rent Disparity.* National Low Income Housing Coalition, 2002 and *Household Food Security in the United States,* 1999. Economic Research Service, U.S. Department of Agriculture.

CHAPTER 6

1. Page 146. "More than 3.5 million brand-new guns have been manufactured since 1990, at the pace of a gun about every 20 seconds." Coalition to Stop Gun Violence. http://www.gunfree.org/resources/res__facts/facts.html.

2. Page 146. "They donated over $3 million during the 2000 election cycle, have 22 million members and have skewed some of their recruitment material." Center for Responsive Politics. www.opensecrets.org.

3. Page 148. All data from the previous two paragraphs were taken from reports published by the Sentencing Project. *Diminishing Returns: Crime and Incarceration in the 1990s.* (2000); *Gender and Justice: Women, Drugs and Sentencing Policy* (1999). The Sentencing Project.

4. Page 148. "According to the National Coalition to Abolish the Death Penalty, we know of twenty-three innocent people who were mistakenly executed this century. Further, over seventy people have been released since 1972 as a result of being wrongly convicted." "Guilty Until Proven Innocent," National Coalition to Abolish the Death Penalty. www.ncadp.org/html/fact4.html.

5. Page 149. "Instead, corporations like Nashville, Tennessee–based Corrections Corporation of America (CCA) or Florida's Wackenhut Corporation have had amazing success: CCA alone currently corners more than half of the United States private prison market." http://web.crim.ufl.edu/pcp/census/2001/Market.html.

6. Page 149. "In 2001, Wackenhut posted revenues of $2.8 billion—a 12.1 percent increase over its 2000 revenues." "Wackenhut Corporation Reports 2001 Fourth Quarter and Year End Results," Wackenhut Corporation, February 8, 2002.

7. Page 149. "Oregon, for example, voted in 1994 to pass a constitutional amendment that mandated that Oregon prisoners work 40 hours per week and require the state to actively market them to private employers." Gordon Lafer, "Captive Labor," The American Prospect. Vol. 10 No. 46, Sept. 1, 1999–Oct. 1, 1999.

CHAPTER 7

1. Page 176. "In the year 2000, for example, the nation experienced a low unemployment rate of 4 percent, which was 3.5 percent for whites and 7.6 for African Americans." Current Population Survey. U.S. Department of Labor Bureau of Labor Statistics, 2001.

2. Page 176. "While 71 percent of whites own their homes, just 46 percent of African American and Latino populations own their own homes." "Homeownership Gap Widens for Blacks," *Sacramento Observer*, March 19, 2002.

3. Page 176–77. "With median annual earnings of $24,229 in 1999, African American women earned more than 91 percent of white women's earnings (Hispanic women earn 72 percent of what white women earn). In contrast, African American men earned 80 percent of what white men earned, while Hispanic men earned 61 percent of white men's earnings." "1999 Median Annual Earnings by Race and Sex." www.infoplease.com.

4. Page 177. "As early as 1910, black women's labor force participation rates were more than double those of white women. One in five black girls worked in 1910, twice

the number of white girls who did." Goldin, Claudia. *Understanding the Gender Gap: An Economic History of American Women*. Oxford University Press: 1990.

5. Page 177. "The percentage of white women who work jumped from 42.6 percent in 1970 to 59.6 percent in 2000. Black women's labor force participation rates didn't rise as sharply, but they increased from 49.5 percent in 1960 to 63.5 percent in 2000." Statistical Abstract of the United States. United States Bureau of the Census, 2001.

6. Page 178. "While 647,000 white women, about 1.4 percent of those with income, earn more than $100,000 a year, just 62,000 African American women, 0.8 percent of black female earners, have six figure salaries." U.S. Bureau of the Census. Current Population Survey, 2001.

7. Page 182. "In California, after the passage of Proposition 209 in 1996, black and brown enrollment dropped by more than 50 percent in parts of the UC System." Rene Sanchez, Black, Hispanic Admissions Plunge at 2 Calif. Campuses." *Washington Post*, April 1, 1998.

8. Page 182. "In Florida, Jeb Bush's One Florida plan reduced enrollment for African American freshmen at the University of Florida by 43 percent in the fall of 2001." "One Florida cuts college enrollment of blacks." The Associated Press, August 13, 2001.

CHAPTER 8

1. Page 190. "Our treatment of children belies conservative's staunch dedication to the fetus: 12 million children are food insecure (*Household Food Security in the United States, 1999,* U.S. Department of Agriculture); approximately 39 percent of fourth grade students read below basic grade level." (National Assessment of Education Progress, National Center for Education Statistics, 2001.)

2. Page 193–94. "Granted, the statistic that just under a quarter of all pregnancies in the United States are terminated by abortion is sobering (even though this number is smaller than the number in other parts of the world, especially Vietnam and central European countries)." *Family Planning Perspectives*, Vol. 25, No. 1. The Alan Guttmacher Institute: March 1999.

CHAPTER 9

1. Page 224. "President Bush projects spending $2 trillion more on defense over the next five years." "Bush presents a $2.1 trillion wartime budget." www.cnn.com/2002/allpolitics/02/04/bush.budget/

2. Page 225. "How can we justify billions of dollars of foreign aid to one country (case in point: Russia, which siphoned off $1.2 billion of IMF aid to a shell corporation in 1996) but only loan guarantees to another (now, I'm thinking South Africa and our more limited economic involvement)?" Brett D. Schaefer, "Why Congress Should Hold Firm on Reducing Foreign Aid." The Heritage Foundation, 1999.

3. Page 227. "When Europe was devastated at the end of World War II, the United States embarked on the Marshall Plan, spending $13.3 billion over three years on developing Europe." *Marshall Plan Fact Sheet*, U.S. Department of State Office of Policy and Public Affairs, Bureau for European and Canadian Affairs. May 12, 1997.

4. Page 230. "Around the world, there is indifference to violence against women. Human Rights Watch reports that 12,000 Russian women die annually as a result of domestic violence. In South Africa there were 49,280 rapes. In the United States, there is a serious problem of sexual abuse of women in state and federal prisons." *Human Rights Watch Backgrounder*, June 2000. www.hrc.org.

CHAPTER 10

1. Page 238. "It should also come as no surprise that asthma accounts for 10 million missed school days, millions of emergency room visits, outpatient visits and hospitalizations and 18 million days of restricted activity every year—with a great many of these victims being inner-city children and adults (whom we know are more likely to be of color), as they have the highest rates for asthma prevalence, hospitalization and mortality." *Asthma: A Concern for Minority Populations*, BlackHealthCare.com. www.blackhealthcare.com/BHC/Asthma/Description.asp.

2. Page 239. "President Bush and EPA Administrator Christine Whitman announced in 2001 that the United States has "no interest" in agreeing to the Kyoto Protocol, fearing the detrimental effect it could have on big energy business and production." "U.S. pulls out of Kyoto Protocol." Environment News Service. www.ens.lycos.com/ens/mar2001/2001L03-28-11.html.

3. Page 240. "And in Atlanta, which has had its federal highway funding snatched away on more than one occasion for its failure to improve air quality, ground-level ozone continues to contribute to its smog problem according to the Environmental Protection Agency." "Atlanta Air Quality," Southern Environmental Law Center, www.selcga.org/originals/atlanta_air/atlanta_air.shtml.

4. Page 240. "The average Washington, D.C.–area resident spends more than an hour in their car per day commuting." "Commute here among the worst." D'Vera Cohn and Katherine Shaver. *The Washington Post*, Nov. 21, 2001.

5. Page 240. "The average San Francisco area resident spends at least an hour in their car per day commuting." Ibid.

6. Page 241–42. "We are 4 percent of the world's population, but we emit 22 percent of its greenhouse gases of its power, produce 37 percent of its garbage." *Planet Out of Balance: Global Warming and a Changing Climate*, Greenpeace USA. www.greenpeaceusa.org/media/factsheets/planetout.htm, and City of Bellevue, Washington, Environmental Facts and Figures. www.ci.bellevue.wa.us.
7. Page 234–235, Pages 274–275—Statistics from Oxfam America.

DEBORAH PERRY

INTRODUCTION

1. Page 10. "One of my heroines in politics is Jeanette Rankin, a less known early pioneer of women's suffrage who was the first women elected to Congress in 1916. *Women in Congress 1917–1990,* Office of the Historian, U.S. House of Representatives, 1991.
2. Page 11. "In 2002, 88 women hold statewide elected executive offices across the country, or 27.4 percent of the 321 available positions." "Women in Elected Office 2001: Fact Sheet Summaries," Center for American Women and Politics, 2001.
3. Page 11. "The same story can be told in state legislatures where women, in 2002, occupy 1,663, or 22.4 percent, of the 7,424 seats." Ibid.
4. Page 11. "Here's a snapshot of how women have exploded onto the business scene today: *Fortune* magazine states we are 46.5 percent of the labor force, 49.5 percent of managers and professionals, and 12.5 percent of corporate officers." *Fortune,* Oct. 15, 2001, p. 190. "Patient But Not Passive," by Patricia Sellers. "Annual Survey of the 50 Most Powerful Women in Business."
5. Page 11. "According to the Department of Labor, from 1964 to 1999, for every two jobs added for men in government, five were added for women." Every industry defined as: mining, construction, durables, nondurables, transportation, wholesale, retail, finance, services, government. *Women's Jobs 1964–1999,* Department of Labor, 2001.
6. Page 12. "In 1999, women represented 44 percent of the freshman class at Yale Medical School." Diana Furchtgott-Roth and Christine Stolba, *Women's Figures: An Illustrated Guide to the Economic Progress of Women in America,* Independent Women's Forum and AEI Press, 1999.
7. Page 13. "In the early 1950s, when the small screen became a staple in every household, television advertising focused on women's role as a domestic caregiver." "Commercial Portrait of a Woman," ABCNews.com, Aug. 17, 2001.

Chapter 1

1. Page 18. "While there was a time in history when it was socially acceptable to pay women less than a male in the same position with the same level of education and experience, women's median earnings have risen over 14 percent since 1979." *The Index of Leading Cultural Indicators 2001,* Empower America.
2. Page 19. "Prior to the 1963 passage of the Equal Pay Act, it was socially acceptable for men to be the breadwinners and heads of household, and therefore they were entitled to make more money." Dr. Christine Lunardini, *What Every American Should Know About Women's History: 200 Events that Shaped Our Destiny,* 1996, p. 306.
3. Page 20. "Consider the Department of Labor statistics, which these women so frequently refer to, stating that in the year 2000 women earned seventy-six cents to the man's dollar." "20 Leading Occupations of Employed Women: 2000 Annual Averages," Department of Labor.

Chapter 2

1. Page 55. "In the fifties, Americans backed postwar prosperity, a baby boom, and the stability of marriage that lasted an average of thirty-one years—the highest rate ever." "Anti-Nuclear Reaction," *The Economist,* Dec. 31, 1999, p. 53.
2. Page 55. "In the forties, 67 percent of households were "traditional" families, as compared to 17 percent today." Denise Venable, "Labor Law Discriminates Against Women," National Center for Policy Analysis, Aug. 2001.
3. Page 56. "Today, only 40 percent of American children reach the age of eighteen with a mother and a father at home." David Blankenhorn, *Fatherless America: Confronting Our Most Urgent Social Problem,* 1996.
4. Page 56. "The consequence of all this confusion is that out-of-wedlock children or children of divorced parents are more likely to experience poverty, crime, abuse, drug and alcohol abuse, behavioral and emotional problems, lower academic achievement, less income over their working lives, and other serious problems." Patrick F. Fagan, "Rising Illegitimacy: America's Social Catastrophe," Heritage Foundation *F.Y.I.,* No. 19/94, June 29, 1994.

Chapter 3

1. Page 66. "During the Clinton years, there was a lot of talk of a heightened federal role in education, which makes great lip service and eye-catching news stories for the morning papers, but our public education system is already plagued by a massive

federal bureaucracy." *Crossroads Project,* a report from the U.S. House Committee on Education and the Workforce, 1998.

2. Page 67. "Even though government spending provides each student with an average of more than $7,000 per year, 40 percent of American fourth graders can't read, and American eighth graders rank last in math and science among students from seven developed nations that administer the International Assessment of Educational Progress." Milton Friedman, "The State of U.S. Public Schools," Educational Choice, 2000.

3. Page 67. "U.S. twelfth graders are behind 95 percent of the children in other countries, and half of the students in urban schools fail to graduate on time, if at all." *Crossroads Project.*

4. Page 67. "A recent National Assessment of Educational Progress (NAEP) test administered to twelfth graders by the federal government to students across the country reveal that . . ." Karl Zinsmeister, "The Quality of Education Has Declined," *Education: Opposing Viewpoints,* 2000, p. 19.

5. Page 70. "The average per pupil expenditure in public school is about $7,000, and the average cost of a parochial school is 3,000." Average cost of parochial school with strong academic component.

6. Page 71. "About eight thousand schoolchildren are benefiting from the voucher plan, which provides each student up to $5,000 per year to the poorest Milwaukee families." Institute for the Transformation of Learning, Marquette University; Institute for Justice; Milton and Rose D. Friedman Foundation.

7. Page 74. "Since 1994, the percentage of public schools with Internet access has increased dramatically: 94 and 98 percent of elementary and secondary schools, respectively." *The Index of Leading Cultural Indicators 2001.*

CHAPTER 4

1. Page 104. "In the eighteenth century, taxes were thwarting people's ability to progress economically, and the common person was powerless to stop it. *What Every American Should Know About Women's History:* p. 10–12.

2. Page 108. "If a woman with children gets divorced, she must literally pass the buck to Uncle Sam." Dr. Emily Card, *The Ms. Money Book,* 1990, p. 220.

3. Page 109. "Widowed women and men face the estate tax, otherwise known as the 'death' tax, but women are more at risk because they tend to outlive their spouses on average by seven years." Dr. Christine Stolba, "Why Women Should Care About the Death Tax," Independent Women's Forum, Feb. 2000.

4. Page 111. "In fact, the United States imports nearly 60 percent of its crude oil, an

all-time high in history." Citizens for a Sound Economy, an open letter to members of Congress, Oct. 2, 2001.

Chapter 5

1. Page 118. "First of all, programs like Social Security were never designed to be permanent, and can be changed or eliminated by Congress at any time." *Economic Report of the President,* Council of Economic Advisers, Feb. 2002.
2. Page 118. "Social Security is the sole source for nearly one in five elderly women, and provides at least 90 percent of income for almost one-third of elderly women." Kathryn H. Porter, et al., "Social Security and Poverty Among the Elderly: A National and State Perspective Executive Summary," Center on Budget and Policy Priorities, Apr. 8, 1999.
3. Page 119. "Unfortunately, today, less than half of American workers have personal savings and about 30 percent of women as compared with 46 percent of men are covered by a private pension." *Economic Report of the President.*
4. Page 122. "It is no wonder that seventy-five percent of working women and 48 percent of unemployed women prefer some investment opportunity with investment accounts." Zogby International Poll, "Majority Support for Social Security Privatization," Sept. 1999.
5. Page 124. "Americans' personal savings rate (personal savings as a percentage of disposable income) has been steadily declining since 1975, and is at its lowest rate (below 1 percent) since World War II." *The Index of Leading Cultural Indicators 2001.*
6. Page 124–25. "Presently, the government is struggling to keep the second-largest entitled program afloat, as Medicare has two major problems: financial health and quality health care in the face of exploding costs." *Economic Report of the President.*

Chapter 6

1. Page 154. "While Representative McCarthy is one of millions of Americans who have been affected by crime and violence in America, crime overall has declined in the United States 27 percent between 1990 and 1999." Total crimes are defined as murder, rape, robbery, and assault and the property crimes of burglary, larceny theft, motor vehicle theft, and arson, Federal Bureau of Investigation, U.S. Crime Index 1960–1999.
2. Page 154. "In 1999, the United States averaged 426.7 crimes per 10,000 residents,

in comparison to 1980 when total crime rates were 595 per 10,000 people." *The Index of Leading Cultural Indicators 2001.*

3. Page 156. "For example, one often referred to, but skewed, statistic used by many nonprofit gun control advocacy groups is that a child dies every thirteen seconds because of a handgun." Iain Murray, "The U.S. Gun-Control Debate: A Critical Look," *Encyclopaedia Britannica,* 2001.

4. Page 158. "Even though public opinion has consistently held a two-to-one ratio in support of the death penalty, national anxiety in recent years has heightened over the constitutionality of the death penalty and making sure that innocent defendants are not being sentenced to death." *Opposing Viewpoints in Social Issues,* Greenhaven Press, 2000.

5. Page 159. "Take the case of Ted Bundy, for example, who confessed to killing twenty-eight women, but is believed to be responsible for raping and killing more than fifty women." Crime Statistics, Bureau of Justice Statistics Clearinghouse, Oct. 2000.

6. Page 160. "While only fifty-four women are currently on death row, the issue is of grave concern to us, because we want to know that violent killers are eradicated off the face of the earth." Jacob Lamar, "I Deserve Punishment," *Time,* Feb. 1989, p. 34.

CHAPTER 7

1. Page 169. "Women played a monumental role in the abolitionist movement at a time when they were not allowed to have much of a voice outside of the home." *What Every American Should Know About Women's History.*

CHAPTER 8

1. Page 198–99. "There has to be regard for the social order of American generations to ensure that populations carry on at a balanced pace so that younger workers can support retired folks." *Economic Report to the President.*

2. Page 199. "No matter where you stand on the issue, abortion by its very definition is an 'induced termination of pregnancy before the fetus is capable of survival as an individual." See *The American Heritage Dictionary.*

3. Page 199. "No one knows for sure how many abortions take place each year, but to the best of our knowledge, there are about 1.4 million." Statistical Assessment Service (STATS).

4. Page 199. "What this figure does not account for are the many women who induce abortions with day-after contraceptives such as RU-486." National Right to Life Committee.

5. Page 199. "Let me summarize what the feminists say about the history of abortion because it runs counter to their principles today." *What Every American Should Know About Women's History.*

6. Page 204. "Most people haven't read the body of literature about health risks of abortions, but there is strong evidence supporting the physical dangers." D. Lazovich, J. A. Thompson, P. J. Mink, T. A. Sellers, and K. E. Anderson, "Induced Abortion and Breast Cancer Risk," *Epidemiol* 11 (2000): pp. 76–80.

7. Page 206. "All aside, we should really just ask ourselves whether we have grown into a culture that has devalued life." "Is Abortion Justifiable," *Opposing Viewpoints in Social Issues,* p. 52.

CHAPTER 9

1. Page 213. "Women and children make up 80 percent of all refugees and displaced persons globally, two out of three of the world's 1.3 billion poor are women, and today 6,000 girls are genitally mutilated." Women for Women International website.

2. Page 214. "It is hard to fathom that some girls are as young as nine and ten years old, and are forced to have sex ten to twenty times a day." WHO Violence Against Women Information Packet, World Health Organization.

3. Page 214. "In lower-rent brothels, four out of five girls contract the AIDS virus." Ibid.

4. Page 214. "For many people not familiar with the practice of female genital mutilation (FGM), it is often compared to a male circumcision during infancy; only it is done to girls and women in a harmful, sometimes deadly manner." Ibid.

CHAPTER 10

1. Page 250. "The Food and Drug Administration estimates that the average adult ingests about fifty-three micrograms of predominately organic arsenic a day." *The Record,* Statistical Assessment Service, STATS, 2001.

2. Page 250. "The Kyoto Protocol, despite the falsified claims put into the public domain, will not prevent global warming—it instead reduces emissions by a mere five percent in industrialized nations only, and only saves the world six years." Bjorn Lomborg, "The Truth About the Environment," *The Economist,* Aug. 4, 2001.

3. Page 250. "There are more important health-related problems that are less costly, such as solving the number one health issue around the world: safe drinking water and sanitation coverage." Ibid.

4. Page 255. "For far too long, the United States has been reliant on foreign energy supply, as we import nearly 60 percent of our crude oil, an all-time high in history." Citizens for a Sound Economy, an open letter to members of Congress, Oct. 2, 2001.

5. Page 256. "The federal government has done little to truly protect endangered species." National Wildlife Institute, "Groundbreaking Study Determines Endangered Species Act to be a Failure," May 20, 1997, p. 1.

CHAPTER 12

1. Page 267. "Voting is the most simple, direct, and powerful way women can affect government." Based on the "The Gender Gap," www.feministcampus.org.

2. Page 267. "Voter turnout in general remains low." "Voter Registration and Turnout in Federal Elections by Gender 1972–1996," Federal Election Commission. www.fec.gov.

3. Page 270. "Even though women make up the majority of the electorate, too few women run for public office." "Women Candidates Can Win . . . When They Run," Center for Voting and Democracy. www.fairvote.org.

INDEX

Page numbers in **bold** indicate tables.